# The AI Trading Edge

*Finding Alpha with NLP and Alternative Data*

Victor Trex

Published by NobleTrex Press


For permissions and other inquiries, write to:
P.O. Box 3132, Framingham, MA 01701, USA

# Contents

# Introduction

Markets have always been stories written in numbers. Today, those stories are told not only in prices and volumes but also in language: filings and earnings calls, news and social media, product reviews and foot traffic, satellite images and digital exhaust. The central premise of this book is simple and pragmatic: when thoughtfully engineered and rigorously validated, natural language processing and alternative data can yield durable trading edges. The path from raw text or sensor streams to tradable alpha is neither linear nor magical; it is a disciplined craft that blends financial intuition with statistical rigor, modern machine learning, and production-grade engineering. This book is a field guide to that craft.

We begin by laying foundations. The opening chapter on quantitative and computational tools refreshes the mathematics that underwrite inference in noisy markets and the optimization principles that govern learning in high dimensions. You will revisit linear algebra and calculus where they matter for model estimation, probability where it matters for uncertainty, and statistics where it matters for risk. Alongside, we standardize a Python research stack-NumPy, Pandas, scikit-learn-and emphasize reproducibility through environment management, visualization discipline, logging, and experiment tracking. These are not academic niceties; they are the scaffolding that keeps research accountable when the stakes are real.

With tools in hand, we turn to the market itself-what is traded, how prices are formed, and which frictions shape realized returns. The treatment of asset classes and microstructure grounds the reader in instruments, order types, liquidity, fragmentation, and cost drivers.

We introduce return conventions and performance metrics so results mean what we think they mean, and we separate genuine alpha from disguised factor bets using risk premia and factor models. Most importantly, we codify a structured research workflow that guards against confirmation bias and p-hacking, establishing the habit of predefining hypotheses, evaluation protocols, and documentation before the first backtest is run.

Data is the lifeblood of modern strategies, and alternative data is both an opportunity and a liability if mishandled. Our data engineering chapters start with compliance, placing MNPI controls, provenance tracking, and privacy safeguards at the gate of every dataset. We discuss vendor selection, licensing, and service agreements with the same seriousness as signal discovery, because operational reliability and legal clarity are components of edge. You will learn to design pipelines that diagnose quality, deduplicate, align timestamps, control survivorship, and label events coherently. We then survey high-impact domains-corporate disclosures and earnings, the fast-twitch world of web and social signals, and real-economy traces from satellite and transactions-always with attention to sampling bias, drift, and data fusion.

From there, we recast unstructured text into quantitative features. We cover preprocessing and tokenization, classical representations and modern embeddings, and the transformer architectures that dominate contemporary NLP. We show how to adapt large language models to finance with domain-aware fine-tuning and parameter-efficient techniques, balancing accuracy with latency, cost, and compliance. Information extraction and sentiment analysis convert narratives into structured facts and measurements; the focus is not novelty for its own sake, but reliability under live constraints.

The bridge from features to finance is explicit. We discuss domain adaptation and sentiment alpha, event extraction paired with event studies, and topic modeling that surfaces evolving narratives for thematic baskets. Practicalities-linking entities to tickers, reconciling issuers across sources, and assembling knowledge graphs-ensure that insights bind to instruments you can trade.

Signal modeling and validation are treated with the skepticism that markets demand. You will build supervised learners and deep models for panel and sequential data, but always inside time-aware cross-validation with purging and embargo to prevent leakage. We emphasize diagnostics, explainability, and causal checks, not as window dressing but as mechanisms to detect spurious correlations, understand failure modes, and communicate with stakeholders who must underwrite model risk.

Strategies live or die in portfolio context. We design backtests that reflect real frictions-transaction costs, slippage, and market impact-and we translate signals into positions subject to capacity, turnover, and risk constraints. Portfolio construction spans mean-variance, Black-Litterman, and turnover-aware optimization, and execution choices-algorithm selection and routing-are treated as first-class determinants of net performance. Finally, we bring the system to production with CI/CD, monitoring for drift and data outages, alerting, and governance aligned to model risk policies. A strategy is not complete when it backtests well; it is complete when it can fail safely.

This book is written for quants, data scientists, and engineers who want to move beyond prototypes to robust trading systems, and for investors who seek to interrogate claims about AI-driven alpha with informed questions. Each chapter is self-contained yet designed to build momentum: from quantitative bedrock, to market structure and disciplined research, to compliant data pipelines, to NLP feature construction, to signal modeling and validation, and finally to portfolios, execution, and production. The destination is not a single recipe but a repeatable practice-a way to ask sharper questions of the data, to measure answers honestly, and to carry them, intact, into the market.

# Chapter 1

# Quantitative & Computational Foundations

*Before we mine alpha from text streams and alternative data, we need a sharp set of tools: the math that governs uncertainty, the time-series intuition for noisy markets, the optimization machinery that actually trains our models, and the Python stack that turns ideas into reproducible code. This chapter is your upgrade from 'coding around in notebooks' to thinking-and building-like a systematic AI trader.*

## 1.1 Quantitative Mathematics for AI Trading

AI trading systems live at the intersection of data, models, and uncertainty. To reason clearly in this environment you need a compact but powerful mathematical vocabulary. This section builds that vocabulary in four parts:

- Linear algebra: how we represent portfolios, features, and covariances as vectors and matrices.

- Calculus and optimization: how we describe sensitivity, change, and local approximations of model behavior.
- Probability: how we formalize randomness in returns and signals.
- Statistical inference: how we decide whether a pattern in data is likely to be real alpha or just noise.

The goal is intuition and fluency, not theorem-proving. We will constantly tie abstract ideas back to concrete trading tasks such as risk modeling, factor exposure analysis, and evaluating a predictive signal.

## Linear Algebra as the Language of Portfolios and Features

### Vectors: from single numbers to portfolios

A *scalar* is a single real number, like a one-day return of 0.4%. A *vector* is an ordered list of scalars. For example, the returns of three stocks on a given day can be written as

$$\mathbf{r} = \begin{bmatrix} r_1 \\ r_2 \\ r_3 \end{bmatrix}.$$

Similarly, a portfolio with weights $w_1, w_2, w_3$ in those three stocks is represented as

$$\mathbf{w} = \begin{bmatrix} w_1 \\ w_2 \\ w_3 \end{bmatrix}.$$

The dot product

$$\mathbf{w}^\top \mathbf{r} = w_1 r_1 + w_2 r_2 + w_3 r_3$$

is the portfolio return for that day. This is the first key idea: *a portfolio, at any point in time, is a vector of weights; its return is a dot product with the vector of asset returns.*

In AI trading, we use vectors not only for returns and weights but also for features (signals). A single observation of features for one asset at one time (e.g., lagged returns, volatility estimate, valuation ratios) is a feature vector $\mathbf{x}_t \in \mathbb{R}^d$.

**Matrices: stacking across assets, times, and features**

A *matrix* is a rectangular array of numbers. You can think of it as a table where rows and columns have specific meanings.

Common examples in trading:

- **Feature matrix** for supervised learning: $X \in \mathbb{R}^{T\times d}$, where each row corresponds to a time (or time-asset pair) and each column to a feature.
- **Covariance matrix** of returns: $\Sigma \in \mathbb{R}^{n\times n}$, where $n$ is the number of assets and
$$\Sigma_{ij} = \text{Cov}(r_i, r_j).$$
- **Factor loading (exposure) matrix**: $B \in \mathbb{R}^{n\times k}$, where $B_{if}$ is the exposure of asset $i$ to factor $f$.

When we estimate a linear model for expected returns,

$$\hat{y} = X\beta,$$

we are multiplying a feature matrix $X$ by a parameter vector $\beta$. Each row of $X$ is a feature vector; the same $\beta$ is applied across all observations. This is exactly how most machine learning libraries view data internally.

**Norms and distances: similarity of market states**

A *norm* is a way to measure the size of a vector. The most common is the Euclidean norm:

$$\|\mathbf{x}\|_2 = \sqrt{x_1^2 + x_2^2 + \cdots + x_d^2}.$$

Given two feature vectors $\mathbf{x}$ and $\mathbf{y}$, their Euclidean distance is

$$\|\mathbf{x} - \mathbf{y}\|_2.$$

Why this matters for AI trading:

- In nearest-neighbor methods or clustering, we group similar market states using distances between feature vectors.
- In regularization (e.g., ridge regression), we penalize the norm of parameter vectors $\|\beta\|_2$ to prevent extreme coefficients.

Another useful measure is the $L_1$ norm:

$$\|\mathbf{x}\|_1 = |x_1| + \cdots + |x_d|.$$

Minimizing $\|\beta\|_1$ encourages many entries of $\beta$ to be exactly zero (sparse models), which we will later connect to feature selection.

**Covariance matrices: quantitative risk maps**

The covariance matrix $\Sigma$ summarizes both the variances of individual assets and the co-movements between them. If $\mathbf{r}$ is the random return vector of $n$ assets with mean $\mathbb{E}[\mathbf{r}] = \boldsymbol{\mu}$, then

$$\Sigma = \mathbb{E}\left[(\mathbf{r} - \boldsymbol{\mu})(\mathbf{r} - \boldsymbol{\mu})^\top\right].$$

Portfolio variance is

$$\mathrm{Var}(\mathbf{w}^\top \mathbf{r}) = \mathbf{w}^\top \Sigma \mathbf{w}.$$

This quadratic form is central to risk modeling:

- If your AI model proposes new portfolio weights $\mathbf{w}$, $\mathbf{w}^\top \Sigma \mathbf{w}$ is a model-based estimate of risk.
- Risk-parity, minimum-variance, and many other allocation rules are built on this formula.

**Eigenvalues, eigenvectors, and principal components**

Covariance matrices have a particularly nice structure. They are symmetric and positive semidefinite, which implies they can be decomposed as

$$\Sigma = Q \Lambda Q^\top,$$

where

- $Q$ is an orthogonal matrix whose columns are eigenvectors (directions in risk space),
- $\Lambda$ is a diagonal matrix of eigenvalues $\lambda_1 \geq \lambda_2 \geq \cdots \geq \lambda_n \geq 0$.

Each eigenpair has a clear interpretation:

- An eigenvector $\mathbf{v}$ is a direction in portfolio space (a particular combination of assets).
- The corresponding eigenvalue $\lambda$ is the variance (risk) associated with that direction.

The first few eigenvectors of $\Sigma$ often correspond to familiar macro factors: overall market, sector tilts, style factors, etc. The technique that computes these dominant eigenvectors is *principal component analysis* (PCA).

In AI trading, PCA and related decompositions are used to:

- Identify dominant risk drivers and reduce dimensionality.
- Build factor models (principal components as artificial factors).
- Diagnose when a model is overly exposed to one risk direction (e.g., most variance explained by a single eigenvalue).

The key mental picture: *the eigenvectors provide a rotated coordinate system in which the covariance matrix becomes diagonal; eigenvalues tell you how much risk lives along each coordinate.*

## Calculus and Optimization: Sensitivity and Local Approximation

Once we represent portfolios and models as functions of parameters and features, we want to know how they respond to small changes. This is the domain of calculus, particularly derivatives and gradients.

**Derivatives and partial derivatives**

A scalar function of one variable, $f(x)$, has derivative

$$f'(x) = \lim_{h \to 0} \frac{f(x+h) - f(x)}{h}.$$

This represents the local slope: how $f$ changes per unit change in $x$.

If $f$ depends on many variables, $f(\theta_1, \ldots, \theta_p)$, the *partial derivative* with respect to $\theta_j$ is

$$\frac{\partial f}{\partial \theta_j} = \lim_{h \to 0} \frac{f(\theta_1, \ldots, \theta_j + h, \ldots, \theta_p) - f(\theta_1, \ldots, \theta_j, \ldots, \theta_p)}{h}.$$

In trading, think of $f$ as a performance metric (e.g., expected P&L, Sharpe ratio, loss function) and $\theta_j$ as a model parameter. Then $\partial f / \partial \theta_j$ is a formal measure of *sensitivity* of performance to that parameter.

**Gradients: direction of steepest change**

Collecting all partial derivatives into a vector gives the *gradient*:

$$\nabla f(\boldsymbol{\theta}) = \begin{bmatrix} \frac{\partial f}{\partial \theta_1} \\ \vdots \\ \frac{\partial f}{\partial \theta_p} \end{bmatrix}.$$

Two key facts:

- The gradient points in the direction of steepest increase of $f$.
- Moving in the opposite direction, $-\nabla f$, most rapidly decreases $f$.

Training a model by gradient descent is simply repeatedly updating

$$\boldsymbol{\theta}_{new} = \boldsymbol{\theta}_{old} - \eta \nabla f(\boldsymbol{\theta}_{old}),$$

where $f$ is the loss function (e.g., mean squared error of return predictions) and $\eta$ is the learning rate. Although the computational details are handled by libraries, conceptually you are following the negative gradient downhill in a high-dimensional surface.

**Taylor approximation: local linear and quadratic views**

Near a point $\boldsymbol{\theta}_0$, a smooth function $f$ can be approximated by its first-order (linear) Taylor expansion:

$$f(\boldsymbol{\theta}) \approx f(\boldsymbol{\theta}_0) + \nabla f(\boldsymbol{\theta}_0)^\top (\boldsymbol{\theta} - \boldsymbol{\theta}_0).$$

Interpretation:

- Close to $\boldsymbol{\theta}_0$, the function behaves approximately like a plane with slope given by the gradient.
- Sensitivity analysis (e.g., how P&L changes if you tweak a parameter) often uses this local linear view.

Including second-order terms yields the quadratic approximation involving the *Hessian* matrix $H$ of second derivatives:

$$f(\boldsymbol{\theta}) \approx f(\boldsymbol{\theta}_0) + \nabla f(\boldsymbol{\theta}_0)^\top (\boldsymbol{\theta} - \boldsymbol{\theta}_0) + \frac{1}{2}(\boldsymbol{\theta} - \boldsymbol{\theta}_0)^\top H(\boldsymbol{\theta}_0)(\boldsymbol{\theta} - \boldsymbol{\theta}_0).$$

Quadratic approximations are important for:

- Understanding curvature of the loss surface (sharp vs. flat minima, which can affect generalization).
- Classical portfolio optimization where the objective is quadratic in weights (mean-variance optimization).

You do not need to compute Hessians by hand to use machine learning in trading, but it is useful to remember: *locally, many optimization problems look quadratic in the parameters or weights*, which explains why methods based on second-order approximations (like Newton's method) can converge quickly under suitable conditions.

## Probability: Modeling Returns and Uncertainty

Financial markets are inherently uncertain. Probability theory gives us a disciplined way to talk about this uncertainty and connect it to trading decisions.

### Random variables, distributions, and moments

A *random variable* $R$ represents a quantity whose value is uncertain, such as next day's return of an asset. Instead of a single number, $R$ has a *distribution* that describes how likely different outcomes are.

Key summaries of a distribution:

- Expectation (mean): $\mathbb{E}[R]$, often interpreted as the average return.
- Variance: $\text{Var}(R) = \mathbb{E}\left[(R - \mathbb{E}[R])^2\right]$, a measure of risk.
- Standard deviation: $\sigma = \sqrt{\text{Var}(R)}$.
- Higher moments: skewness (asymmetry), kurtosis (tail thickness).

If **R** is a random vector of returns, we also care about covariance and correlation:

$$\text{Cov}(R_i, R_j) = \mathbb{E}\left[(R_i - \mathbb{E}[R_i])(R_j - \mathbb{E}[R_j])\right],$$

$$\text{Corr}(R_i, R_j) = \frac{\text{Cov}(R_i, R_j)}{\sqrt{\text{Var}(R_i)\,\text{Var}(R_j)}}.$$

Correlations drive diversification benefits: low (or negative) correlation between assets reduces portfolio variance.

### Conditional probability and updating with new information

AI trading models operate in a conditional world: predictions are always of the form "given features $X$, what is the distribution of return $R$?".

The conditional probability $\mathbb{P}(R \in A \mid X = x)$ expresses the chance that $R$ falls in set $A$ given that we observe $X = x$. Conditional expectation $\mathbb{E}[R \mid X = x]$ is the expected return given features $x$.

Bayes' rule is the fundamental formula for updating beliefs:

$$\mathbb{P}(A \mid B) = \frac{\mathbb{P}(B \mid A)\mathbb{P}(A)}{\mathbb{P}(B)},$$

where $A$ is a hypothesis (e.g., "a regime shift has occurred") and $B$ is new evidence (e.g., "observed volatility spiked this week").

While explicit Bayesian modeling is only one approach among many, the underlying idea is universal in AI trading: *new data modifies your beliefs about hidden states of the world and about future returns.*

**Independence and dependence structures**

Two random variables $R$ and $S$ are independent if knowing one gives no information about the other. In financial time series this is rarely strictly true, but the concept is important:

- Many theoretical results (e.g., simple law of large numbers) assume independent observations.
- In practice, returns may be weakly dependent, and residuals of a well-specified model are often treated as approximately independent noise.

For time series, we are especially interested in dependence across time. Autocorrelation (introduced in detail in the time-series fundamentals section) measures correlation of a variable with its own lagged values, such as $\mathrm{Corr}(R_t, R_{t-1})$. Nonzero autocorrelation can signal momentum or mean reversion.

**Scenarios and risk measures**

Probability provides the language for scenario analysis:

- Simulated scenarios: generate many possible paths of returns $\{R_t^{(s)}\}$ from a probabilistic model or bootstrap; evaluate P&L under each scenario.
- Risk measures: value-at-risk (VaR) and expected shortfall (ES) are quantiles and tail expectations of the P&L distribution.

Even when your AI model is not explicitly probabilistic, you can still interpret its outputs probabilistically (e.g., classification probabilities, predictive distributions for Bayesian or ensemble models) to inform scenario-based risk management.

## Statistical Inference: From Data to Belief about Alpha

So far we have treated distributions and expectations as if we knew them. In reality, we only see *samples* from the underlying processes: a finite history of prices and returns. Statistical inference is about going from data to conclusions while quantifying uncertainty.

**Samples, estimators, and sampling variability**

Suppose we observe $T$ daily returns of an asset: $r_1, \ldots, r_T$. A natural estimator of the mean return is the sample average

$$\hat{\mu} = \frac{1}{T} \sum_{t=1}^{T} r_t.$$

Similarly, we estimate variance by the sample variance

$$\hat{\sigma}^2 = \frac{1}{T-1} \sum_{t=1}^{T} (r_t - \hat{\mu})^2.$$

An *estimator* is a rule that maps data to a numerical estimate of some parameter (here, mean and variance). The crucial insight:

> If you repeated the sampling experiment (collecting new data of length $T$) many times, the estimator would take different values each time.

This variability leads to confidence intervals and hypothesis tests.

**Confidence intervals: how much uncertainty?**

A $(1-\alpha)$-level confidence interval for a parameter is a range that, under repeated sampling, would contain the true parameter value in approximately a fraction $1-\alpha$ of the samples.

For example, a 95% confidence interval for the mean return might be of the form

$$\hat{\mu} \pm 1.96 \cdot \frac{\hat{\sigma}}{\sqrt{T}}.$$

Intuition in a trading context:

- A small $\hat{\mu}$ relative to its standard error $\hat{\sigma}/\sqrt{T}$ implies high uncertainty about whether the mean is truly positive.
- For short samples or noisy signals, the confidence interval may easily include zero, suggesting that the data do not strongly support a nonzero mean.

When evaluating an alpha signal (e.g., average return conditional on a signal decile), wide confidence intervals should trigger skepticism.

### Hypothesis testing: is the alpha real?

Hypothesis testing frames questions like "does this signal have nonzero predictive power?" in a structured way. The typical steps:

- **Null hypothesis** $H_0$: there is no alpha (e.g., mean conditional return is zero, or information coefficient is zero).
- **Alternative hypothesis** $H_1$: there is some alpha (e.g., mean is positive).
- **Test statistic**: a number computed from data that tends to be large in magnitude when $H_1$ is true. For a mean, this is often a $t$-statistic:
$$t = \frac{\hat{\mu}}{\hat{\sigma}/\sqrt{T}}.$$
- ***p*-value**: the probability, under $H_0$, of observing a test statistic at least as extreme as what you computed. A small $p$-value suggests the data are unlikely under $H_0$.

In practice for trading:

- A large positive $t$-statistic (e.g., greater than 3 in absolute value, depending on context) is evidence that the signal may be genuine.
- However, you must adjust your intuition for multiple testing: if you try hundreds of signals, some will show large $t$-stats by luck alone.

Hypothesis testing is a tool, not an oracle. It is useful to calibrate how surprising your backtest results are under a "no alpha" world, but it does not replace out-of-sample testing and robust validation.

**Correlation, causation, and backtest pitfalls**

Statistical tools can easily mislead if interpreted naively. A few recurring issues:

- **Correlation vs. causation**: a strong historical correlation between a signal and returns does not mean the signal causes returns. It might be driven by a hidden common factor, structural break, or data artifact.
- **Overfitting**: with many parameters or flexible models, it is easy to fit noise in the training data. The in-sample statistics (high Sharpe, low loss) then overstate true performance.
- **Look-ahead bias and leakage**: using future information in your features or labels (even indirectly, e.g., via improperly constructed rolling windows) produces spuriously good results.

Statistical inference provides some defenses:

- Confidence intervals and tests remind you how uncertain your estimates are, especially with short histories.
- Penalized models (regularization) and cross-validation, introduced in later sections, reduce degrees of freedom and expose overfitting.
- Explicitly modeling the dependence structure of time series (autocorrelation, volatility clustering) helps you avoid underestimating uncertainty.

## Bringing It Together for AI Trading

The four mathematical domains we have covered are tightly interwoven in AI trading practice:

- **Linear algebra** provides the structures (vectors, matrices, eigen-decompositions) in which we represent portfolios, features, and risk.
- **Calculus and optimization** explain how we adjust model parameters to minimize loss functions and how sensitive P&L is to changes in those parameters and in inputs.
- **Probability** lets us describe uncertain returns, scenario distributions, and dependence structures across assets and time.
- **Statistical inference** lets us move from finite samples to beliefs about true performance, quantify uncertainty, and test whether apparent alpha is likely to be real.

As you move into the next sections on time-series fundamentals, optimization principles for model training, and the Python toolkit, keep these core concepts in mind. They are the mental scaffolding that will let you interpret model outputs, debug strange behaviors, and design trading strategies that respect both the geometry of feature spaces and the probabilistic nature of markets.

## 1.2 Time-Series Fundamentals

In the previous section we built the mathematical vocabulary of vectors, matrices, probability, and inference. We now apply that vocabulary to the special case that dominates trading: *time series.*

A time series is simply data indexed by time: prices every second, returns every day, volatility estimates every month. But financial time series are not generic. They exhibit characteristic patterns and pathologies—non-stationarity, dependence over time, volatility clustering, heavy tails, and calendar structure—that strongly influence how you should engineer features, design models, and evaluate AI trading strategies.

This section introduces those defining characteristics in a structured way:

- Prices, returns, and log-returns: the basic objects and notation.

- Stationarity and regime shifts: how distributions move over time.
- Temporal dependence: autocorrelation, mean reversion, and momentum.
- Volatility clustering and heavy tails: why risk is time-varying and extreme moves are common.
- Seasonality and calendar effects: predictable patterns in time.
- Implications for feature design and evaluation: how to respect time order and avoid subtle biases.

Throughout, keep in mind the mental model from the previous section: a time series is a sequence of random variables, and we care about both their marginal distributions and their dependence structure over time.

## Prices, Returns, and Log-Returns

Let $P_t$ denote the price of an asset at (discrete) time $t$, for example the closing price each day. The raw price series $\{P_t\}_{t=1}^T$ is what you see on a typical chart, but it is usually *not* what you should model directly.

### Simple returns

The *simple (arithmetic) return* from $t$ to $t+1$ is

$$R_{t+1} = \frac{P_{t+1} - P_t}{P_t} = \frac{P_{t+1}}{P_t} - 1.$$

If you invest \$1 at time $t$, you have $1 + R_{t+1}$ at $t+1$. Chaining returns over multiple periods corresponds to multiplying the gross returns:

$$(1 + R_{t+1})(1 + R_{t+2}) \cdots (1 + R_{t+h}) = \frac{P_{t+h}}{P_t}.$$

### Log-returns

The *log-return* is defined as

$$r_{t+1} = \log\left(\frac{P_{t+1}}{P_t}\right) = \log P_{t+1} - \log P_t.$$

For small returns, $\log(1 + R_{t+1}) \approx R_{t+1}$, so log-returns and simple returns are numerically close in daily or intraday data.

Log-returns are often preferred because:

- They are *additive*: summing log-returns over a horizon gives the total log-return:

$$r_{t+1} + \cdots + r_{t+h} = \log\left(\frac{P_{t+h}}{P_t}\right).$$

- Many stochastic models (e.g., geometric Brownian motion) naturally assume that log-prices behave like a random walk.

In matrix notation, if you have returns for $n$ assets across $T$ days, you can arrange them in a return matrix

$$R = \begin{bmatrix} r_{1,1} & \cdots & r_{1,n} \\ \vdots & & \vdots \\ r_{T,1} & \cdots & r_{T,n} \end{bmatrix},$$

where row $t$ is the return vector $\mathbf{r}_t \in \mathbb{R}^n$. This is the core numeric object that feeds AI models.

**Why we model returns, not prices**

Modeling prices directly tends to mix two phenomena:

- *Scale*: a stock that went from \$10 to \$50 over several years has a different price level than one that went from \$500 to \$550, even if their *percentage* moves are similar.
- *Trend and drift*: long-run growth or decline in the price can overwhelm subtler predictive signals.

Returns normalize out scale and focus on relative changes. For supervised learning, they provide a more stable and stationary-like target. Nearly all AI trading workflows therefore use some notion of return (simple, log, or more elaborate excess returns) as the dependent variable.

## Stationarity and Regime Shifts

In the previous section we treated random variables with fixed distributions. In time series, the key question is: does the distribution of $r_t$ stay the same over time, or does it drift?

### Strict and weak stationarity

A time series $\{X_t\}$ is *strictly stationary* if the joint distribution of $(X_{t_1}, \ldots, X_{t_k})$ is the same as that of $(X_{t_1+h}, \ldots, X_{t_k+h})$ for all time shifts $h$ and all sets of indices. Intuitively, the probabilistic behavior does not change over time.

This is a strong requirement. In practice we often work with *weak (or covariance) stationarity*: a process is weakly stationary if

- $\mathbb{E}[X_t] = \mu$ is constant over time.
- $\text{Var}(X_t) = \sigma^2$ is constant over time.
- $\text{Cov}(X_t, X_{t-k})$ depends only on the lag $k$, not on $t$.

For returns, the stationarity question is: can we treat the mean, variance, and autocorrelations as roughly stable over the horizon we care about (e.g., a few years)?

### Non-stationarity in prices and returns

Most financial price series are *non-stationary* in levels: price distributions drift, and the variance often grows over longer horizons. A classic example is a random walk:

$$P_t = P_{t-1} + \epsilon_t,$$

where $\epsilon_t$ are independent shocks. Here, the increments $R_t = P_t - P_{t-1}$ may be stationary, but the price itself is not.

Even returns are not perfectly stationary:

- Average returns can change between bull and bear markets.
- Volatility regimes can shift sharply (crises, policy changes).
- Market microstructure evolves (tick sizes, liquidity).

However, returns are often *locally* stationary: over a limited window, assuming roughly constant mean and variance is a reasonable approximation. Many AI models implicitly rely on this idea by training on rolling or recent windows.

### Regime shifts and structural breaks

A *regime shift* or *structural break* is a change in the underlying data-generating process. Examples:

- A central bank announces a new policy framework, altering interest rate dynamics.
- A company enters a new business line, changing its volatility and correlation structure.
- A market transitions from floor trading to high-frequency electronic trading.

From a modeling perspective, regime shifts can invalidate parameters learned from older data. The covariance matrix you compute over the last ten years may be a poor guide to risk in the next year if a structural break has occurred.

For AI trading, this motivates:

- Emphasizing recent data in feature engineering and training.
- Including regime indicators (e.g., volatility state, macro regime) as features.
- Using backtesting and validation schemes that test robustness across multiple historical regimes, not just one favorable period.

## Temporal Dependence: Autocorrelation, Momentum, and Mean Reversion

In independent data, each observation tells you nothing about the next. Time series are different: the past often contains information about the future.

### Autocovariance and autocorrelation

For a (weakly) stationary series $\{X_t\}$, the *autocovariance* at lag $k$ is

$$\gamma(k) = \mathrm{Cov}(X_t, X_{t-k}).$$

The *autocorrelation function (ACF)* at lag $k$ is

$$\rho(k) = \frac{\gamma(k)}{\gamma(0)} = \frac{\mathrm{Cov}(X_t, X_{t-k})}{\mathrm{Var}(X_t)}.$$

$\rho(k)$ lies between $-1$ and $1$ and summarizes how strongly the series is linearly related to its own lagged values.

### Momentum-like and mean-reverting patterns

Two stylized behaviors are particularly important for trading:

- **Momentum**: positive autocorrelation (e.g., $\rho(1) > 0$) indicates that above-average returns tend to be followed by above-average returns, and vice versa. This is the statistical fingerprint of trend-following strategies.
- **Mean reversion**: negative autocorrelation ($\rho(1) < 0$) suggests that above-average returns tend to be followed by below-average returns, pulling the process back toward its mean. This underpins many statistical arbitrage and mean-reversion strategies.

In practice, the autocorrelation structure can vary by horizon and asset class. Daily returns of large liquid equities often exhibit weak autocorrelation at lag 1, but stronger patterns at longer lags or in constructed signals (e.g., moving averages, residual spreads).

### Partial autocorrelation

The *partial autocorrelation function (PACF)* at lag $k$ measures the correlation between $X_t$ and $X_{t-k}$ after removing the linear effects of the intermediate lags $1, \dots, k-1$.

Intuitively:

- A large partial autocorrelation at lag 1 means that yesterday's value directly helps predict today's value.

- If the partial autocorrelation at lag 2 is small but the ordinary autocorrelation at lag 2 is not, it suggests that the lag-2 effect is mostly mediated through lag 1.

PACF is useful for diagnosing the appropriate lag structure in autoregressive (AR) models and, by extension, for deciding how many lagged returns to include as features in an AI model.

## Volatility Clustering and Heavy Tails

If you plot returns over time, you will notice that large moves tend to cluster: quiet periods with small fluctuations alternate with stormy periods of high volatility. This *volatility clustering* is one of the most robust properties of financial time series.

**Realized and rolling volatility**

A common way to estimate volatility over a window of length $m$ is via a rolling standard deviation. For a series of returns $\{r_t\}$, define rolling volatility at time $t$ as

$$\hat{\sigma}_t = \sqrt{\frac{1}{m-1}\sum_{j=0}^{m-1}(r_{t-j} - \bar{r}_t)^2},$$

where $\bar{r}_t$ is the sample mean over the same window.

This gives a time series $\{\hat{\sigma}_t\}$ that tracks the "local" volatility. High, persistent values indicate a high-volatility regime.

In more advanced settings, models like GARCH (Generalized Autoregressive Conditional Heteroskedasticity) explicitly model conditional variance as a dynamic process, but the basic intuition is the same: volatility is not constant; it moves and clusters.

**Heavy tails and extreme moves**

Empirically, return distributions often have *heavy tails*: the probability of large absolute returns is much higher than under a normal (Gaussian) distribution with the same variance. Consequences include:

- Extreme losses (and gains) are more common than a normal model would predict.

- Sample estimates of higher moments (e.g., kurtosis) and even variance can be unstable, especially with short histories.

For AI trading, heavy tails and volatility clustering matter because:

- Models trained to minimize squared error can be disproportionately influenced by a few extreme observations.

- Backtests that ignore volatility dynamics will misestimate risk and Sharpe ratios.

- Position sizing and risk management features (e.g., volatility-scaled positions) must adapt to changing volatility to avoid blow-ups.

## A Visual Tour of Core Time-Series Properties

We now consolidate the concepts of non-stationarity, returns vs. prices, volatility clustering, and autocorrelation in a single synthetic example.

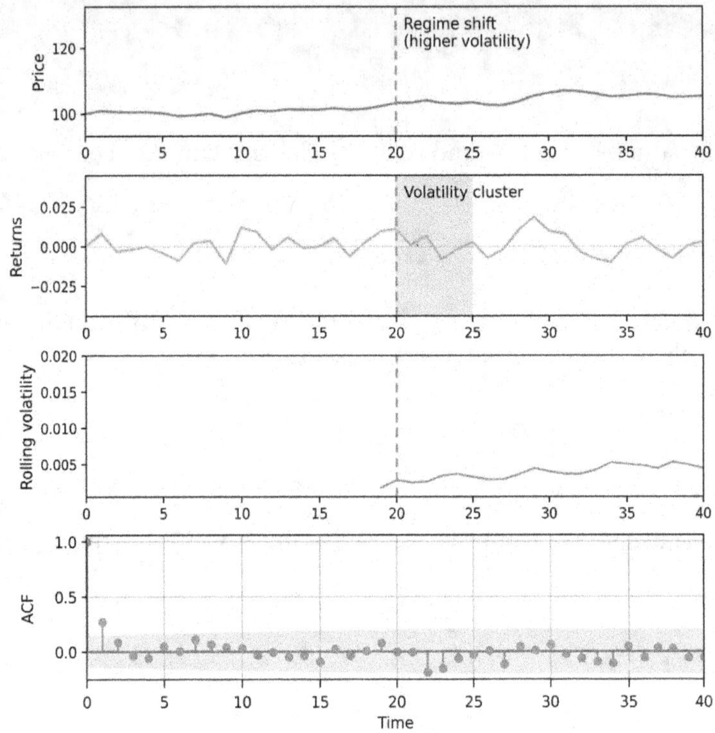


This synthetic example illustrates several key points:

- The price level is clearly non-stationary, drifting upward and changing behavior around the regime shift.
- Returns fluctuate around zero but with a visible volatility cluster in the later regime.
- Rolling volatility spikes and stays elevated in the high-volatility regime.
- The autocorrelation function shows small but non-zero dependence at short lags, consistent with mild momentum or mean-

reversion effects.

When you work with real data, you will see noisier but conceptually similar patterns.

## Seasonality and Calendar Effects

Beyond generic dependence, financial time series often show systematic patterns tied to the calendar:

- **Day-of-week effects**: average returns or volatility on Mondays may differ from Fridays.
- **Intraday patterns**: liquidity, spreads, and volatility follow characteristic shapes over the trading day (e.g., U-shaped volatility: high at open and close, lower mid-day).
- **Event-driven spikes**: earnings announcements, macro releases, and option expiries can create predictable bursts of volatility or volume.

These patterns are double-edged:

- As *features*, they can add predictive power (e.g., encoding time-of-day or days to earnings as inputs).
- As *nuisances*, they can induce overfitting: a model may learn to exploit a spurious intraday or calendar pattern that is not robust or has already been arbitraged away.

A practical approach is to:

- Visualize seasonality (e.g., average intraday volatility profile).
- Decide whether to normalize it away (e.g., divide returns by typical intraday volatility) or to model it explicitly as a feature.
- Ensure that backtests include all relevant calendar structures so the model sees realistic environments.

## From Characteristics to Features and Models

The properties described so far drive concrete decisions in AI trading workflows. We highlight a few direct links.

**Feature engineering guided by time-series structure**

Some common, time-series-aware features include:

- **Lagged returns**: $r_{t-1}, r_{t-2}, \ldots$ capture momentum or mean reversion. The number of lags should be informed by observed autocorrelation and partial autocorrelation.
- **Rolling statistics**: moving averages of returns or prices, rolling volatility, rolling skewness, or rolling correlations between assets. These capture local trends and regimes.
- **Regime indicators**: binary or continuous features that encode states such as "high volatility" vs. "low volatility", bull vs. bear regime, or spread between realized and implied volatility.
- **Calendar features**: day-of-week, time-of-day, days since last earnings, or days until options expiry.

Mathematically, each feature at time $t$ is a function of the past path $\{P_s, r_s, \cdots : s \leq t\}$ and possibly exogenous data (news, macro series). Good features respect the causal structure: nothing at time $t$ should depend on future information beyond $t$.

**Model choices shaped by dependence and non-stationarity**

Different model classes make different implicit assumptions:

- **Static linear models** (e.g., linear regression with lagged features) assume that the mapping from features to returns is stable over the training horizon. They can handle autocorrelation via features but are less adaptive to regime shifts unless you retrain frequently or use short windows.
- **Time-series models** (ARIMA, state-space models, GARCH) directly model temporal dependence and changing volatility. They are well-suited to capturing simple low-dimensional dynamics

but may miss rich nonlinear interactions in high-dimensional feature spaces.

- **Sequence models** (RNNs, LSTMs, Transformers) ingest entire histories or windows and can, in principle, learn complex temporal patterns and nonlinear interactions. However, they are more prone to overfitting, especially in noisy financial data, and demand careful regularization and validation.

Your understanding of stationarity, autocorrelation, and volatility clustering should guide:

- How long a history window you provide to the model.
- Whether you model levels, differences, or returns.
- Whether you explicitly normalize or de-volatilize inputs.

### Evaluation and backtesting with time order in mind

Unlike i.i.d. data, you cannot shuffle financial time series arbitrarily when splitting into training and test sets:

- **No look-ahead**: the test period must come strictly after the training period. Using future data to inform training or features leads to inflated performance.
- **Walk-forward (rolling) evaluation**: train on an initial window, test on the next period, then roll the window forward. This mimics how a live strategy would be updated and reveals sensitivity to regime changes.
- **Time-series cross-validation**: instead of random folds, you use forward-expanding or sliding windows that respect chronological order. This is crucial for hyperparameter tuning.

Moreover, risk and performance metrics (drawdowns, rolling Sharpe, turnover) should be computed as time series themselves, not just as single summary numbers. This helps you see how a strategy behaves in different volatility regimes and structural environments.

Financial time series are not generic datasets; they are sequences with structure:

- Prices are typically non-stationary, while returns are closer to stationary but still exhibit regime shifts.
- Temporal dependence shows up as autocorrelation, momentum, and mean reversion.
- Volatility clusters and tails are heavy, making risk time-varying and extreme events frequent.
- Seasonality and calendar effects introduce systematic patterns at daily and intraday horizons.

These characteristics shape every stage of an AI trading pipeline: what you predict (returns vs. prices), which features you construct (lags, rolling statistics, regimes), which models you choose (static vs. sequence), and how you evaluate them (walk-forward tests that respect time).

In the next section, we will connect these time-series realities to the mechanics of optimization: how to train models on noisy, dependent, and regime-shifting financial data in a way that balances in-sample fit with out-of-sample robustness.

## 1.3 Optimization Principles for Model Training

The previous sections gave you the mathematical vocabulary (vectors, gradients, expectations) and an understanding of how financial time series behave (non-stationarity, autocorrelation, volatility clustering). We now bring these together to study *optimization*: the process of choosing model parameters to fit historical data.

Whenever you train an AI model—from a simple linear predictor of returns to a deep network processing order book states—you are solving an optimization problem. The details of that optimization, and how it interacts with noisy, regime-shifting market data, strongly influence whether the resulting strategy is robust or brittle.

This section focuses on three pillars:

- **Loss functions and optimization landscapes**: what you are minimizing and what the geometry of that objective looks like.
- **Gradient-based algorithms and regularization**: how parameters are updated and how complexity is controlled.
- **Convergence diagnostics and validation**: how to tell if optimization has "worked" in the sense relevant for trading, not just for in-sample fit.

Throughout, keep the core practical question in mind: *how do my optimization choices affect out-of-sample Sharpe, drawdowns, and stability?*

## Loss Functions: What Are We Optimizing For?

A loss function maps model predictions and observed outcomes into a scalar that we seek to minimize. Formally, if $f_\theta(x)$ is a model with parameters $\theta$ and input $x$, and $y$ is the target (e.g., future return), then the loss on a single observation is

$$\ell(\theta; x, y).$$

Over a dataset $\{(x_t, y_t)\}_{t=1}^{T}$, the empirical loss is typically

$$L(\theta) = \frac{1}{T} \sum_{t=1}^{T} \ell(\theta; x_t, y_t).$$

### Standard regression losses

For predicting continuous outcomes such as next-period return or spread, the most common choice is squared error:

$$\ell(\theta; x_t, y_t) = \big(y_t - f_\theta(x_t)\big)^2.$$

This penalizes large prediction errors heavily and is mathematically convenient: its gradient and Hessian are simple.

However, squared error implicitly assumes that large positive and negative residuals are equally undesirable and that residuals are roughly Gaussian. In heavy-tailed financial data, you may prefer more robust losses, such as the Huber loss (quadratic near zero, linear in the tails) or absolute error:

$$\ell(\theta; x_t, y_t) = |y_t - f_\theta(x_t)|.$$

These alternatives reduce the influence of outliers (e.g., crisis days) on parameter estimates.

### Classification and ranking losses

If you only care about direction (up vs. down) or a discrete label (e.g., decile bucket), classification losses are natural. For binary direction prediction with labels $y_t \in \{0, 1\}$ and predicted probabilities $p_t = f_\theta(x_t)$, a standard loss is cross-entropy:

$$\ell(\theta; x_t, y_t) = -\big(y_t \log p_t + (1 - y_t) \log(1 - p_t)\big).$$

For portfolios constructed via ranking or sorting (e.g., long top-decile predicted returns, short bottom-decile), you might optimize a ranking loss such as pairwise hinge loss or a differentiable approximation to the information coefficient.

### Trading-aware custom objectives

Crucially, the loss need not be purely statistical. You can embed trading considerations directly into the objective. Examples include:

- **Risk-adjusted loss**: incorporate variance of model-driven P&L into the objective, approximating a negative Sharpe ratio.
- **Transaction costs and turnover**: penalize parameter configurations that induce excessively frequent position changes.
- **Asymmetric penalties**: weight downside prediction errors more heavily than upside, reflecting risk aversion.

Mathematically, you might define

$$L(\theta) = \mathbb{E}\Big[\underbrace{\ell_{pred}(\theta; x_t, y_t)}_{\text{predictive error}} + \lambda_{risk} \cdot \underbrace{g_{risk}(\theta; x_{\leq t})}_{\text{risk term}} + \lambda_{tc} \cdot \underbrace{g_{tc}(\theta; x_{\leq t})}_{\text{turnover/cost}}\Big],$$

and approximate the expectation with a time-series average. The choice of $\lambda_{risk}, \lambda_{tc}$ becomes part of your model design.

## Convexity, Non-Convexity, and Landscape Geometry

Once you define a loss function, you have implicitly defined a surface $L(\theta)$ in parameter space. The geometry of this surface influences how easy optimization is and how interpretable the solution is.

### Convex objectives

A function $L(\theta)$ is convex if for all $\theta_1, \theta_2$ and $\alpha \in [0, 1]$,

$$L(\alpha\theta_1 + (1 - \alpha)\theta_2) \leq \alpha L(\theta_1) + (1 - \alpha)L(\theta_2).$$

Geometrically, the line segment between any two points on the graph lies above the graph.

Why convexity matters:

- Any local minimum is a global minimum.
- Gradient-based methods are guaranteed (under mild conditions) to converge to the global optimum.
- Solutions are typically unique or lie in a convex set, aiding interpretability.

Linear models with convex losses (e.g., squared error) plus convex regularizers (e.g., L1, L2) are classic examples. For instance, ridge regression and lasso are convex optimization problems.

In trading, convex models are attractive as baseline predictors or risk models: you understand exactly what loss you are minimizing, and there are fewer "mystery" local minima.

### Non-convex landscapes

Deep networks, tree-based ensembles, and many custom architectures common in AI trading create highly non-convex objectives. These landscapes may contain:

- Many local minima and saddle points.
- Flat regions (plateaus) where gradients are small.
- Sharp valleys where the loss changes quickly along some directions and slowly along others.

Yet, in large-scale machine learning people still find good solutions with gradient-based methods. Why?

- In high dimensions, many local minima can be "good enough" in terms of out-of-sample performance.
- Stochastic gradient noise (due to sampling mini-batches) helps escape shallow local minima and saddle points.

For trading, the key point is that a near-optimal *in-sample* minimum is not necessarily desirable if it corresponds to a sharp, overfit solution that generalizes poorly. The shape of the minimum (sharp vs. flat) and the amount of regularization become more important than reaching the absolute lowest possible loss.

## Gradient-Based Algorithms Under Market Noise

With a loss function in hand, the workhorse of modern optimization is gradient descent and its variants. You rarely need to implement these manually, but understanding the mechanics helps you choose hyperparameters and interpret behavior.

### Batch, stochastic, and mini-batch gradient descent

For an empirical loss

$$L(\theta) = \frac{1}{T}\sum_{t=1}^{T} \ell(\theta; x_t, y_t),$$

the full gradient is

$$\nabla L(\theta) = \frac{1}{T}\sum_{t=1}^{T} \nabla_\theta \ell(\theta; x_t, y_t).$$

- **Batch gradient descent**: compute the gradient over the entire dataset at each step and update

  $$\theta^{(k+1)} = \theta^{(k)} - \eta \nabla L(\theta^{(k)}),$$

  where $\eta$ is the learning rate. This is stable but expensive for large datasets.

- **Stochastic gradient descent (SGD)**: at each step, sample a single observation $t$ and use

  $$\theta^{(k+1)} = \theta^{(k)} - \eta \nabla_\theta \ell(\theta^{(k)}; x_t, y_t).$$

  This is noisy but cheap per step.

- **Mini-batch SGD**: compromise using a small batch $\mathcal{B}_k$ of observations:

  $$\theta^{(k+1)} = \theta^{(k)} - \eta \frac{1}{|\mathcal{B}_k|} \sum_{t\in\mathcal{B}_k} \nabla_\theta \ell(\theta^{(k)}; x_t, y_t).$$

In financial time series, observations are temporally dependent and often autocorrelated. This has several implications:

- Randomly shuffling time series for mini-batching can break temporal structure if you are not careful with features (e.g., leakage via overlapping windows). However, when features at time $t$ only depend on past information, shuffling inputs for optimization is usually acceptable as long as evaluation respects time order.

- Nearby observations carry similar information. Updating several times in a row on highly correlated data can lead to redundant steps and slow learning.

A common compromise in practice is to form mini-batches from consecutive time blocks across many instruments, or from non-overlapping time windows, to reduce correlation within batches.

### Adaptive methods: Adam and friends

Simple SGD uses a fixed learning rate $\eta$. Adaptive methods like Adam maintain per-parameter learning rates based on moving averages of past gradients and squared gradients. The update rule schematically is

$$\theta^{(k+1)} = \theta^{(k)} - \eta \frac{\hat{m}^{(k)}}{\sqrt{\hat{v}^{(k)}} + \epsilon},$$

where $\hat{m}^{(k)}$ and $\hat{v}^{(k)}$ are bias-corrected estimates of the first and second moments of gradients.

Advantages in trading contexts:

- Parameters with consistently large gradients (sensitive directions) receive smaller effective step sizes.
- Parameters with small gradients (flat directions) can be updated more aggressively.
- Training becomes less sensitive to the choice of a global learning rate.

However, adaptive methods can sometimes overfit small noisy datasets more easily if not regularized and validated carefully. It is good practice to compare adaptive optimizers to plain SGD with momentum for your specific problem.

### Learning rate schedules

The learning rate $\eta$ controls the step size in parameter space:

- Too large: updates overshoot minima and cause divergence or oscillation.
- Too small: convergence is painfully slow and may get stuck in shallow regions.

Because financial data are noisy and often scarce at high quality, you rarely benefit from very long training times with minuscule learning rates. Instead, simple schedules work well:

- Fixed $\eta$ tuned by validation.
- Step decay: reduce $\eta$ by a factor (e.g., 0.1) after validation loss plateaus.
- Cosine or exponential decay over epochs.

Always tune $\eta$ and schedule with a time-series-aware validation scheme; what looks like convergence under one regime may deteriorate sharply when evaluated on another.

## Regularization: Guarding Against Overfitting Scarce Alpha

Optimization algorithms will happily minimize in-sample loss, even if the resulting model chases noise. Regularization modifies the objective to discourage overly complex or unstable solutions.

### L2 (ridge) and L1 (lasso) penalties

Suppose your base loss is $L(\theta)$. An *L2-regularized* objective is

$$L_\lambda^{(L2)}(\theta) = L(\theta) + \lambda \|\theta\|_2^2,$$

where $\lambda \geq 0$ is the regularization strength.

Interpretation:

- Penalizes large weights; shrinks coefficients toward zero.

- Distributes shrinkage smoothly across parameters.
- For linear models, often improves stability of predictions, especially when features are correlated (a common situation in finance).

An *L1-regularized* objective is

$$L_{\lambda}^{(L1)}(\theta) = L(\theta) + \lambda\|\theta\|_1 = L(\theta) + \lambda \sum_j |\theta_j|.$$

L1 has the important property of inducing sparsity: many coefficients become exactly zero. In an AI trading context:

- Sparse linear models effectively perform feature selection, which can be useful when you have many candidate signals (factors) but limited data.
- Sparse models are easier to interpret and may be more robust if many features are weak or redundant.

The *elastic net* combines both:

$$L_{\lambda_1,\lambda_2}^{(EN)}(\theta) = L(\theta) + \lambda_1\|\theta\|_1 + \lambda_2\|\theta\|_2^2,$$

balancing sparsity and smooth shrinkage.

### Regularization beyond penalties

Other forms of regularization are embedded in model structure or training protocol:

- **Dropout** in neural networks: randomly zero out activations during training to prevent co-adaptation.
- **Weight constraints**: explicitly bounding weights or using spectral norm constraints to limit sensitivity to inputs.
- **Data augmentation**: in non-textual contexts (e.g., order book images), augmenting the training data to encourage invariance.

- **Smaller models**: choosing architectures with fewer parameters or shallower depth.

In noisy financial data with limited truly independent observations, simpler models with strong regularization often outperform complex ones with weak regularization, once transaction costs and implementation frictions are accounted for.

### Early stopping as regularization

Early stopping views optimization as a path: as you iterate, the model moves from underfitting (high training and validation loss) through a sweet spot (lower validation loss) to overfitting (training loss continues to decrease while validation loss worsens).

The procedure:

- Train the model and monitor loss on a validation set that respects time order (e.g., train on earlier data, validate on a subsequent period).
- Track the epoch $k^*$ where validation loss is minimized.
- Stop training when validation loss has not improved for a prespecified patience window, and keep parameters from epoch $k^*$.

Interpretation in trading terms:

- Early stopping limits the model's capacity to fit idiosyncratic noise in the training history, much like an implicit L2 penalty.
- It adapts to the effective noise level of your data: noisier series tend to reach the overfitting point earlier.

Crucially, validation sets must be chronologically later than training data. Using future data to tune stopping time introduces look-ahead bias.

## Convergence Diagnostics: Did Training "Work"?

Optimization is not an end in itself. You care about whether the resulting model generalizes and produces acceptable trading performance. Still, it is important to assess whether optimization has reached a sensible region of the loss landscape.

### Training vs. validation curves

Plotting the loss (or an equivalent metric) over epochs for both training and validation sets provides deep insight:

- **Underfitting**: both training and validation loss remain high and decrease only slowly. The model is too simple or the learning rate too low.
- **Good fit**: training loss decreases; validation loss decreases and then levels off around a reasonably low value.
- **Overfitting**: training loss continues to decrease while validation loss bottoms out and then increases. The model is fitting noise in the training data.

In finance, you should complement generic losses with trading metrics:

- Track information coefficient (IC) or rank correlation between predictions and realized returns over time.
- Track approximate out-of-sample Sharpe or hit rate on the validation period.

You may find that the epoch with minimum validation loss does not correspond to maximum validation Sharpe, especially if your loss does not directly encode risk. In that case, you might define a composite validation metric or use multi-objective criteria.

### Gradient and parameter diagnostics

Beyond loss curves, inspect:

- **Gradient norms**: if they explode (very large) or vanish (near zero) early in training, your learning rate or initialization may be problematic.
- **Parameter norms**: very large weights often signal overfitting or an unregularized model chasing noise.
- **Sensitivity to initialization**: if different random seeds produce wildly different validation performance, the optimization landscape may have many qualitatively distinct minima, and your procedure may be unstable.

Simple checks like clipping gradients, reducing learning rates, or increasing regularization often stabilize training.

## Time-Series-Aware Validation and Robustness

Because financial data are sequential and non-stationary, classical i.i.d. cross-validation (randomly shuffling observations into folds) is inappropriate. Your convergence diagnostics and model selection must reflect time order.

### Rolling and expanding window schemes

Two common validation patterns are:

- **Expanding window**: train on data from times $1$ to $t$, validate on $t+1$ to $t+h$; then expand the training set to $1$ to $t+h$, validate on the next block, and so on.
- **Rolling window**: train on a fixed-length window $t-w+1$ to $t$, validate on $t+1$ to $t+h$; then roll both windows forward.

These schemes mimic how a live strategy would be trained and deployed and allow you to see:

- How sensitive optimization is to the choice of training window.
- How hyperparameters (e.g., regularization strength, learning rate) perform across regimes.

### Hyperparameter tuning with time-respecting splits

Hyperparameters such as $\lambda$ in regularization, network depth, or learning rate schedule should be chosen using multiple out-of-sample validation periods, not just a single split. A typical workflow:

- Define a grid or search space over hyperparameters.
- For each candidate, run a walk-forward evaluation over several contiguous time blocks.
- Aggregate a trading-relevant metric (e.g., median Sharpe across blocks) and choose configurations that perform consistently, not just spectacularly in one period.

This process is computationally demanding, but it is essential for avoiding subtle overfitting to a single historical regime.

## From Optimization to Trading Outcomes

Finally, link back to what really matters: the behavior of the live trading strategy.

Optimization choices influence:

- **Out-of-sample Sharpe**: aggressive, weakly regularized models may achieve lower in-sample loss but often deliver lower or unstable Sharpe out-of-sample.
- **Turnover and costs**: if the loss ignores costs and regularization does not penalize rapid changes, optimization may favor highly volatile predictions, leading to excessive trading.
- **Drawdowns and tail risk**: models that ignore volatility clustering or heavy tails may be calibrated to typical conditions and fail badly in crises; incorporating volatility-aware losses or constraints can mitigate this.

A useful mindset is to treat optimization as a controlled experiment:

- Change one aspect (e.g., add L2 regularization, alter learning rate schedule).
- Re-run time-series-aware backtests.
- Examine not only average metrics (mean return, Sharpe) but also distributional properties (drawdowns, sensitivity to regimes).

Over time, you will develop intuition for how different optimization and regularization settings imprint themselves on the trading characteristics of your strategies.

In this section, we reframed model training as an optimization problem shaped by:

- The **loss function**, which encodes what you care about (prediction accuracy, risk, costs).
- The **optimization landscape**, convex or non-convex, which determines how difficult it is to find good parameters.
- **Gradient-based algorithms** and **regularization**, which control how you traverse that landscape and how complex a model you allow.
- **Convergence diagnostics** and **time-series-aware validation**, which tell you whether training has produced a model that generalizes across regimes rather than memorizing a single historical path.

Armed with these principles, you can move beyond "push-button" training and start to deliberately shape your optimization procedure to produce AI trading models that are not only statistically sound but also operationally robust and economically meaningful. The next section will connect these ideas to a concrete computational environment in Python, showing how to implement reproducible, scalable workflows that respect both the mathematics and the time-series realities we have covered so far.

# 1.4 Python Toolkit for Quant Research

The previous sections developed the mathematical language of AI trading and showed how optimization operates on noisy financial time series. We now turn to the practical question: *how do you implement all of this in a way that is efficient, reproducible, and scalable?*

In modern quantitative research, the de facto standard stack is:

- **Python** as the high-level orchestration language.
- **NumPy** for fast numerical operations on arrays.
- **Pandas** for labeled time-series and panel data.
- **scikit-learn** for classical machine learning models and pipelines.

This section explains how these tools fit together into a disciplined workflow. We start with environment and project structure, then move through each library in turn, and finish with a cohesive example.

## A Robust Python Environment for Research

Before writing a single line of model code, it is worth standardizing your computational environment. This reduces "it works on my machine" problems and makes backtests reproducible months later.

### Virtual environments and dependency pinning

A *virtual environment* isolates the Python interpreter and installed packages for a given project. Common choices are venv, conda, or tools like pipenv and poetry.

In a terminal, you might create and activate a venv environment as follows:

```
python -m venv env
source env/bin/activate # On Windows: env\Scripts\activate
pip install numpy pandas scikit-learn matplotlib
```

To make your work reproducible:

- Record exact versions of packages in a requirements.txt or environment.yml.
- Commit this file to version control (e.g., git).
- When rerunning an old experiment, recreate the environment from this file.

This is especially important in AI trading, where small changes in dependencies (e.g., a different scikit-learn version) can change model defaults and subtly alter backtest results.

**Project structure: separating research and production**

A simple project layout that scales well is:

```
project_root/
  data/
    raw/
    processed/
  notebooks/
  src/
    features/
    models/
    backtests/
    utils/
  config/
  results/
    logs/
    figures/
    reports/
  requirements.txt
```

Guiding principles:

- Keep *one-off exploration* in notebooks under notebooks/.
- Put *reusable code* (feature builders, model wrappers, evaluation utilities) in importable Python modules under src/.
- Store *intermediate datasets* (e.g., aligned returns and features) in data/processed/ so you can decouple data preparation from modeling.
- Save *experiment artifacts* (metrics, plots, configuration files) in results/.

This structure makes it straightforward to rerun a backtest, change a single component (e.g., a model), and compare results in a controlled way.

## NumPy: Fast Numerical Foundations

NumPy provides the multidimensional array type and vectorized operations that underlie most performance-critical work in Python-based quant research.

### Arrays as the basic numeric container

Conceptually, a NumPy array ndarray is the concrete implementation of the vectors and matrices we discussed earlier. For example, a matrix of returns with shape $(T, n)$ can be represented as:

```
import numpy as np

# T days, n assets
returns = np.random.randn(T, n) * 0.01 # synthetic daily returns
```

Key properties:

- returns.shape gives the dimensions $(T, n)$.
- Operations like np.mean(returns, axis=0) compute the mean by column (per-asset).
- Broadcasting rules let you apply transformations across portfolios or features without explicit Python loops.

### Vectorized computations and broadcasting

Vectorization replaces slow Python loops with compiled C operations. For example, computing portfolio returns given an array of weights:

```
# weights shape: (n,)
portfolio_ret = returns @ weights # shape: (T,)
```

NumPy also supports broadcasting—automatically expanding arrays with compatible shapes. This is particularly useful for portfolio-level transforms:

```
# De-mean each asset's returns
demeaned = returns - returns.mean(axis=0, keepdims=True)

# Volatility-scale each asset's returns
vol = returns.std(axis=0, ddof=1, keepdims=True) # shape: (1, n)
scaled = returns / vol
```

Broadcasting allows these operations to be written in a concise, mathematically transparent way that mirrors formulas like

$$\tilde{\mathbf{r}}_t = \frac{\mathbf{r}_t - \mu}{\sigma}.$$

### Random number generation for simulations

Many backtesting and risk analyses rely on Monte Carlo simulation (e.g., simulating return paths, bootstrapping blocks of historical data). NumPy's random module provides high-quality pseudorandom numbers:

```
rng = np.random.default_rng(seed=42)
simulated_returns = rng.normal(loc=0.0005, scale=0.01, size=(T, n))
```

By fixing the seed, you make simulations reproducible: the same script will generate identical random sequences, which is crucial for comparing strategies fairly.

## Pandas: Labeled Time-Series and Panel Data

While NumPy excels at raw numerical speed, it lacks labels for rows and columns. Pandas builds on NumPy to provide *Series* and *DataFrame* objects that understand time indices and asset identifiers.

### Series and DataFrames with time indices

A Series is a one-dimensional labeled array; a DataFrame is a two-dimensional table with labeled rows and columns.

For example, daily prices for one asset:

```
import pandas as pd

dates = pd.date_range("2020-01-01", periods=T, freq="B") # business days
price = pd.Series(data=some_price_array, index=dates, name="XYZ")
```

Multiple assets form a DataFrame:

```
prices = pd.DataFrame(data=price_matrix, index=dates, columns=asset_ids)
```

Advantages over raw NumPy:

- Time alignment is automatic when you add, subtract, or join series.
- Missing data is handled explicitly with NaN values.
- Time-based indexing and slicing (e.g., by date ranges) is intuitive.

### Multi-index for cross-section and time

In AI trading, you often work with panel data: returns and features for many assets across many dates. Pandas supports a *MultiIndex* (hierarchical index) to organize such data:

```
tuples = [(date, asset) for date in dates for asset in asset_ids]
index = pd.MultiIndex.from_tuples(tuples, names=["date", "asset"])

df = pd.DataFrame({
    "return": returns.flatten(),
    "feature1": feature1.flatten(),
}, index=index)
```

Now you can:

- Slice by date: df.loc["2020-03-16"] gives the cross-section on that day.
- Slice by asset: df.xs("AAPL", level="asset") gives the time series for one asset.
- Group by asset or date to compute aggregated statistics:

```
# Per-asset mean return
mean_by_asset = df["return"].groupby("asset").mean()

# Cross-sectional std of a feature each day
cs_std = df["feature1"].groupby("date").std()
```

This structure maps naturally to the way we think about returns matrices $R_{t,i}$ and feature matrices $X_{t,i,j}$.

### Resampling and rolling windows

Resampling changes the frequency of a time series (e.g., from daily to monthly). Rolling operations compute windowed statistics (e.g., 20-day volatility):

```
# Monthly returns from daily prices
monthly_ret = prices["XYZ"].resample("M").last().pct_change()

# 20-day rolling volatility
rolling_vol = returns["XYZ"].rolling(window=20).std(ddof=1)
```

For panel data with a MultiIndex, you typically group by asset and then apply rolling:

```
def rolling_volatility(x, window=20):
    return x.rolling(window).std(ddof=1)

df["roll_vol"] = (
    df["return"]
    .groupby("asset")
    .apply(rolling_volatility, window=20)
)
```

These operations are the building blocks of many features (moving averages, volatility estimates, rolling betas).

### Aligning features and labels without look-ahead

Pandas' alignment behavior encourages explicit handling of time shifts. For example, to create a one-day-ahead return as a label:

```
df["ret_fwd_1d"] = (
    df["return"]
    .groupby("asset")
    .shift(-1) # move one day earlier: label at t is return at t+1
)
```

By using shift and grouping by asset, you avoid accidentally leaking future information into features. When you later drop rows with missing labels (NaN at the end of each series), you ensure all sample pairs (features at time $t$, label at time $t+1$) are causal.

## scikit-learn: Models and Pipelines

scikit-learn provides a consistent interface for classical supervised learning algorithms and preprocessing. It is particularly useful for baseline models, feature scaling, and time-series-aware cross-validation.

### The estimator API

Most scikit-learn models follow a simple pattern:

- est = ModelClass(**hyperparams)
- est.fit(X_train, y_train)
- y_pred = est.predict(X_test)

Here, $X$ is a 2D NumPy array or Pandas DataFrame of shape $(n_{samples}, n_{features})$, and $y$ is a 1D array of labels.

For example, a ridge regression predicting next-day returns from features:

```
from sklearn.linear_model import Ridge

model = Ridge(alpha=1.0)
model.fit(X_train, y_train)
y_pred = model.predict(X_test)
```

The internal optimization (e.g., solving a convex least-squares problem) is handled by scikit-learn.

### Preprocessing with Pipelines

Scaling and transforming features consistently across training and test sets is critical. Pipeline chains preprocessing steps with a final estimator:

```
from sklearn.pipeline import Pipeline
from sklearn.preprocessing import StandardScaler
from sklearn.linear_model import Lasso

pipe = Pipeline(steps=[
    ("scale", StandardScaler()),
    ("model", Lasso(alpha=0.001)),
])
```

```
pipe.fit(X_train, y_train)
y_pred = pipe.predict(X_test)
```

Advantages:

- Ensures that scaling is fit only on training data and then applied to test data (no leakage).
- Simplifies hyperparameter tuning; you can vary both preprocessing and model parameters in one object.
- Makes the entire transformation and prediction process serializable (e.g., via joblib) for deployment.

### Time-series-aware cross-validation

Standard scikit-learn cross-validation utilities assume i.i.d. data and random splits, which are inappropriate for time series. Instead, use TimeSeriesSplit or custom generators that respect chronological order:

```
from sklearn.model_selection import TimeSeriesSplit
from sklearn.metrics import r2_score

tscv = TimeSeriesSplit(n_splits=5)

scores = []
for train_idx, test_idx in tscv.split(X):
    X_tr, X_te = X[train_idx], X[test_idx]
    y_tr, y_te = y[train_idx], y[test_idx]

    pipe.fit(X_tr, y_tr)
    y_pred = pipe.predict(X_te)
    scores.append(r2_score(y_te, y_pred))
```

This pattern can be adapted to trading-specific metrics by replacing r2_score with, for example, a function that computes information coefficient or pseudo-Sharpe on the validation slice.

## Putting It All Together: A Minimal Research Workflow

To illustrate how these tools interoperate, consider a stripped-down but realistic workflow:

- Load raw prices for multiple assets.
- Compute returns and basic time-series features.
- Align features and future returns into a supervised learning dataset.
- Train a regularized linear model using time-series cross-validation.
- Evaluate out-of-sample performance and store results.

### Step 1–2: Data loading and feature construction

```
import numpy as np
import pandas as pd
from pathlib import Path

data_dir = Path("data")

# Example: prices.csv with columns: date, asset, price
prices = pd.read_csv(data_dir / "prices.csv", parse_dates=["date"])
prices = prices.pivot(index="date", columns="asset", values="price")

# Compute daily returns
returns = prices.pct_change().dropna(how="all")

# Construct a MultiIndex DataFrame
df = returns.stack().to_frame("return")
df.index.names = ["date", "asset"]

# Add 5-day and 20-day moving averages of returns as features
for window in [5, 20]:
    df[f"ma_ret_{window}"] = (
        df["return"]
        .groupby("asset")
        .rolling(window)
        .mean()
        .reset_index(level=0, drop=True)
    )

# Add 20-day rolling volatility
df["vol_20"] = (
    df["return"]
    .groupby("asset")
    .rolling(20)
    .std(ddof=1)
    .reset_index(level=0, drop=True)
)
```

### Step 3: Labels with proper alignment

```
# One-day-ahead return as label
df["ret_fwd_1d"] = (
    df["return"]
    .groupby("asset")
    .shift(-1)
)

# Drop rows with missing features or labels
df = df.dropna()
```

At this point, each row corresponds to an (date, asset) pair with feature values computed from information up to that date and a label equal to the next day's return.

### Step 4: Model training with time-series cross-validation

```
from sklearn.pipeline import Pipeline
from sklearn.preprocessing import StandardScaler
from sklearn.linear_model import Ridge
from sklearn.model_selection import TimeSeriesSplit

# Convert to design matrix (flatten MultiIndex)
X = df[["ma_ret_5", "ma_ret_20", "vol_20"]].values
y = df["ret_fwd_1d"].values

pipe = Pipeline([
    ("scale", StandardScaler()),
    ("model", Ridge(alpha=10.0)),
])

tscv = TimeSeriesSplit(n_splits=5)
val_ic = []

for train_idx, test_idx in tscv.split(X):
    X_tr, X_te = X[train_idx], X[test_idx]
    y_tr, y_te = y[train_idx], y[test_idx]

    pipe.fit(X_tr, y_tr)
    y_pred = pipe.predict(X_te)

    # Compute simple information coefficient (Pearson correlation)
    ic = np.corrcoef(y_te, y_pred)[0, 1]
    val_ic.append(ic)

avg_ic = np.mean(val_ic)
print("Average validation IC:", avg_ic)
```

This small example demonstrates:

- NumPy arrays as the underlying numeric representation.
- Pandas for alignment, rolling features, and label construction

without look-ahead.

- scikit-learn pipelines for standardized preprocessing and modeling.
- Time-series-aware cross-validation for a more realistic assessment of predictive power.

**Step 5: Logging results for reproducibility**

Even in early research, you should log key artifacts:

- Hyperparameters (e.g., ridge alpha, look-back windows).
- Validation metrics (e.g., average IC, per-split ICs).
- Code version (e.g., git commit hash).

This can be as simple as writing a JSON or CSV file under results/logs/, or as elaborate as integrating with experiment tracking tools. The goal is that you can later answer: "What exactly produced this backtest?"

Python, NumPy, Pandas, and scikit-learn form a powerful, coherent toolkit for AI trading research:

- Python provides the glue language and rich ecosystem.
- NumPy implements the array operations that realize the linear algebra and probability concepts from earlier sections.
- Pandas brings time and asset labels, enabling clean construction of returns, rolling features, and aligned labels while avoiding look-ahead.
- scikit-learn offers a consistent interface for models, preprocessing, and time-series cross-validation.

Combined with a disciplined environment setup, clear project structure, and careful logging, these tools let you translate mathematical ideas into reproducible backtests and, eventually, deployable AI trading strategies. In later chapters, we will build on this foundation to incorporate richer signals, including NLP-based features and alternative data, into the same standardized research pipeline.

# Chapter 2

# Market Structure, Alpha, and Research Framework

*Most AI trading projects fail not because the models are weak, but because the market story behind them is shallow. In this chapter, you will learn what is actually being traded, how prices emerge from the microstructure of modern markets, and how professional researchers frame, test, and harden alpha ideas. By the end, you will see that a robust research workflow-not a clever notebook-is what separates a fragile backtest from a durable trading edge.*

## 2.1 Asset Classes and Market Microstructure

Before we can talk about alpha, models, or NLP signals, we need to be precise about what we are trading and how trades are actually executed. An AI model never interacts with "the market" in the abstract. It interacts with a specific instrument (say, a large-cap U.S. stock or a Bitcoin perpetual swap), through a specific market structure (a limit order book, a dealer, or an RFQ system), with specific frictions (spreads, depth, fees, and latency). This section introduces the main asset classes and instruments, then connects them to the plumbing of modern markets—the microstructure that determines whether a seemingly profitable signal can be monetized in practice.

## The Investable Universe: Major Asset Classes and Instruments

At a high level, most AI-driven strategies in practice operate in one or more of the following asset classes:

- **Equities** (stocks and equity indices)
- **Fixed income** (bonds and interest-rate products)
- **Derivatives** (options, futures, swaps)
- **Foreign exchange** (FX spot and forwards)
- **Cryptoassets** (tokens, stablecoins, DeFi governance coins)

Each asset class has its own conventions, payoff structures, liquidity patterns, and typical trading venues. Understanding these differences is essential when you design a prediction target (returns over 5 minutes, 1 day, or 1 month) and choose an execution strategy that your models can actually support.

**Equities.**

Equities represent ownership in a company. The simplest instruments are common stocks such as large-cap U.S. names (Apple, Microsoft) or microcap stocks with smaller market capitalization and thinner trading. You may also trade equity indices (e.g., S&P 500) via index futures or ETFs.

From an AI-research perspective, equities are attractive because:

- They usually trade on centralized limit order book exchanges.
- Data (prices, volumes, news, filings) is rich and relatively clean.

- There is a long history of cross-sectional and time-series predictability at daily and intraday horizons.

However, liquidity varies widely: a signal that works on large-cap stocks might be impossible to trade in microcaps without large price impact.

**Fixed income.**

Fixed income instruments are promises to pay cash flows in the future. The basic building block is a bond, with:

- *Coupon payments* at fixed intervals.
- *Principal repayment* at maturity.

Within bonds, we often distinguish:

- **On-the-run** government bonds: the most recently issued bond for a given maturity (e.g., the current 10-year U.S. Treasury). These tend to be very liquid.
- **Off-the-run** bonds: older issues with the same or similar maturity, typically less liquid and with wider bid–ask spreads.

Corporate bonds, municipal bonds, and securitized products (MBS, ABS) broaden the universe, but many trade in dealer or RFQ markets, not on a central order book. For AI strategies, this means limited intraday price transparency and episodic liquidity: your model may predict long-term relative value but cannot assume instant, frictionless execution.

**Derivatives.**

Derivatives are contracts whose value depends on an underlying asset or index. Common examples:

- **Futures** on equity indices, interest rates, commodities, or crypto. These are standardized, centrally cleared contracts with defined expiries.

- **Options** (listed or OTC) that give the right, but not the obligation, to buy (call) or sell (put) an underlying asset at a strike price before or at expiry.
- **Swaps** (often OTC) that exchange cash flows, such as fixed-for-floating interest payments.

Derivatives often amplify leverage and offer richer payoff structures (convexity, optionality), but they also introduce additional microstructure features: margin requirements, funding rates, exchange-specific rules, and sometimes discrete trading hours.

**Foreign exchange (FX).**

The FX market is the market for currency pairs, such as EUR/USD or USD/JPY. Key instruments:

- **Spot FX**: standard settlement (e.g., T+2) of currencies.
- **Forwards** and **swaps**: agreements to exchange currencies at a future date at a pre-agreed rate.

FX is predominantly an OTC market with a hybrid structure: major currencies are traded on electronic platforms with limit order books and also via dealers and RFQ systems. Liquidity is deep for major pairs, but fragmented across venues and idiosyncratic for emerging markets.

**Cryptoassets.**

Crypto markets trade digital tokens on public blockchains. Examples:

- **Layer-1 tokens** (e.g., BTC, ETH) that secure a base blockchain.
- **DeFi governance coins** that confer voting rights over decentralized protocols.
- **Stablecoins** pegged to fiat currencies.

Many crypto instruments trade on centralized exchanges with limit order books, while others trade via automated market makers (AMMs) on decentralized exchanges. Crypto is typically 24/7, globally accessible, and often highly volatile, which has direct implications for latency-sensitive strategies and risk management.

## From Asset Classes to Market Plumbing

So far, we have focused on "what" you can trade. Now we connect that to "how" it is traded: the market microstructure. Two strategies with identical predictive skill can have very different realized performance depending on:

- where orders are sent (exchange vs. dealer),
- how they are expressed (market vs. limit orders, RFQs),
- and what kind of liquidity is available (depth, spreads, frequency of trades).

In AI-driven trading, this connection is critical. NLP or alternative data signals often have a short shelf life: if your microstructure assumptions are unrealistic, the edge evaporates between prediction and fill.

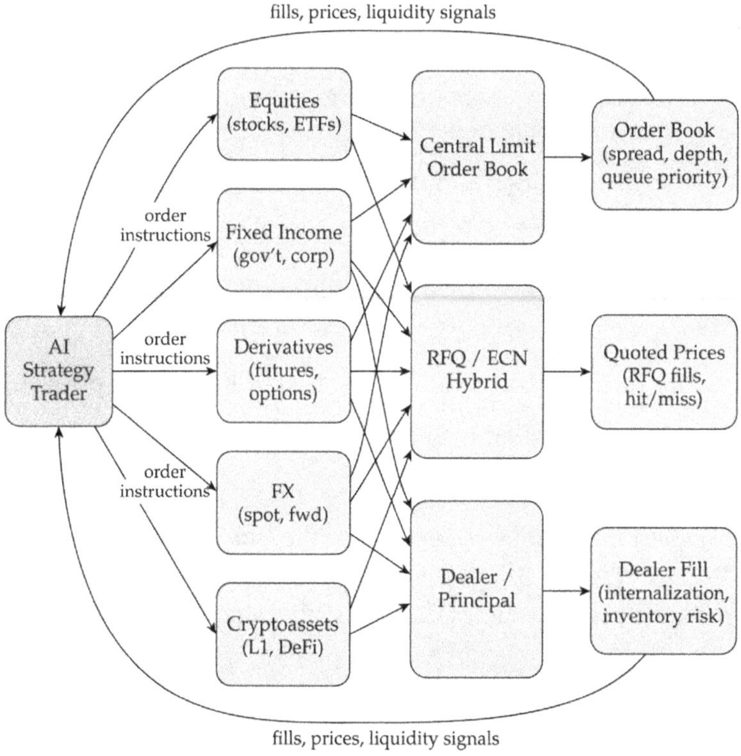


## Core Market Structures

Broadly, modern markets implement trading via three archetypal structures:

- Central limit order books (CLOBs)
- Request-for-quote (RFQ) and hybrid platforms
- Dealer or principal markets

Most real markets are hybrids, but thinking in these pure types helps you reason about what your strategy actually faces.

### Central Limit Order Books

In a CLOB, all participants can submit:

- **Limit orders**: "Buy 1,000 shares at $100 or better" or "Sell 500 shares at $100.50 or better."
- **Market orders**: "Buy 1,000 shares now at the best available prices."

The exchange aggregates all active limit orders into an *order book*, with:

- *Bids* on one side (buy interest, sorted by descending price).
- *Asks* (or offers) on the other (sell interest, sorted by ascending price).

The highest bid and lowest ask define the **bid–ask spread**. Trades occur whenever incoming orders match against resting orders.

Two microstructure concepts are especially important for AI strategies:

**Depth.**

Depth measures how much quantity is available at each price level. A signal that predicts a 5 bps move in the midprice is attractive only if you can trade your desired size against available depth without pushing the price further (market impact).

**Queue priority and latency.**

In most CLOBs, orders at a given price are executed in *time priority*: first-in, first-out. If many traders place buy limit orders at $100, the earliest orders get filled first when a seller arrives. Low-latency participants can quickly cancel and re-post orders to maintain queue position. For fast AI strategies that depend on news or order book dynamics, your fill probability depends not just on your price but on how quickly you can respond to information and how crowded the queue already is.

### RFQ and Hybrid Markets

In RFQ systems, typical in corporate bonds and some derivatives, the trading workflow is:

- The buy-side trader sends a quote request to multiple dealers for a specific instrument and size.
- Dealers respond with indicative or firm quotes (prices).
- The trader chooses which quote to hit or lift, or decides not to trade.

Here, there is no public continuous order book showing depth at each price. Instead, liquidity manifests as:

- The number of dealers willing to quote.
- The tightness of the best quotes.
- The probability that a dealer honors a quote for the requested size.

For AI research, this has two implications:

- High-frequency, tick-level prediction is less relevant: you simply do not have a transparent, continuous tape with visible queues.
- Instead, models may focus on medium-horizon pricing of illiquid bonds or derivatives, balancing estimated alpha against the expected cost and uncertainty of execution via RFQs.

Hybrid electronic platforms in FX and rates blend order books and RFQs: some participants post limit orders; others request quotes from designated market makers. Your execution logic must understand which mode you are using.

### Dealer / Principal Markets

In dealer markets, you trade bilaterally with a market maker who stands ready to buy or sell from their own inventory. The dealer quotes two-sided prices (bid and ask) and:

- earns the spread as compensation for providing liquidity,
- manages inventory risk and hedges in other markets.

Execution quality depends heavily on your relationship with the dealer, your size, and current market conditions. When volatility spikes, dealers may:

- Widen spreads,
- Reduce the maximum size they are willing to quote,
- Or withdraw quotes entirely for certain names.

In such environments, an AI model that predicts long-run mispricing is necessary but not sufficient. You must also model the *availability* and *cost* of liquidity, which are state-dependent.

## Order Types: How Instructions Reach the Market

Regardless of market structure, an AI strategy's predictions must eventually be turned into specific order instructions. Even in simple CLOB markets, the choice of order type materially changes realized P&L.

**Market orders.**

A market order instructs: "Execute now for the full size at the best available prices." It maximizes execution certainty but leaves the price unspecified. Costs include:

- Paying the full bid–ask spread (you cross the spread).
- Potential *slippage* if the visible depth at the top of the book is insufficient and your order walks the book.

Latency-sensitive alpha based on fresh news may justify market orders: speed is more valuable than a marginal reduction in costs.

**Limit orders.**

A limit order sets a maximum buy price or minimum sell price. For example, "Buy 10,000 shares at $100 or better." If the market trades through your limit, you will be filled; otherwise, you may wait in the queue. Advantages:

- You control the worst price at which you trade.
- You may *earn* the spread if your limit order provides liquidity and is hit or lifted by an impatient counterparty.

The downside is *fill uncertainty*: you might not be executed, especially if the market moves away. For AI strategies, this introduces a subtle modeling issue: your backtest must decide how to simulate whether a given limit order would actually have been filled, given historical order book data and queueing behavior.

**Other order types.**

Many venues support richer order types:

- **Stop orders**: trigger a market or limit order when price crosses a threshold.
- **Iceberg orders**: show only part of the order size in the book, hiding the rest.
- **Pegged orders**: automatically adjust price relative to the current best bid or ask.

While these can be powerful tools, they also complicate modeling: the state of the book you observe may hide significant hidden liquidity, and your strategy's own orders can change other participants' behavior.

## Liquidity: Spreads, Impact, and Capacity

Liquidity is the bridge between a model's predicted return and the realized performance of a trading strategy. Informally, a market is liquid if you can buy or sell significant size quickly, at low cost, without moving the price too much.

Three simple, intuitive dimensions help organize your thinking:

**Tightness.**

Tightness captures how close transaction prices are to the "fair" price at any point in time. The primary measure is the **bid–ask spread**: the difference between the best ask (lowest sell price) and best bid (highest buy price). A narrower spread implies tighter markets and lower costs for crossing the spread.

For small, infrequent trades, your expected cost per trade is roughly one-half of the spread (because you buy at the ask and sell at the bid). A daily rebalancing equity strategy that is insensitive to seconds-level timing may treat this as a constant cost. A high-frequency strategy cares about micro-changes in spread throughout the day.

**Depth.**

Depth measures how much volume is available at different prices. If the top of the book in a stock shows:

```
Bid: 100.00 x 1,000
Ask: 100.02 x 500
```

then an order to buy 10,000 shares will consume all visible asks at 100.02 and likely several levels above, pushing the price up. The greater your trade size relative to available depth, the greater your **market impact**.

For AI research, this leads directly to the concept of **capacity**: the maximum capital or average trade size your strategy can deploy before its own trading materially erodes its alpha. A brilliant NLP sentiment signal that yields a 2 bps edge on a thinly traded microcap may be capacity-constrained to a few hundred thousand dollars, whereas the same predictive edge applied to a liquid index future could support much larger flows.

**Resiliency.**

Resiliency refers to how quickly markets recover from trades or shocks. After a large trade, does the order book refill at similar prices, or does it remain thin and wide? In resilient markets, temporary price deviations created by large orders might invite liquidity providers to step in; in fragile markets, the same trade could induce persistent dislocation.

Resiliency is especially relevant for strategies that either provide liquidity (posting limit orders) or depend on mean reversion. If your model is calibrated on a regime with high resiliency, but the live market becomes fragile (for example, during a crisis), the realized path of returns and drawdowns can be quite different from your backtest.

## Why Microstructure Matters for AI and Alternative Data

Once you begin building AI or NLP signals, microstructure becomes an explicit part of your research design rather than a background detail.

Consider three examples:

- A news-based equity strategy that trades large, liquid U.S. stocks intraday.
- A credit-spread strategy using alternative data (e.g., web-scraped indicators) applied to off-the-run corporate bonds.
- A cross-exchange crypto arbitrage using order book imbalances between two venues.

In each case, the same conceptual steps—predict return, compare to risk and cost, decide to trade—play out in radically different microstructural environments:

- **Latency vs. horizon.** In large-cap equities and crypto, fresh NLP signals derived from news or order flow might decay in seconds or minutes. Your infrastructure (data ingestion, feature computation, order routing) must be fast enough that a meaningful fraction of the predicted edge remains by the time your order reaches the book. In corporate bonds, by contrast, latency measured in seconds may be irrelevant; days or weeks matter more.
- **Execution model.** In liquid CLOB markets, you can explicitly model spreads, depth, and queue dynamics. Your backtests can replay historical order books and simulate fills. In RFQ or dealer markets, you may have only indicative quotes or trade prints; your execution assumptions must be more conservative and scenario-based.
- **Capacity and turnover.** High-frequency strategies that trade frequently with small edges are extremely sensitive to trading costs and impact. Small misestimation of spreads or fees can

flip an apparently profitable strategy to unprofitable. Medium-horizon strategies with lower turnover have more room for modeling error in execution costs but must still respect capacity constraints in less liquid instruments.

A central theme of this book is that no alpha claim is complete until it passes through a realistic microstructure lens. For AI-driven strategies, this implies:

- When you define prediction targets (e.g., next-5-minute return), you must also define the *execution window* and typical order type.
- When you construct features using alternative data (e.g., social media sentiment, search trends), you must align their timestamps to when a trade could plausibly be executed, not when the model is evaluated in hindsight.
- When you simulate strategy performance, you must incorporate explicit models of spreads, fees, and impact appropriate to the asset class and venue.

In the following sections, we will formalize how returns, risk, and performance are measured and evaluated. Those metrics—Sharpe ratios, drawdowns, turnover, capacity—only make sense when interpreted through the lens of the market structures described here. An AI edge that looks compelling in a spreadsheet but cannot survive the journey from model output to executed trade is not an edge at all.

## 2.2 Measuring Returns, Risk, and Performance

In the previous section we focused on *where* and *how* you trade: asset classes, venues, order types, and liquidity. We now turn to how you *measure* what your strategy delivers once it interacts with that market plumbing.

An AI model, no matter how sophisticated, ultimately produces a sequence of trades and a corresponding sequence of portfolio values. To judge whether the model is adding value, we need a common quantitative language that everyone—researchers, portfolio managers, risk committees, and external investors—can understand. This section builds that language in three steps:

- Return conventions: how to define and manipulate returns.
- Risk measures: how to summarize the variability and path of those returns.
- Performance metrics: how to combine return and risk into interpretable diagnostics.

Throughout, keep in mind that *every* AI or NLP signal you design will eventually be evaluated using some subset of these metrics. Understanding them up front prevents you from over-optimizing on the wrong objective or misinterpreting what your backtest is actually saying.

## Return Conventions

A *return* measures how much a price or portfolio value changes relative to its starting point over a given period. Even this simple idea has several standard conventions, each suited to different tasks.

## Simple vs. Log Returns

Suppose an asset has price $P_t$ at time $t$ and $P_{t+1}$ at the next observation.

**Simple return.** The simple (or arithmetic) return over the interval is

$$R_{t+1} = \frac{P_{t+1} - P_t}{P_t} = \frac{P_{t+1}}{P_t} - 1.$$

If $P_t = 100$ and $P_{t+1} = 103$, then $R_{t+1} = 3\%$.

Simple returns are intuitive: they map directly into percentage gain or loss. They also add naturally when you form portfolios: the portfolio return is the weighted sum of asset returns.

**Log return.** The log (or continuously compounded) return is

$$r_{t+1} = \ln\left(\frac{P_{t+1}}{P_t}\right).$$

For small moves (a few percent or less), $r_{t+1} \approx R_{t+1}$, but log returns have two technical conveniences:

- They *add* over time: if you have multiple periods, the multi-period log return is the sum of single-period log returns.
- They are symmetric with respect to up and down moves: a $+10\%$ move followed by a $-10\%$ move yields a net log return close to zero, reflecting the fact that prices nearly return to their starting point.

In cross-sectional equity research (daily or monthly horizons), many practitioners use simple returns. In high-frequency or theoretical work, log returns are often preferred because of their nice aggregation properties.

## Price Return vs. Total Return

So far we implicitly assumed that all gains come from price changes. In reality, many assets pay coupons, dividends, or other cash flows. We distinguish:

- **Price return:** measures change in price only.
- **Total return:** includes both price changes and reinvested cash distributions.

For example, a stock might trade from $100 to $102 over a year and pay a $3 dividend.

- Price return: $(102 - 100)/100 = 2\%$.
- Total return: $(102 + 3 - 100)/100 = 5\%$, assuming the dividend is reinvested.

For longer-horizon evaluation of AI strategies (e.g., monthly or quarterly), you almost always want total returns for fairness: a model that tilts into high-dividend stocks should not be penalized simply because your summary statistics ignore dividends.

## Gross vs. Net of Costs

Backtests in AI research often begin with *gross* returns: they assume that you can trade at mid-prices with no fees or slippage. In reality, execution costs chip away at returns. We therefore distinguish:

- **Gross return:** return ignoring trading costs and management fees.
- **Net return:** return after subtracting explicit costs (commissions, fees, borrow costs) and implicit costs (spreads, market impact).

As a rule of thumb:

- Use gross returns in early-stage model development to compare features or algorithms quickly.
- Shift to net returns as soon as you start taking a signal seriously, incorporating realistic estimates of spreads, fees, and impact that reflect the microstructure features discussed in the previous section.

A strategy that looks phenomenal on a gross basis but collapses once costs are included is not a robust candidate for live deployment—especially if it relies on short-lived, high-turnover AI or NLP signals.

## Risk: Volatility, Drawdowns, and Dependence

Return alone is not enough. Two strategies may both deliver 10% per year on average, but one might do so with gentle month-to-month fluctuations, while the other whip-saws with large gains and losses. Risk measures capture this variability and the *shape* of the return path.

## Volatility and Variance

The most common risk measure is **volatility**, typically defined as the standard deviation of returns:

$$\sigma = \sqrt{\mathbb{E}[(R - \mu)^2]},$$

where $R$ is the return over a fixed horizon (e.g., daily) and $\mu$ is its mean. In practice, we estimate $\sigma$ from a time series of returns $\{R_1, \dots, R_T\}$:

$$\hat{\sigma} = \sqrt{\frac{1}{T-1} \sum_{t=1}^{T} (R_t - \bar{R})^2},$$

where $\bar{R}$ is the sample mean.

Key points:

- Volatility is *scale-dependent*. If you double the holding period (e.g., from daily to weekly), volatility does not simply double; under certain assumptions it scales with the square root of time.
- Volatility does not distinguish between upside and downside moves; both increase the standard deviation.

Despite its limitations, volatility is widely used because it is easy to compute and compare across strategies.

## Drawdown and Path-Dependent Risk

Volatility summarizes dispersion around an average, but investors care deeply about *losses from previous peaks*. This is captured by **drawdown**.

Let $V_t$ denote the portfolio value at time $t$, and define the running maximum up to time $t$ as

$$M_t = \max_{s \le t} V_s.$$

Then the drawdown at time $t$ is

$$D_t = \frac{V_t - M_t}{M_t},$$

which is a negative number (or zero at peaks). The **maximum drawdown** over a period is the minimum of $D_t$:

$$\text{MaxDD} = \min_t D_t.$$

Drawdown is intuitive:

- It measures the worst peak-to-trough decline an investor would have experienced.
- It reflects both the magnitude and the duration of losses: a deep, long-lasting drawdown is more painful than a shallow, quickly recovered one.

For AI strategies, drawdowns have two roles:

- They serve as a risk constraint (e.g., the strategy must be sized such that historical max drawdown remains within a target range).
- They help detect regime sensitivity: a model that collapses into an unprecedented drawdown in specific environments (e.g., volatility spikes, liquidity crises) may be overfitted or overly dependent on a narrow regime.

## Downside Risk and Tail Sensitivity

Volatility treats upside and downside moves symmetrically, but many investors are more sensitive to losses. **Downside deviation** focuses only on returns below a threshold, often zero or a risk-free rate $R_f$:

$$\sigma_{down} = \sqrt{\mathbb{E}\left[(\min(0, R - R_f))^2\right]}.$$

This measure grows when a strategy experiences large negative returns, but is unaffected by large positive surprises. It underpins the Sortino ratio, a downside-focused performance metric discussed below.

Tail risk can also be summarized via percentiles:

- **Value-at-Risk (VaR):** a quantile of the loss distribution over a fixed horizon.
- **Expected Shortfall (ES):** the average loss in the worst $q\%$ of scenarios.

We will not dwell on technical definitions here, but conceptually, these measures emphasize rare, extreme events, which can be especially important for strategies that use leverage or trade illiquid instruments.

## Correlation and Beta

Risk is not just about a strategy in isolation; it is also about how it co-moves with other assets or benchmarks.

**Correlation.** The correlation between two return series $R^{(1)}$ and $R^{(2)}$ is

$$\rho = \frac{\mathrm{Cov}(R^{(1)}, R^{(2)})}{\sigma_1 \sigma_2},$$

where Cov is covariance and $\sigma_1, \sigma_2$ are the standard deviations. Correlation ranges from $-1$ (perfect opposite moves) to $+1$ (perfect co-movement).

**Beta.** With a benchmark (e.g., a broad equity index), we often summarize sensitivity via **beta**. If we regress strategy returns $R^{strat}$ on benchmark returns $R^{mkt}$:

$$R_t^{strat} = \alpha + \beta R_t^{mkt} + \varepsilon_t,$$

then $\beta$ represents the expected change in strategy return for a one-unit change in the benchmark.

An "absolute return" AI strategy is often designed to have a low correlation and low beta to traditional risk factors, so that its performance is not just a leveraged expression of broad market moves.

## Performance Metrics: Combining Return and Risk

With returns and risk measures in hand, we can define performance metrics that summarize how efficiently a strategy transforms risk into return. These metrics form the backbone of professional evaluation: investment committees routinely scrutinize them before allocating capital.

## Sharpe Ratio

The **Sharpe ratio** is the workhorse risk-adjusted return measure. Over a given horizon (e.g., daily, monthly), define excess returns over a risk-free rate $R_f$:

$$X_t = R_t - R_f.$$

Then the Sharpe ratio $S$ is

$$S = \frac{\mathbb{E}[X_t]}{\sigma_X},$$

where $\sigma_X$ is the standard deviation of $X_t$.

In sample, we estimate

$$\hat{S} = \frac{\bar{X}}{\hat{\sigma}_X},$$

where $\bar{X}$ is the average excess return and $\hat{\sigma}_X$ its sample standard deviation, then annualize as appropriate (typically by multiplying numerator and denominator to a common annual scale).

Intuitively, Sharpe tells you how many units of excess return you earn per unit of volatility:

- A Sharpe of 1 means your average excess return equals your volatility.
- A Sharpe of 2 is considered strong for liquid strategies.

AI strategies with high turnover often exhibit decent raw returns but also high volatility; Sharpe helps you see whether the reward justifies the risk.

## Sortino Ratio and Downside Focus

The **Sortino ratio** modifies Sharpe by focusing on downside deviation $\sigma_{down}$ instead of total volatility:

$$\text{Sortino} = \frac{\mathbb{E}[R_t - R_f]}{\sigma_{down}}.$$

If a strategy exhibits frequent small gains and occasional large losses, its volatility may look moderate, but downside deviation will be large, pulling down the Sortino ratio. This makes Sortino particularly relevant for strategies with asymmetric payoffs or exposure to rare but severe tail events.

## Information Ratio and Benchmarking

When a strategy is explicitly benchmarked to a reference portfolio (e.g., an equity index), we care about *active* risk and return:

- Active return: $A_t = R_t^{strat} - R_t^{bench}$.
- Active risk: volatility of active returns.

The **information ratio** (IR) is

$$\text{IR} = \frac{\mathbb{E}[A_t]}{\sigma_A}.$$

While the Sharpe ratio compares a strategy to a risk-free asset, the information ratio compares it to a specific benchmark. For AI strategies that layer incremental signals on top of an existing portfolio (e.g., alpha overlays on a factor portfolio), IR is often more relevant than Sharpe: it tells you how efficiently the model adds value relative to the baseline.

## Hit Rate, Payoff Ratio, and Turnover

A few additional metrics help interpret the *structure* of returns:

- **Hit rate:** fraction of trades or periods with positive returns. A strategy could have a low hit rate but high profitability if its winners are much larger than its losers.

- **Payoff ratio:** average gain on winning trades divided by average loss on losing trades.

- **Turnover:** trading volume relative to portfolio size over a period. High turnover strategies are more sensitive to costs and operational constraints; low turnover strategies may be more robust but slower to react.

AI and NLP strategies often generate frequent, small signals. A high hit rate with modest payoff ratios can still produce attractive Sharpe ratios, provided that costs are under control and the strategy's capacity is not exceeded.

## Equal Returns, Different Paths

Two strategies can deliver the same cumulative return but with very different risk and path characteristics. This is where the visual shape of the equity curve complements summary statistics.

Consider Strategy A and Strategy B, each starting at value 1.0 and ending at 1.5 over several years (a total return of 50%). Strategy A climbs steadily with small fluctuations; Strategy B oscillates wildly, with deep drawdowns before recovering. Both have the same terminal value, but Strategy B has higher volatility and larger maximum drawdowns, and thus a lower Sharpe ratio.

This contrast is often missed when you look only at start and end points. In investment committees, it is common to present both a table of metrics (Sharpe, max drawdown, etc.) and a plot of equity curves to make these differences concrete.

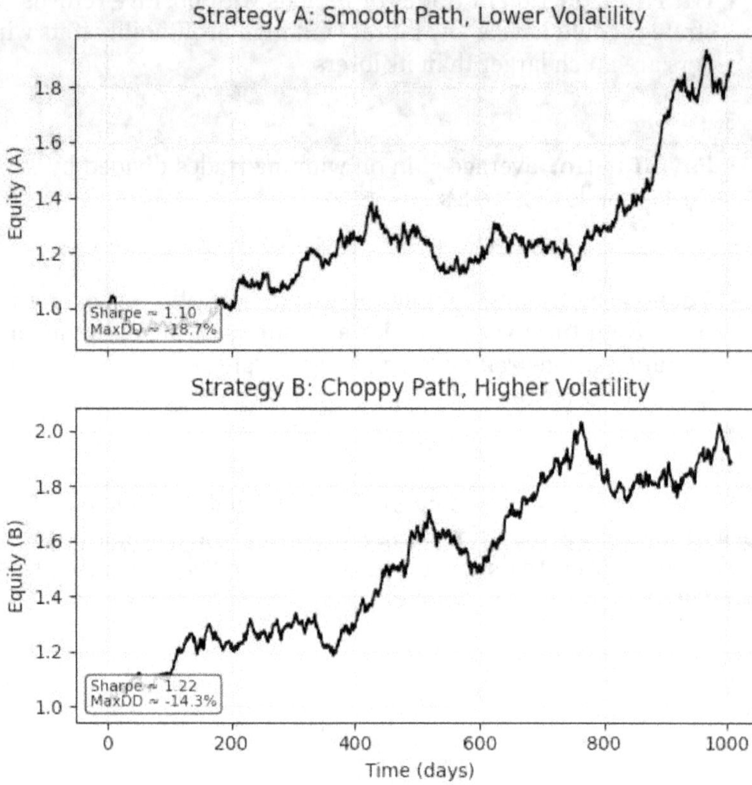


Figure 2.1: Two equity curves with similar total return but different volatility and drawdowns. Strategy B experiences larger swings and deeper drawdowns, resulting in lower risk-adjusted performance despite the same terminal value.

## From Metrics to Research Constraints

The metrics introduced here are more than descriptive statistics. In a professional AI research process, they become explicit *constraints* and *objectives*. For example:

- A portfolio manager might require that any new NLP-based alpha model achieve an out-of-sample Sharpe ratio above a threshold (say, 0.8 annualized) with maximum drawdown below 15%.

- A risk committee might cap the strategy's beta to equity markets (e.g., $|\beta| < 0.3$) to ensure it truly provides diversification.
- An execution team may impose turnover and capacity limits to keep trading costs within a given fraction of gross alpha.

In other words, when you iterate on model architectures, feature sets, or alternative data sources, you are not just chasing higher raw returns. You are trying to shape the entire profile of returns, risk, and path so that the resulting strategy can live comfortably within the firm's risk budget and client expectations.

The next sections will extend this language to factor models and structured research workflows. There we will see how these basic metrics plug into more advanced tools: decomposing returns into systematic risk premia and true alpha, and designing backtests and validation protocols that respect microstructure, control for overfitting, and keep reported performance aligned with what can realistically be achieved in live trading.

## 2.3 Factor Models and Alpha Drivers

The previous sections equipped us with two essential pieces of groundwork. First, we saw how different markets and microstructures shape the implementation of any trading idea. Second, we established a common language for returns, risk, and performance—Sharpe ratios, drawdowns, volatility, and so on. We now add a third layer: an organizing framework for understanding *why* returns occur in the first place.

In practice, most of what looks like "performance" can be explained by broad, systematic forces that affect many assets at once. These forces are called *risk premia* or *factors*. Only the portion of returns that cannot be plausibly attributed to such factors is called *alpha*.

This section explains:

- What we mean by systematic risk premia and style factors.

- How factor models decompose portfolio returns into factor-driven components and residual alpha.
- How AI and NLP-based strategies often load on existing factors, sometimes unintentionally.
- How to distinguish genuine alpha from compensated risk exposure and from overfitting.

The goal is not to turn you into a factor theorist, but to give you a practical lens: every AI signal you build should be evaluated in the context of factor models if you want to make credible alpha claims.

## Systematic Risk Premia: Getting Paid for Bearing Risk

A *risk premium* is the extra return investors demand, on average, for bearing certain types of risk. The classic example is the **equity risk premium**: over long periods, stocks tend to outperform government bills, compensating investors for the possibility of large drawdowns and high volatility.

Empirically, researchers have documented that certain characteristics of securities are associated with returns in many markets and periods. These characteristics are often called *factors* or *styles*. Common examples in equities include:

- **Size:** small-cap vs. large-cap stocks.
- **Value:** cheap vs. expensive stocks (e.g., high book-to-price vs. low).
- **Momentum:** recent winners vs. recent losers.
- **Quality:** high vs. low profitability and balance-sheet strength.
- **Low risk:** low-volatility or low-beta stocks versus the market.

In macro and cross-asset contexts, we see similar patterns:

- **Carry:** assets with higher yields or forward discounts tend to earn higher returns (e.g., high-yield currencies in FX, high carry in bond or futures curves).
- **Value and momentum in commodities or rates:** cheap or trending contracts often earn excess returns relative to others.

Two points are crucial:

- These premia are often *systematic*: they involve broad portfolios (e.g., all small vs. all large companies), not idiosyncratic bets on single names.
- They can be understood as compensation for risks that are unpleasant but bearable for some investors: drawdowns concentrated in bad times, funding risk, liquidity dry-ups, and so on.

From an AI-research perspective, this means: if your model simply tilts a portfolio toward cheap, small, or trending stocks, it may indeed earn extra return—but that is not necessarily "secret" alpha. You are harvesting known risk premia.

## Linear Factor Models: Decomposing Returns

To formalize these ideas, we use *linear factor models*. At a high level, a factor model expresses asset or portfolio returns as a combination of:

- Sensitivity to systematic factors (size, value, momentum, etc.).
- A residual component that is specific to the asset or strategy.

### Single-Factor (CAPM) Intuition

The simplest example is the Capital Asset Pricing Model (CAPM). In its empirical form, for a portfolio with returns $R_t$ and a market index with returns $R_t^{mkt}$, we write:

$$R_t - R_t^f = \alpha + \beta \left( R_t^{mkt} - R_t^f \right) + \varepsilon_t,$$

where:

- $R_t^f$ is the risk-free return (e.g., Treasury bill).
- $\beta$ measures the sensitivity of the portfolio to the equity market.
- $\alpha$ is the intercept, interpreted as *excess* return unexplained by the market.
- $\varepsilon_t$ is residual noise.

In this view:

- A mutual fund with $\beta \approx 1$ and $\alpha \approx 0$ is essentially just giving you market exposure—its returns are explained by equity risk alone.
- A strategy with $\beta \approx 0$ and significantly positive $\alpha$ appears to deliver returns uncorrelated with the broad market—a candidate for genuine alpha (subject to statistical and structural scrutiny).

### Multi-Factor Models

Realistic evaluation uses multiple factors. For an AI-driven equity strategy, you might regress its returns on a set of standard equity factors:

$$R_t - R_t^f = \alpha + \beta_{mkt} F_t^{mkt} + \beta_{size} F_t^{size} + \beta_{value} F_t^{value} + \beta_{mom} F_t^{mom} + \cdots + \varepsilon_t,$$

where each $F_t^{\cdot}$ is the return on a tradable factor portfolio (e.g., long small / short large, long value / short growth).

Interpreting this regression:

- The $\beta$ coefficients tell you how much your strategy behaves like each factor. For example, $\beta_{mom} = 1.2$ indicates a strong positive exposure to momentum.
- The residual $\alpha$ is what remains after accounting for these standard exposures.

Practically, this decomposition serves three purposes:

- **Attribution:** You can explain past performance: was it mostly due to a big bet on momentum during a momentum-friendly period?
- **Risk management:** You can control unintended factor exposures by constraining or hedging certain $\beta$s.
- **Alpha validation:** You can test whether your AI strategy adds value beyond what a simple factor tilt would deliver.

## When Alpha is Really a Factor Tilt

AI and NLP-based strategies are particularly prone to inadvertently loading on existing factors, because many textual or alternative data signals correlate with fundamental characteristics already captured by factor models.

**Examples in Equities**

Consider three stylized cases:

**Case 1: Text sentiment as momentum.**

Suppose you build a news sentiment model that scores stocks based on recent headlines and articles. You then go long the most positively scored stocks and short the most negatively scored.

It is very plausible that such a portfolio:

- Overlaps heavily with recent *winners* (stocks that have gone up tend to attract positive coverage).
- Avoids recent *losers* (which receive negative sentiment).

If you regress the strategy's returns on a standard momentum factor, you might find:

$$\beta_{mom} \approx 1.0 \quad \text{and} \quad \alpha \approx 0,$$

meaning that your "sophisticated" AI sentiment signal is, in effect, a noisy and perhaps more expensive way of implementing the momentum factor. The apparent backtest success was a story of momentum doing well, not of secret text-based insight.

**Case 2: ESG or controversy scores as quality/low risk.**

An NLP model that penalizes companies with frequent controversy-related headlines and rewards those with stable, positive coverage may systematically favor:

- High-quality firms (strong governance, consistent earnings).
- Lower-risk stocks (less likely to be involved in scandals or extreme events).

A factor regression might reveal strong exposures to quality and low-volatility factors. If the strategy's $\alpha$ is small and insignificant once these exposures are accounted for, then most of its "alpha" is really the well-known quality premium.

**Case 3: Web-traffic or app-usage data as growth/size bets.**

Alternative data on web traffic or app usage may lead your models to overweight high-growth, tech-oriented firms with strong user metrics, which are often:

- Large-cap or mid-cap growth names.
- Stocks with high price-to-earnings or price-to-sales ratios (i.e., expensive on value metrics).

The resulting strategy may have:

- Positive exposure to growth (negative exposure to value).
- Possibly a size tilt (toward larger firms).

If growth outperforms in your backtest period, your model looks brilliant; but out-of-sample, if value recovers, the strategy's performance may deteriorate sharply. A factor model would have warned you: you were largely making a one-way style bet, not discovering a robust, orthogonal AI edge.

## Alpha Drivers Beyond Standard Factors

If so much can be explained by systematic factors, where does true alpha come from, and why might AI and alternative data help to capture it?

Three broad mechanisms are particularly relevant:

### Behavioral Biases

Human investors are not perfectly rational. Well-documented biases include:

- **Overreaction and underreaction:** Prices may overreact to sensational news or underreact to complex, hard-to-parse information.
- **Attention constraints:** Investors have limited bandwidth; they may ignore or slowly process certain signals.
- **Herding and feedback loops:** Crowd behavior can push prices away from fundamentals.

AI and NLP can help identify and exploit these biases by:

- Parsing large volumes of textual information that humans cannot fully process in real time.
- Distinguishing between sentiment-driven noise and information-rich content.
- Detecting patterns in how different investor groups react over time.

For example, a model that identifies when markets underreact to complex, technical disclosures (e.g., footnotes in regulatory filings) might systematically buy mispriced stocks before the broader market catches up.

### Information-Processing Frictions

Even sophisticated institutions face frictions in how quickly and efficiently they can process new data:

- **Latency of human workflows:** Analyst reports and committee decisions take time.
- **Siloed data:** Different desks or systems may not share information effectively.
- **Constraints on model complexity:** Many firms rely on relatively simple, explainable models, leaving more complex patterns under-exploited.

AI systems that can ingest alternative data (social media, web traffic, transaction-level data) and convert it into real-time signals have the potential to anticipate price moves that traditional pipelines will only reflect days or weeks later. This "speed-of-processing" edge can generate alpha, particularly on short to medium horizons.

### Slow-Moving Capital and Limits to Arbitrage

Even when mispricings are visible, not everyone is willing or able to exploit them immediately. Obstacles include:

- Mandate restrictions (e.g., long-only, sector limits).
- Regulatory or risk constraints (e.g., leverage caps, shorting limits).
- Funding and career risks (e.g., underperforming peers in the short term).

These frictions create room for specialized investors to harvest alpha by bearing certain types of transient risk that others avoid. Many AI strategies, particularly those leveraging niche datasets, effectively monetize such slow-moving capital: they step into gaps where traditional capital reacts only gradually.

## Distinguishing Genuine Alpha from Overfitting

Even after accounting for known factors, we must be cautious: an apparent residual $\alpha$ in a backtest can still be illusory due to *overfitting*—finding patterns in noise that will not repeat out of sample.

Several practical principles help distinguish robust alpha from statistical mirages:

### Out-of-Sample and Cross-Validation Discipline

As will be discussed more fully in the research workflow section, a credible alpha claim requires:

- Clear separation between training, validation, and test periods.
- No look-ahead bias or data leakage (especially acute with textual and alternative data, where timestamps and availability lags must be handled carefully).
- Time-series aware cross-validation techniques that respect temporal ordering.

An AI model that shows strong $\alpha$ in backtests but fails to maintain it in true out-of-sample tests is likely overfitted, regardless of how impressive its in-sample factor-adjusted metrics look.

### Parsimony and Economic Intuition

A model boasting hundreds of parameters and dozens of loosely motivated features will almost always find some pattern in historical data. To guard against this:

- Favor simpler models unless the added complexity demonstrably delivers out-of-sample benefits.
- Seek economic or behavioral stories that plausibly explain why your signal should persist.
- Examine whether the signal survives across different markets, time periods, and market regimes.

In factor terms, robust alpha should not flip sign dramatically with small changes in sample period or minor alterations in implementation. If it does, what you have is likely noise.

### Factor-Neutral and Hedged Implementations

One practical way to test whether your AI signal truly adds value beyond known premia is to implement it in a factor-neutral way and compare:

- Construct one portfolio that applies your signal naively.
- Construct another portfolio that is explicitly neutral to key factors (e.g., via optimization or matching, you ensure $\beta_{mkt}$, $\beta_{value}$, $\beta_{mom}$, etc., are near zero).

If the naive portfolio looks excellent but the factor-neutral portfolio's performance collapses, much of your apparent edge may be just a factor tilt. If the factor-neutral version still shows reasonable Sharpe and alpha, you have stronger evidence of genuine signal content.

## AI Features as Overlays, Not Magic Boxes

The central message of this section is conceptual discipline: think of AI and NLP-derived features as *layers* on top of an existing factor and risk framework, not as black boxes that replace it.

- Your starting point should be: what known risk premia and factors are relevant in my asset class and horizon?
- Next: how might my AI features refine, time, or complement these premia? For example, using text sentiment to dynamically adjust exposure to momentum, or using alternative data to detect when value opportunities are more likely to realize.
- Finally: how does the resulting strategy look through the lens of a factor model—what are its $\beta$s, its residual $\alpha$, and its behavior under different regimes?

By embedding AI innovations within a transparent factor framework, you gain several advantages:

- **Interpretability:** You can explain performance and risk to stakeholders in a familiar language.
- **Risk control:** You can limit unintended exposures and design hedges systematically.
- **Scientific rigor:** You can subject your alpha claims to the same standards used to evaluate more traditional strategies.

The next section will translate these ideas into a structured research workflow: from hypothesis and data acquisition through modeling, backtesting, factor-adjusted evaluation, and finally to production. There we will see how microstructure, performance metrics, and factor models all come together in a coherent pipeline for discovering and validating AI-driven alpha.

## 2.4 Structured Alpha Research Workflow

The previous sections have given us the key ingredients for serious AI-driven trading: an understanding of market structure and trading frictions, a common language for returns and risk, and a factor framework to separate true alpha from systematic exposures. What we still need is a disciplined way to put all of this into practice.

Without a structured workflow, it is dangerously easy to fool yourself. You can p-hack your way to impressive backtests, accidentally leak future information into your features, or test so many ideas that some will look good purely by chance. A robust research process acts as a scaffold: it constrains bias, encourages rigor, and ensures that any claimed alpha has a clear path from hypothesis to live deployment.

In this section we lay out an end-to-end workflow for AI and NLP-based alpha discovery:

- Problem framing and hypothesis design.
- Data acquisition, cleaning, and alignment.
- Feature engineering and label construction.
- Model development and validation.
- Backtesting with realistic trading assumptions.
- Factor-adjusted evaluation and risk diagnostics.
- Implementation, paper trading, and live monitoring.

The steps are sequential but also iterative: new findings feed back into better hypotheses, data choices, and models.

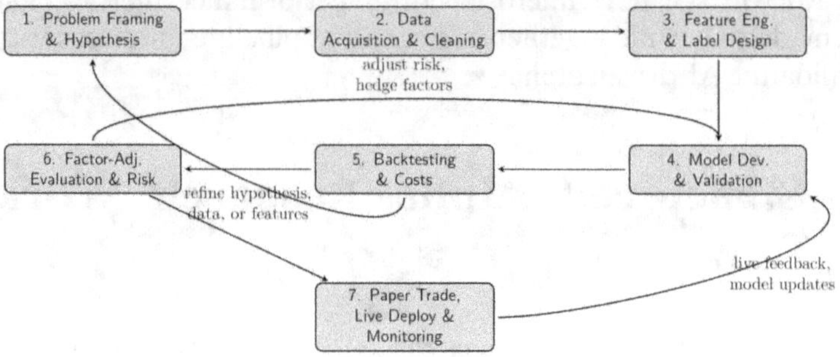


## Step 1: Problem Framing and Hypothesis Design

Every serious research project starts by answering four concrete questions:

- **What is the decision or prediction task?** For example, "predict next-day excess return of large-cap equities" or "decide whether to enter a long/short position in a credit index over the next week."
- **Over what horizon?** Your microstructure assumptions (latency, spreads, impact) depend critically on whether you trade over seconds, hours, days, or months.
- **On which investable universe?** Large-cap U.S. equities, on-the-run Treasury futures, major FX pairs, liquid crypto pairs, etc. This ties back to the *Asset Classes and Market Microstructure* discussion.
- **Under what constraints?** Position limits, leverage, turnover caps, factor exposure limits, and risk budgets.

Alongside, you articulate an initial *economic or behavioral hypothesis*. For an NLP strategy this might be:

- "Firms receiving unusually positive language in earnings call transcripts subsequently outperform, because the market underreacts to nuanced tone."
- "Crypto tokens with deteriorating developer-community sentiment exhibit negative medium-horizon returns, reflecting slow-moving capital exiting the ecosystem."

A well-formed hypothesis does not guarantee alpha, but it anchors your choices about data, features, and model complexity. It also makes it easier later to judge whether results are plausible or just artifacts.

## Step 2: Data Acquisition, Cleaning, and Alignment

AI and NLP strategies are data-hungry. The quality of your inputs sets a ceiling on the quality of your outputs.

## Data Types and Sources

Typical inputs include:

- **Market data:** prices, volumes, order book snapshots, corporate actions.
- **Reference data:** identifiers, sector classifications, accounting fields.
- **Textual data:** news, social media posts, earnings call transcripts, regulatory filings, research reports.
- **Alternative data:** web traffic, app usage metrics, credit card transaction aggregates, satellite imagery, developer activity metrics for blockchains.

Each dataset comes with quirks: missing values, inconsistent identifiers, changing coverage over time, and—critically—timestamp conventions.

## Timestamp Integrity and Lag

For predictive modeling, it is not enough to know when an event occurred; you must know when the information was *available for trading*. For text and alternative data, you should:

- Use the earliest reliable timestamp at which the text or signal could be observed by your systems.
- Add realistic processing lag if your pipeline would take time to parse and score documents.
- Align labels (future returns) so that no information from time $t+1$ contaminates features at time $t$.

Misalignment here leads to *look-ahead bias*, a subtle but fatal flaw where your model is allowed to "see" the future in backtests.

## Cleaning and Survivorship

Data cleaning should be systematic and documented:

- Handle missing or erroneous prices, splits, and corporate actions.
- Ensure you include delisted or bankrupt securities when constructing historical universes (avoid survivorship bias).
- For text, filter spam, duplicates, and extremely short or non-informative documents.

All cleaning steps should be reproducible—ideally implemented as code with version control, not one-off manual edits.

## Step 3: Feature Engineering and Label Construction

With data in place, you construct:

- **Features** (inputs): summaries of past information at time $t$.
- **Labels** (targets): the quantity you aim to predict, typically some future return or classification outcome.

## Labels Anchored in Market and Risk Conventions

Labels must reflect realistic trading and evaluation:

- Define returns consistently (simple vs. log, excess vs. raw, total vs. price-only) and at a horizon compatible with your execution assumptions.
- Respect holding periods and turnover: for example, a next-$k$-day return label implicitly assumes you hold the position over that period.
- Consider risk-adjusted labels: predicting Sharpe-like measures or volatility-adjusted returns can sometimes align better with portfolio objectives.

## NLP Features: From Raw Text to Signals

For textual data, common feature families include:

- **Lexicon-based sentiment:** counts or scores of positive/negative words.
- **Embeddings:** vector representations from language models (e.g., sentence-level embeddings of headlines or paragraphs).
- **Topic distributions:** probabilities over latent topics (e.g., "regulatory risk", "earnings quality").
- **Style and tone metrics:** measures of uncertainty, optimism, or complexity in language.

Key principles:

- Aggregate appropriately over time and across documents (e.g., daily sentiment per stock).
- Normalize features to avoid look-ahead (e.g., z-scores within a rolling window).
- Track coverage: a firm with no news is different from a firm with neutral news.

## Leakage Checks

Before moving on, you systematically check for leakage:

- Ensure that features use only information timestamped at or before $t$.
- Exclude variables that directly encode future outcomes (e.g., restated earnings that incorporate later information).
- For alternative data, confirm that data vendor delivery lags are correctly modeled historically.

Leakage can easily inflate in-sample performance, especially in complex feature spaces typical of AI models.

## Step 4: Model Development and Validation

With features and labels defined, you select and train models. Options range from linear regressions and gradient boosting to deep neural networks and specialized architectures for sequences or graphs.

## Baselines and Incremental Value

You should always begin with simple baselines:

- Mean or median forecasts.
- Linear models using a small, interpretable feature set.

- Existing factor models or commodity strategies as benchmarks.

The question is not just "can a large model fit the data?" but "how much incremental value does the AI model add beyond simple alternatives?" This keeps complexity in check and clarifies whether it is the modeling technique or the data that carries most of the edge.

## Time-Series Aware Validation

Standard random cross-validation is inappropriate for time series. Instead:

- Split data into training, validation, and test sets respecting chronology (e.g., train on 2012–2017, validate on 2018–2019, test on 2020–2022).
- Use rolling or expanding-window schemes: train on an initial window, validate on the following period, then roll forward.
- Avoid peeking into the future when tuning hyperparameters.

Performance metrics at this stage are typically predictive, not yet trading-specific: mean squared error of returns, directional accuracy, or rank correlations. However, you should already favor models whose predictive gains plausibly outweigh the additional complexity and risk of overfitting.

## Step 5: Backtesting with Realistic Trading Assumptions

A predictive model is not yet a strategy. To know whether it can generate alpha in live markets, you must translate predictions into positions and trades, then simulate their performance under realistic microstructure constraints.

## Signal-to-Portfolio Mapping

You specify a mapping from model outputs to portfolio weights or orders:

- **Ranking strategies:** go long the top decile of predicted returns, short the bottom decile, and stay neutral in the middle.
- **Regression-based sizing:** map predicted returns to position sizes subject to risk and concentration limits.
- **Classification-based rules:** take or close positions only when the model's classification confidence exceeds a threshold.

At this point, you must embed position constraints (max weight per asset, sector caps, leverage limits) and turnover constraints, all consistent with your earlier problem framing.

## Trading Costs, Slippage, and Capacity

Next, you incorporate the microstructure elements discussed earlier:

- **Spreads and commissions:** model explicit and implicit costs per trade, varying by asset class and liquidity.
- **Market impact:** estimate how trading larger size relative to volume moves prices, reducing realized alpha.
- **Latency and execution horizon:** ensure that you are using the prices your orders could realistically capture, given delays between signal computation and execution.

Capacity analysis is critical: simulate performance at different capital scales. Many promising signals degrade rapidly once you size up.

## Path and Regime Analysis

Beyond point estimates, inspect:

- Equity curves, drawdowns, and time-under-water.
- Performance across volatility regimes, liquidity conditions, and macro environments.
- Sensitivity to parameter choices: rebalance frequency, universe definitions, or cost assumptions.

Backtesting should be adversarial: you try to break your strategy by asking "what if costs were worse? what if my best period is excluded? what if liquidity dries up?"

## Step 6: Factor-Adjusted Evaluation and Risk Diagnostics

Once you have a backtested return series, you interpret it through the lens of factor models and risk metrics from earlier chapters.

### Factor Attribution

Run regressions of strategy returns on relevant factors (equity market, size, value, momentum, carry, etc.). Examine:

- Which factor betas are significant and economically large.
- Whether the residual alpha remains positive and statistically meaningful after accounting for these exposures.
- How stable the betas and alpha are across sub-periods.

If your AI strategy's returns are largely explained by one or two factors, you may choose to:

- Embrace it as a deliberate risk-premium strategy, or
- Neutralize those factors (through portfolio construction) to isolate the pure AI-driven edge.

## Risk and Robustness Checks

Apply the performance metrics discussed earlier:

- Sharpe and Sortino ratios, information ratio vs. relevant benchmarks.
- Maximum drawdown and other path-dependent statistics.
- Turnover, tail risk measures, and exposure to stress scenarios.

Robust strategies show:

- Reasonable risk-adjusted returns across different regimes.
- No extreme concentration in a handful of trades or periods.
- Sensible trade-level behavior (e.g., no massive unintended bets driven by outliers in the model output).

## Step 7: Implementation, Paper Trading, and Live Monitoring

Only after a strategy has cleared all prior gates should you consider implementation. Even then, you proceed in stages.

## From Research Code to Production System

Productionizing an AI trading strategy involves:

- Translating research pipelines (data ingestion, feature computation, model inference) into robust, monitored systems.
- Ensuring that the same code and parameters used in research are deployed, or that any differences are fully documented and tested.
- Implementing safeguards: input validation, fallback behaviors if data is missing or models fail, and explicit version control for models and configuration.

Reproducibility is non-negotiable: you must be able to recreate the inputs and decisions that led to any trade.

## Paper Trading (Shadow Mode)

Before risking capital, run the strategy in *paper trading* or *shadow* mode:

- Generate real-time signals and hypothetical orders as if trading live.
- Record not only the implied P&L but also operational metrics: latency, fill estimates, coverage of data feeds, and system stability.
- Compare paper-trade performance to backtest expectations, recognizing that small deviations are normal but large, systematic differences point to modeling gaps.

Paper trading serves as a bridge between idealized historical simulations and messy reality.

## Live Deployment and Ongoing Monitoring

Once live with real capital, monitoring focuses on three layers:

- **Operational health:** data feed integrity, model inference timing, execution system performance.
- **Risk and exposure:** adherence to limits, factor exposures, leverage, and liquidity usage.
- **Performance attribution:** decomposing live P&L into contributions from signals, market moves, and idiosyncratic events.

Crucially, you maintain:

- A clear separation between *research* and *production* changes.

- A disciplined model update process: new versions are tested, backtested, and paper-traded before being promoted.
- A feedback channel: insights from live behavior feed back into hypothesis refinement, data acquisition, and model improvements (as indicated by the feedback arrows in the flowchart).

## Putting It All Together

A structured alpha research workflow might feel heavy compared to quick experimentation, but it is the only reliable way to turn AI and NLP innovations into durable trading strategies. Each stage plays a specific role:

- Problem framing anchors your work in realistic markets and constraints.
- Data handling and feature design protect you from hidden biases and leakage.
- Model development and time-aware validation guard against overfitting.
- Backtesting with costs and capacity ensures feasibility under real microstructure.
- Factor-adjusted evaluation keeps you honest about what is alpha and what is just compensated risk.
- Implementation and monitoring close the loop, enforcing reproducibility and giving you continuous feedback.

As the rest of this book explores more sophisticated AI architectures and richer alternative datasets, this workflow should serve as your mental checklist. No matter how advanced the model, an alpha claim is only as strong as the process that produced and tested it.

# Chapter 3

# Data Engineering and Alternative Data

*Most funds now have access to machine learning and cloud compute; far fewer have clean, compliant, battle-tested data. This chapter shows how to turn noisy alternative data-news, web traffic, satellite feeds, transaction traces-into a strategic asset. You'll learn how to gate every dataset through rigorous compliance controls, negotiate and evaluate data vendors, industrialize quality and governance, and engineer research pipelines that consistently yield reproducible signals instead of one-off backtest miracles.*

## 3.1 Compliance Foundations for Alternative Data

In traditional quant research, the main question about a new dataset used to be: *"Does it help my Sharpe ratio?"* With alternative data, that question is no longer first. The first question must be:

> *"Are we allowed to use this data for investment decisions at all?"*

Compliance is not a box to tick after you have built a profitable signal. It is a hard constraint that shapes which signals you are allowed to trade, how you can process the underlying data, who may access it, and how you must document its use. A dataset that violates legal or ethical boundaries can create regulatory, reputational, and even criminal risk that dwarfs any expected alpha.

In this section, we build a practical framework for deciding *which* alternative datasets may enter your research environment and *under what conditions*. We will:

- Clarify the key legal concepts, especially material non-public information (MNPI).
- Walk through gray zones common in alternative data: web scraping, app exhaust, and location traces.
- Design an intake workflow where compliance is a gate, not an afterthought.
- Translate legal and policy requirements into concrete data-engineering controls.

Throughout, think of every dataset as an asset with three attributes: *information value*, *cost*, and *compliance risk*. The art of alternative data is maximizing the first while keeping the last strictly within your firm's risk appetite.

## What Counts as Material Non-Public Information?

Most regulatory frameworks around securities trading prohibit the use of *material non-public information*. To use alternative data safely, you must have an intuitive grasp of both words: *material* and *non-public*.

**Material.** An item of information is typically considered material if a reasonable investor would view it as important in making an investment decision. You do not need to prove that it *definitely* moves the price; it is enough that it *could* significantly influence decisions. Examples include:

- Unannounced earnings results or guidance.

- Major mergers, acquisitions, or divestitures.
- Product recalls or regulatory enforcement actions not yet disclosed.

**Non-public.** Information is non-public if it has not been widely disseminated through accepted channels (e.g., regulatory filings, press releases, widely accessible media) and is not otherwise readily available to the general investing public. Restricted-access or selectively shared information can retain a non-public character even if "some people know."

**MNPI in Alternative Data.** Alternative data is attractive precisely because it can reveal economic activity before it appears in official disclosures. That proximity to real-world behavior is also what can push a dataset into MNPI territory if:

- It originates from insiders or people bound by confidentiality (e.g., employees, consultants with access to company internals).
- It is obtained via breached systems, unauthorized scraping, or misrepresentation (e.g., posing as a customer or partner).
- It reconstructs corporate performance so precisely and so quickly that it effectively front-runs formal disclosure, especially when the provider had special access.

Compliance review focuses on *source and rights*, not on signals or models. If the upstream pipeline is tainted, no amount of downstream aggregation or modeling can "wash" the data.

## Common Alternative Data Gray Zones

Most alternative data used in practice falls into gray zones rather than clear-cut legal categories. Understanding these gray zones is essential when designing guardrails.

### Web-Scraped Content

Web scraping ranges from clearly acceptable to clearly prohibited, depending on:

- **Access control:** Scraping content behind logins, paywalls, or technical protections (e.g., CAPTCHAs) is far riskier than scraping publicly accessible pages.
- **Terms of service (ToS):** Many sites explicitly forbid automated collection or commercial reuse. Violating ToS can breach contract law and, in some jurisdictions, computer misuse statutes.
- **Robots.txt and rate limits:** Even if not legally binding everywhere, ignoring them can be treated as evidence of bad faith.

From a trading perspective, web-scraped data must be vetted for:

- *Source provenance:* Which sites? What access mechanisms? Any logins or tokens?
- *Rights:* Do the sites' ToS permit scraping? Do you have a license?
- *Data content:* Are you inadvertently capturing user identifiers, private messages, or non-public corporate information?

### App Exhaust and Product Usage Data

"Exhaust" data is generated as a byproduct of using a digital service: clickstreams, in-app events, device metadata, and so forth. In the alternative-data ecosystem, vendors often aggregate exhaust from many apps and sell it as indicators of product adoption or engagement.

Key issues:

- **User consent:** Did end-users meaningfully consent to their data being used for analytics and resale to third parties, including financial institutions?
- **Scope of consent:** Was the consent limited to "improving the app" or did it include "sharing with partners for marketing and analytics"? Explicit reference to resale or financial use is rare and thus must be scrutinized.

- **Vendor-to-vendor chains:** Data can pass through multiple intermediaries. You must understand the chain from original collection to your firm and ensure that rights travel lawfully with the data.

### Location Traces and Sensor Data

Location pings from mobile devices, GPS sensors, Wi-Fi, or Bluetooth beacons can reveal store visits, commuting patterns, and logistics flows. This is powerful, but especially sensitive.

Risk drivers:

- **Re-identification risk:** Even if device identifiers are hashed, sparse location patterns can re-identify individuals. Re-identification risk increases with spatial and temporal precision.
- **Regulatory regimes:** Laws such as GDPR (EU) and CCPA/CPRA (California) impose requirements on consent, minimization, purpose limitation, and user rights (access, deletion).
- **Aggregation level:** Data aggregated to, say, daily store-visit counts by postal code is generally safer than raw device-level pings with timestamps.

For such data, compliance review often insists on strong aggregation or on-device processing before data reaches your environment, along with documented privacy assessments from the vendor.

## Designing a Compliance-Gated Intake Workflow

To embed these concerns into daily practice, you need a structured intake workflow where each alternative dataset passes explicit compliance gates *before* it touches any research or production system.

At a high level, the stages are:

- **Initial idea and source triage.**

- **Compliance due diligence and red-flag screening.**
- **Formal approval or rejection (possibly with remediation requirements).**
- **Technical onboarding: ingestion and cataloging.**
- **Monitored usage and periodic re-review.**

Right after establishing this principle, it is useful to visualize the process.

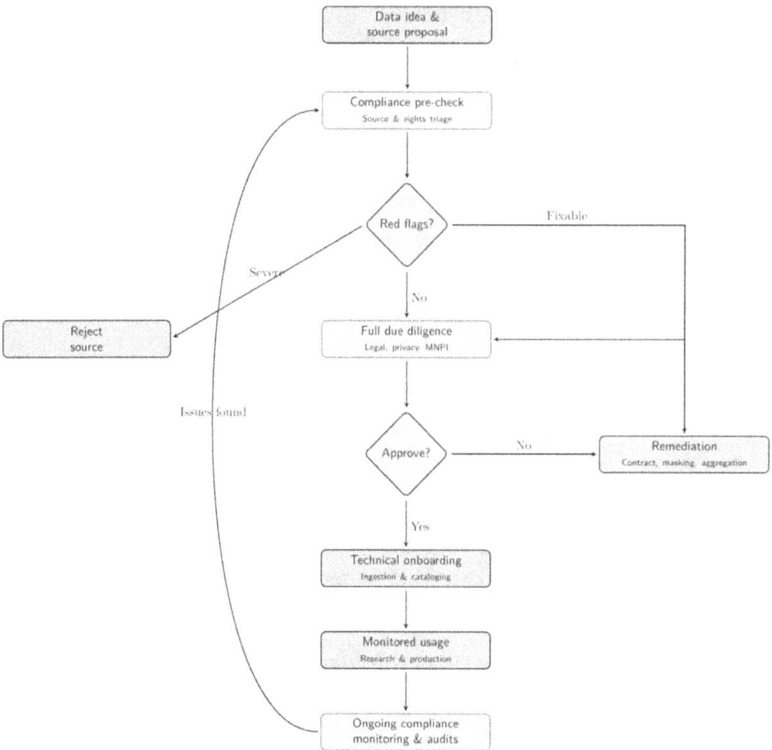


This diagram encodes the core philosophy: no dataset moves from "idea" to "usage" without passing through explicit, documented compliance checkpoints, and monitoring feeds back into earlier stages.

### Stage 1: Initial Idea and Source Triage

At this earliest stage, the goal is to quickly rule out obviously impermissible ideas and to prepare structured information for deeper review. You typically capture:

- **Business purpose:** What hypothesis does the dataset serve? Which asset classes or strategies?
- **Source description:** Who collects the data? Through what interfaces (APIs, SDKs, scraping, partnerships)?
- **Data content:** High-level fields and granularity (e.g., "daily store-level foot traffic" versus "raw device-level GPS pings").
- **Geographic coverage:** Which jurisdictions' data protection laws apply?

At this point, researchers and data engineers should be able to recognize obvious red flags and bring in compliance early rather than after technical work has begun.

### Stage 2: Compliance Due Diligence and Red-Flag Screening

Once a dataset passes initial triage, compliance and legal teams perform deeper due diligence. Typical questions include:

- **Collection practices:** How is the data collected in practice? Are there screenshots of consent dialogs, privacy notices, or ToS?
- **User consent and rights:** Does the consent explicitly allow third-party sharing? Are there mechanisms for opt-out and data deletion?
- **Vendor controls:** Does the vendor have its own compliance function, data-security certifications, and documented privacy assessments?
- **MNPI assessment:** Could the dataset reflect information that originated from insiders or confidential relationships?

The outcome is typically one of three:

- **Reject:** The source is fundamentally flawed (e.g., obtained via ToS violations, evident lack of consent, or ties to insiders).
- **Approve with conditions (remediation):** The dataset is usable only if specific mitigations are in place (e.g., aggregation, field suppression, contractual limitations).
- **Approve:** The dataset meets requirements under defined policies and can proceed to onboarding.

### Stage 3: Formal Approval, Contracts, and Policy Alignment

Formal approval usually requires:

- **Contractual rights:** Clear language on what you can do (research, backtesting, live trading) and cannot do (redistribute, re-identify, or combine with certain other sources).
- **Jurisdictional mapping:** Confirmation that data from specific regions complies with local privacy laws and cross-border transfer restrictions.
- **Retention and deletion rules:** How long you may store the data and under what conditions you must delete it.

Crucially, you must link the approval to your internal policies. For instance, your "Alternative Data Policy" might state that all user-level data must be aggregated to an entity or regional level before being used in models; the contractual terms and the technical implementation should reflect that.

### Stage 4: Technical Onboarding and Lineage

Once a dataset is approved, technical onboarding must be done in a way that preserves a clear *chain of evidence* from the legal approval to the actual bytes in storage. Good practices include:

**Versioning at Acquisition.** Treat each initial load and each subsequent vendor refresh as a versioned snapshot. At minimum, record:

- Dataset identifier and version.
- Acquisition date and time.

- Vendor name and contact.
- Contract or approval ID associated with this version.

**Data Lineage and Cataloging.** In your data catalog, every dataset should include:

- **Origin:** Source system or vendor, jurisdictions, and collection method.
- **Update cadence:** How frequently the data is refreshed.
- **Transformation history:** Major processing steps from raw ingestion to curated tables.
- **Approved use cases:** Research-only, paper trading allowed, or fully approved for production.
- **Restrictions:** Fields that must not be exported, shared, or used in certain models.

Engineers thus know not only *what* the data is, but also *how* they are permitted to use it.

### Stage 5: Monitored Usage and Periodic Re-Review

Compliance is not a one-time event. Laws, vendor practices, and platform policies evolve; so do your internal strategies and models. It is therefore essential to:

- **Log usage:** Record which teams, projects, and models access each dataset and when. This supports audits and incident investigations.
- **Monitor anomalies:** Sudden changes in vendor behavior (e.g., schema shifts exposing more granular data) should trigger review.
- **Schedule periodic audits:** Re-validate that consent forms, ToS, and contractual rights still cover your use cases.

In effect, every dataset has a "compliance lifecycle" parallel to its technical lifecycle.

## From Legal Guidance to Engineering Controls

So far we have discussed the *process*. To make this operational for researchers and engineers, you must translate high-level legal and policy guidance into concrete technical controls. Three families of controls are central: *access control, data minimization and masking*, and *automated policy checks*.

### Access Tiers and Role-Based Permissions

Not everyone should see every dataset. A simple but powerful pattern is to define *access tiers*.

- **Tier 0: Prohibited.** Datasets that have been rejected; no copies may exist in the environment.
- **Tier 1: Restricted raw data.** Highly sensitive data (e.g., semi-anonymized user-level events) used only by a small, designated engineering team that applies aggregation and de-identification.
- **Tier 2: Curated research data.** Aggregated or masked data approved for broader research use.
- **Tier 3: Production-safe features.** Final feature tables approved for use in live trading models.

With role-based access control (RBAC), you then map user roles (e.g., "vendor-integration engineer", "quant researcher", "production engineer") to specific tiers. Access changes (granting or revoking) should be logged and periodically reviewed.

### Data Minimization, De-Identification, and Aggregation

Data minimization means storing and using only the data necessary for your purpose. Common techniques include:

- **Field dropping:** Discard direct identifiers (names, emails, device IDs) as early as feasible.
- **Aggregation:** Convert user-level events into entity-level or regional metrics (e.g., per-store daily footfall).

- **Truncation and binning:** Reduce temporal or spatial precision (e.g., rounding coordinates to large grids, binning timestamps to hours or days).

*Anonymization* is frequently misunderstood. Simply hashing identifiers is often not enough; if the combination of other fields (timestamps, locations, behavior patterns) can re-identify individuals, the data may still be considered personal data under privacy laws. Therefore, technical de-identification must be accompanied by *re-identification risk assessment* and documented as part of the compliance record.

### Automated Policy Checks and Guardrails

To prevent accidental policy violations, you can embed simple automated checks into your pipelines:

- **Schema validators:** Assert that raw datasets do not contain forbidden fields (e.g., email, phone, precise coordinates) unless stored in a restricted tier.
- **Lineage-aware queries:** When researchers query data, the system can require that they only access approved, curated tables rather than raw restricted datasets.
- **Usage alerts:** Notify compliance if a dataset marked "research-only" is used in a pipeline that writes to a production feature store.

These controls do not replace human compliance review, but they greatly reduce the risk of unintentional drift outside the compliance perimeter.

## Jurisdictional Nuances and Global Portfolios

Most institutional investors operate portfolios exposed to multiple regions, and many alternative datasets are global. This interaction raises subtle issues.

**GDPR-Style Regimes.** In jurisdictions with strict data protection laws, personal data collection and processing require:

- A clearly defined legal basis (consent, contractual necessity, legitimate interest, etc.).
- Purpose limitation: you cannot repurpose data for incompatible ends without fresh consent.
- Data subject rights: access, correction, deletion, and portability.

Even if your firm has no physical presence in such a jurisdiction, handling data about its residents may trigger obligations. This can influence which subsets of a global dataset you are willing to ingest and how you must store them.

**Cross-Border Transfers.** Moving data across borders (e.g., from EU-based systems to US-based cloud infrastructure) may require specific safeguards (standard contractual clauses, adequacy decisions, or localization). Researchers need not be experts in these mechanisms, but the data catalog should clearly indicate any geographical or infrastructure constraints on each dataset.

## Why Strong Compliance is an Alpha Enabler

It is tempting to think of compliance as a tax on research velocity. In practice, disciplined compliance foundations can accelerate your work:

- **Faster approvals:** Standardized intake forms and clear policies reduce ambiguity and rework.
- **Reusable patterns:** Once you establish acceptable templates (e.g., for web-scraped news, aggregated location data), future vendors can be onboarded by analogy.
- **Defensible backtests:** When you know exactly what rights you had and how data was transformed and used, you can defend your models under regulatory scrutiny years later.
- **Strategic focus:** Eliminating non-viable datasets early lets you focus scarce engineering time on sources that are both legally sound and economically promising.

In other words, robust compliance foundations are not a barrier to competitive alternative-data trading; they are a prerequisite. In the next sections, we will build on this foundation to discuss how to acquire and manage data vendors, engineer high-quality datasets, and design research pipelines that respect these guardrails end-to-end.

## 3.2 Data Acquisition and Vendor Management

In the previous section we treated compliance as a hard constraint on *whether* a dataset is admissible for research and trading. We now turn to a more practical question:

> *Given those constraints, how do you actually find, evaluate, and manage data vendors so that your research roadmap is fed with reliable, legally sound, and economically rational data?*

Alternative data acquisition is often messy in practice: ad-hoc trials, one-off CSVs, forgotten contracts, and overlapping feeds that no one quite owns. The goal of this section is to replace that chaos with a disciplined acquisition process that links investment hypotheses to concrete data needs, and then to rigorously selected vendors.

We will proceed in four steps:

- Start from investment hypotheses and translate them into explicit data requirements.
- Run a structured search and evaluation process for potential vendors.
- Understand and negotiate the key commercial and legal terms.
- Build a portfolio-level vendor management approach to avoid waste and maintain quality.

Throughout, keep in mind the central theme: data is not free. Cost, complexity, and risk all compound. Vendor management is therefore as much a *portfolio construction* problem as selecting securities.

## From Investment Hypothesis to Data Requirement

A common anti-pattern in alternative data is "shopping for data": attending conferences, hearing vendor pitches, and buying feeds opportunistically because they *might* be useful. This rarely produces a coherent research program. Instead, you should start from the trading side.

## Clarifying the Information Edge

Every proposed dataset should answer a specific question about the world. You can think of this question as an *information edge hypothesis*. Examples:

- **Consumer demand timing:** "We believe that daily credit-card transactions around key holidays predict retail earnings surprises one quarter ahead."
- **Product adoption:** "We believe that early app-download and active-usage trends anticipate revenue growth for SaaS companies."
- **Operational stress:** "We believe that changes in shipping traffic around major ports signal bottlenecks that affect commodity prices and industrial firms."

Each hypothesis implies several data requirements:

- **Entities:** Which tickers, sectors, or macro variables must the data link to?
- **Frequency and latency:** How fresh must the data be to support the strategy? Intraday, daily, weekly?
- **History:** How many years of back history do you need to run statistically meaningful backtests?
- **Granularity:** Do you need store-level, region-level, or only country-level data? Company-level or user-level?

Documenting these elements up front has two benefits. First, it narrows your vendor search. Second, it gives compliance and legal a clear statement of purpose, which is important for privacy and regulatory assessments.

## Writing a Data Requirements Brief

In practice, it is useful to write a short data requirements brief for each potential acquisition. A simple template might include:

- Business owner and research owner.
- Investment hypothesis and target strategies.
- Required data characteristics (entities, frequency, latency, history, coverage).
- Sensitivity assessment (e.g., likely presence of personal data or location traces).
- Success metrics: what would count as a worthwhile signal improvement?

This document becomes the anchor for vendor conversations and later for evaluating whether the dataset delivered what you expected.

## Finding and Shortlisting Vendors

With a clear brief, you can now search for vendors who plausibly meet your needs. Sources include:

- Industry conferences and alternative-data marketplaces.
- Broker and bank research teams that curate vendor lists.
- Direct outreach to companies whose products generate relevant exhaust (e.g., e-commerce platforms, logistics providers).
- Open data and public datasets (government statistics, regulatory filings aggregators) that can complement paid feeds.

The goal at this stage is to assemble a *shortlist* of vendors for deeper evaluation, not to sign contracts yet. For each candidate, gather high-level facts:

- Data type and domain (web, transactions, mobility, news, ESG, etc.).
- Stated coverage (regions, sectors, instruments).
- High-level collection method and privacy posture.
- Typical clients (other asset managers, corporates, etc.).

Even this early, you should apply a basic compliance filter based on the previous section: discard vendors whose collection methods or rights look fundamentally misaligned with your firm's standards.

## Evaluating Vendors: Technical and Coverage Criteria

Once you have a shortlist, the next step is structured evaluation. You want to avoid being swayed by polished sales narratives; instead, compare vendors along a set of objective criteria.

## Coverage, History, and Stability

**Coverage.** Ask:

- Does the dataset cover the instruments you trade? For equities, what portion of your investable universe has non-trivial signal?
- Are there geographical gaps (e.g., strong US coverage but weak Asia)?
- Are there sector biases (e.g., strong for consumer discretionary, weak for industrials)?

**History.** For serious research you typically want:

- At least one full market cycle of data, and ideally several years of history.
- History that is representative of how the data is collected today, not a fundamentally different legacy product.

**Stability.** Data that constantly changes schema or methodology is expensive to maintain and dangerous for backtesting. Ask vendors:

- How often has the schema changed in the last few years?
- Have there been major methodological breaks (e.g., new collection channels, changes in how entities are mapped)?
- Do they provide change logs and versioning when they update methodologies?

## Latency and Update Frequency

Trading strategies are extremely sensitive to timing. A dataset can be economically useless if it arrives too late or with inconsistent delays.

Key questions:

- **Update frequency:** Is the data updated intraday, daily, weekly, or monthly?
- **Publication latency:** How long after real-world events is the data available? For example, "T+1 by 10:00 New York time" is very different from "within three business days."
- **Calendar alignment:** Are updates aligned with trading calendars, or can they arrive on weekends and holidays? Does the vendor provide clear timestamps in UTC or another standard?

In your research environment, you will later need to incorporate these latencies into backtests to avoid look-ahead bias. Evaluating them upfront prevents you from buying datasets that are structurally misaligned with your intended use.

## Engineering Maturity and Integration Effort

From a data engineering standpoint, some vendors are remarkably easy to work with and others create constant friction. Important dimensions include:

- **Delivery mechanism:** Well-designed REST APIs or S3-style file drops are easier to automate than ad-hoc email attachments or proprietary desktop tools.
- **Data formats:** Standardized formats (CSV with clear delimiters, Parquet, JSON with schemas) are preferable to Excel files or unstructured text.
- **Documentation quality:** Good vendors provide data dictionaries, field-level descriptions, sample code, and realistic examples that cover edge cases.
- **Entity mapping:** Do they provide robust mappings to tickers, ISINs, or other security identifiers, or will you need to build and maintain complex crosswalks?

A vendor with lower list prices but weak engineering support may cost more overall, once you factor in internal integration and maintenance work.

## Compliance and Privacy Posture

Building on the previous section, you should assess:

- How transparent is the vendor about data collection? Are there clear statements about consent, ToS, and legal reviews?
- Do they have internal compliance and legal teams with which your own teams can engage?
- Can they provide documentation, such as privacy impact assessments or summaries of legal opinions (where appropriate)?

This is not a one-time checkbox: your choice of vendors influences your ability to withstand regulatory scrutiny if your trading strategies are ever questioned.

## Commercial Terms and Total Cost of Ownership

Once technical and compliance evaluation is promising, you must confront economics. Alternative data is often priced in opaque ways, and naive buyers can end up with cost structures that overpower any potential alpha.

## Pricing Models

Common pricing models include:

- **Per seat:** Charged by named user or seat. This can be acceptable for visualization tools but is often misaligned with systematic research teams that rely on shared infrastructure.
- **Per symbol or universe slice:** Charged based on the number of tickers, regions, or sectors you access. This gives you control but may complicate experiment design if each incremental slice adds cost.
- **Per data volume:** Charged by gigabyte or row count. Useful when you only need a small subset; risky if you underestimate volumes.
- **Flat license:** A fixed annual fee for defined use cases. Simpler to manage but requires careful scoping.
- **Revenue share or performance-based:** Rare but occasionally offered; the vendor is paid a share of alpha or profits. These models pose complex valuation and conflict-of-interest questions.

The "cheapest" structure depends on your usage. For systematic teams that expect to integrate deeply and run many experiments, flat licenses or universe-based pricing often make more sense than per-seat models.

## Trials and Evaluation Periods

You should almost always insist on:

- A meaningful trial period (often 3–6 months) with enough history access to run backtests.
- Clear rules about what you can do with data during and after the trial (e.g., must you delete it if you do not proceed? Can you keep derived features?).
- Support during the trial: timely help with integration issues and explanation of quirks in the data.

A trial that only gives you a few weeks of sample data is rarely sufficient for robust evaluation and may be more of a marketing tool than a serious offering.

## Service Level Agreements (SLAs)

For production use, SLAs are critical. They should cover:

- **Uptime and availability:** Especially for API-based delivery.
- **Delivery timeliness:** Concrete commitments, such as "daily files available by 09:00 UTC" with remedies if repeatedly missed.
- **Schema stability:** Advance notice and documentation for any schema or methodology change.
- **Support responsiveness:** Expected response times for tickets, especially for production-impacting issues.

Well-crafted SLAs reduce operational risk and make it easier to integrate the dataset into automated pipelines.

## Estimating Total Cost of Ownership

To judge whether a dataset is economically rational, you must go beyond license fees and estimate *total cost of ownership* (TCO):

- Direct license cost (including any per-user, per-symbol, or per-volume components).
- Internal engineering time for initial integration and ongoing maintenance.
- Storage and compute costs, especially for high-volume feeds like tick-level data or raw location pings.
- Compliance and legal overhead, including reviews and audits.

A simple way to frame this is to ask: *What improvement in risk-adjusted performance (e.g., Sharpe ratio, drawdown statistics) do we need from this dataset to justify its annualized TCO?* You will not know the exact number upfront, but this discipline keeps you from collecting data for its own sake.

## Contracts, Rights, and Exit Strategies

Legal agreements with vendors express, in binding form, the rights and constraints that compliance has deemed acceptable. As a researcher or data engineer, you do not need to write contracts, but you must understand their implications.

## Usage Rights

Contracts usually specify:

- **Permitted uses:** Research, backtesting, paper trading, live trading, distribution to affiliates, etc.
- **Prohibited uses:** Redistributing raw data, providing it to clients, or reverse engineering certain aspects.

- **Scope:** Which legal entities within your firm can use the data.

Practically, this means your pipelines might need to separate research-only datasets from those cleared for live trading, even if they come from the same vendor.

## Retention and Termination

Key points include:

- How long you may keep historical data if you terminate the contract.
- Whether you may retain derived features or models trained on the data.
- Procedures for secure destruction of data on termination or at the end of retention periods.

These provisions matter for backtesting reproducibility. If you must delete all history upon termination, you should design your research logs and feature stores accordingly.

## Vendor Failure and Exit

Vendors merge, pivot, or go out of business. As part of vendor management, consider:

- What happens if the vendor stops delivering data or materially changes the product?
- Do you have rights to a final extract or to self-host infrastructure for a period?
- Do you maintain contingency plans (e.g., secondary vendors or open-data fallbacks)?

Thinking about exit at the beginning prevents you from becoming overly dependent on a single fragile data source.

## Standardized Onboarding Checklists

To ensure consistency across teams and years, it is helpful to implement a standardized onboarding checklist for every data vendor. A typical checklist might include sections for:

- **Business and hypothesis:** Completed data requirements brief, expected value.
- **Compliance:** Collection methods, consent documentation, MNPI assessment, jurisdictional issues.
- **Technical:** Delivery mechanism, formats, sample data validation, entity mapping, latency characterization.
- **Commercial:** Pricing model, SLAs, trial arrangements, retention and termination terms.
- **Operational:** Initial ingestion jobs, data catalog entries, assigned data owner, monitoring and alerting.

You can treat this checklist as a stage-gate: the dataset only becomes "available for research" in your catalog once all relevant boxes are ticked and signed off by the appropriate owners (research, engineering, compliance, legal).

## Portfolio-Level Vendor Management

As your organization matures, you will likely work with dozens of vendors. Managing them individually is not enough; you need a portfolio-level view, much like in asset management.

## Avoiding Redundant Coverage

Multiple datasets can cover the same economic phenomenon (e.g., web traffic, app usage, card transactions). It may be appropriate to maintain redundancy—for example, to mitigate vendor risk or combine complementary views. But redundancy can easily become wasteful.

To manage this:

- Maintain a simple inventory that maps each dataset to key *signals* or economic concepts (e.g., "US retail demand", "global mobility").
- Periodically review which datasets deliver unique alpha versus those that mostly replicate others.
- Be willing to prune underperforming feeds based on a combination of signal value and TCO.

## Measuring Vendor Performance

You can define key performance indicators (KPIs) for vendors, such as:

- Delivery timeliness adherence to SLA.
- Frequency and quality of communication about changes.
- Responsiveness to support inquiries.
- Stability of schema and methodology.

These KPIs can feed into renewal decisions and negotiations, just as you would reallocate capital from underperforming managers to better ones.

## Governance and Ownership

For each vendor and dataset, assign clear ownership:

- A business owner who is responsible for justifying the dataset economically.
- A technical owner who is responsible for integration and operational reliability.
- A compliance contact who monitors legal and regulatory aspects.

This mirrors the data governance themes we will develop in the next section. Without ownership, datasets tend to become "orphans"—still costing money, but with unclear usage and accountability.

### Putting It All Together

Data acquisition and vendor management sit at the intersection of strategy, engineering, compliance, and economics. A disciplined process:

- Begins with a clear investment hypothesis and corresponding data requirements.
- Shortlists and rigorously evaluates vendors on coverage, latency, engineering maturity, and compliance posture.
- Negotiates commercial terms and SLAs that reflect realistic usage and risk.
- Onboards datasets with standardized checklists, strong documentation, and clear ownership.
- Manages the vendor portfolio over time, pruning, renewing, or expanding based on value delivered relative to cost and risk.

With such a framework, adding a new data source is no longer a speculative gamble but a deliberate capital allocation decision. In the next section, we will turn inward and examine what happens once the data is in the door: how to measure and improve its quality, create useful labels for machine learning, and implement governance structures that keep your growing data lake coherent and trustworthy.

## 3.3 Data Quality, Labeling, and Governance

By this point in the chapter, we have focused on *which* data you are allowed to use (compliance) and *how* to bring it in the door (vendor management). Now we turn inward and ask a different question:

> *Once the data lands in your environment, how do you turn raw, messy feeds into reliable research assets that you can trust in backtests and, eventually, in production models?*

Alternative data is unusually noisy. Web logs contain bot traffic, card-transaction feeds have missing merchants, and location data is sparse and irregular. Naively feeding such data into sophisticated models is like building a skyscraper on swampy ground: the structure may look impressive, but it is not safe.

This section develops three pillars that stabilize that ground:

- **Data quality:** systematic checks and processes to detect and correct problems.
- **Labeling:** constructing clear targets and semantic tags that make data usable for supervised learning and organized exploration.
- **Governance:** assigning ownership and implementing controls so that every dataset and transformation is auditable and accountable.

Together, these turn raw feeds into trustworthy research assets with clear semantics and well-understood limitations.

## 3.4 What Do We Mean by Data Quality?

"Data quality" is often used loosely, but for trading applications it is useful to think of it along several concrete dimensions. A dataset that fails badly on any one of these can silently poison model performance or create false alpha in backtests.

**Key Quality Dimensions**

**Completeness.** Are the expected records present?

- For a daily panel keyed by (date, ticker), are there gaps in time (missing days) or cross-section (missing tickers)?
- For alternative data, do you have observations for all firms in a sector, or only for those with certain apps, websites, or physical footprints?

Incomplete coverage can create subtle biases: for example, if smaller firms are systematically missing, models may systematically misestimate risk or alpha for that part of the universe.

**Accuracy.** Are the values correct and plausible?

- Are there obvious errors (e.g., negative counts, impossible coordinates, prices off by factors of 100)?
- Are there duplicated entries that double-count events?

Accuracy problems may not show up as simple outliers; they can also appear as consistent but mis-scaled data (e.g., percentages represented as 0–1 in one period and 0–100 in another).

**Timeliness.** Is the data available in time to support your decision points?

- For daily strategies, can you reliably access the data before your order-cutoff time?
- For backtests, do the timestamps faithfully reflect when the information was *knowable*, not when your system ingested it?

Timeliness affects both feasibility in production and the integrity of historical simulations (avoiding look-ahead bias).

**Consistency.** Are definitions and units stable over time and across entities?

- Are field meanings consistent across regions, products, or vendors?
- Have definitions changed (e.g., which transactions are included in a "sales" metric), and are such changes versioned and documented?

Inconsistent definitions can create apparent regime shifts in models that are in fact data artifacts.

**Stability of the feed.** Does the data behave in predictable ways?

- Are delivery times, file naming conventions, and schema updates relatively stable?
- Does the data acquisition process itself change frequently (e.g., vendor adds/removes collection partners), leading to step-changes in coverage?

For trading, stability is almost as important as the quality of any single snapshot, because models and monitoring rely on predictable patterns.

## 3.5 Designing Automated Quality Checks

Good data quality cannot rely on heroics or ad-hoc inspection. You need automated checks that run every time new data arrives and that surface anomalies quickly and reproducibly.

At a minimum, consider three layers of checks: *schema*, *statistical*, and *cross-source*.

**Schema and Structural Checks**

These ensure that the incoming data matches your expectations about shape and fields.

- **Schema validation:** Verify that required columns are present, have the expected types (e.g., dates, floats, enumerated categories), and that there are no unexpected new fields that might indicate a vendor-side change.
- **Primary key constraints:** Check for uniqueness of keys such as (date, ticker) or (timestamp, device_id) after appropriate grouping. Duplicate keys can imply double-counting or upstream data replication.
- **Basic missingness checks:** Ensure that key identifiers (tickers, dates) and critical fields (e.g., counts, amounts) are not systematically missing.

These checks are cheap to run and can automatically block ingestion or raise alerts if violated.

### Statistical and Distributional Checks

Here you treat data values as a time series and examine whether new data is "reasonable" given historical patterns.

Typical examples:

- **Range checks:** Are numeric fields within plausible ranges (e.g., fraction of active users between 0 and 1, number of visits non-negative and below a large but realistic maximum)?
- **Distribution drift:** Compare summary statistics (mean, variance, percentiles) of the latest batch to recent history. Large shifts might indicate vendor changes, seasonal effects, or real-world events—all of which may require further investigation.
- **Volume checks:** Monitor row counts per day, per ticker, or per region. Sudden drops or spikes in record volumes can reveal outages, new collection channels, or changes in user behavior.

These checks should not automatically discard data based on simple rules; instead, they act as an early warning system that prompts human review when something unusual happens.

### Cross-Source and Reconciliation Checks

When multiple datasets speak about the same underlying reality, they can cross-validate each other.

For example:

- Compare vendor-reported web-traffic indices with public Alexa-style rankings or with another vendor's data.
- Compare aggregated card-transaction trends for a retailer with its reported revenues (shifted appropriately to match reporting lag).
- Check that company identifiers and entity mappings are consistent across feeds (same store or ticker appears under the same ID).

Discrepancies do not necessarily mean one source is "wrong," but they highlight where definitions or coverage differ, which is crucial context for modeling.

## 3.6 Deduplication and Conflict Resolution

Alternative data often comes from overlapping sources: two vendors may observe the same app usage, different brokers may provide similar analyst estimates, or your internal systems might generate attributes that overlap with external data.

**Identifying and Removing Duplicates**

Duplicates can arise from:

- Vendor-side replication (e.g., re-sending the same file with a new timestamp).
- Internal processing (e.g., accidentally loading the same file twice).
- Genuine re-observations of the same real-world event.

A robust deduplication process involves:

- Defining a canonical primary key at the right granularity (e.g., (event_id) or (timestamp, user_id, action) for event logs).
- Deciding how to treat near-duplicates (e.g., same timestamp and location but different noisy IDs).
- Logging how many records were dropped and why, so that changes in duplication rates can be tracked over time.

**Reconciling Conflicting Values**

Sometimes multiple sources give different values for what appears to be the same quantity: one vendor says store visits were 1000 on a given day, another says 1200.

Resolution strategies include:

- **Source hierarchy:** Define a priority order (e.g., regulatory filings > internal systems > external vendors) and choose the highest-priority source where conflicts occur.
- **Statistical combination:** Take averages, medians, or more sophisticated ensemble estimates, especially when each source has known biases.
- **Segmentation:** Use different sources for different segments (e.g., one vendor for US, another for Europe) if that reflects their strengths.

Whatever approach you choose, record it as part of the dataset's documented methodology so that modelers understand what they are consuming.

## 3.7 Introducing Labels: Targets and Semantic Tags

So far we have focused on input quality. To train models and to organize your data lake, you need clear *labels*. In trading, labels serve two main purposes:

- **Targets for supervised learning:** outcomes the model tries to predict.
- **Semantic tags for structure:** classifications or annotations that help discover, filter, and analyze data.

### Constructing Targets for Trading Models

A target is typically a function of future returns or events. For example:

- Next-day or next-week excess return of a stock.
- Realized volatility over a given horizon.

- Indicator that a firm will announce an earnings surprise above a certain threshold.

The construction of such targets must respect time-series structure:

- Use information *available at decision time* to define the target horizon. If your model trades at the close based on information up to that day's 15:00 time, your target might be the return from today's close to tomorrow's close.
- Avoid label leakage: do not inadvertently use future corporate events, index rebalancings, or revisions to data when defining targets.

In alternative data, the key challenge is to correctly align the timestamp at which the alternative signal becomes available with the financial target horizon.

**Labels for Text and Behavioral Data**

For NLP and behavioral signals, labels often take the form of annotations:

- **Sentiment:** positive, negative, or neutral tone of a news article or social-media post.
- **Relevance:** whether a piece of text actually pertains to the company or asset you care about.
- **Event type:** classification into categories such as product launch, regulatory action, management change, or macro announcement.

Creating these labels can involve:

- Manual annotation by domain experts or crowd workers.
- Weak supervision (e.g., using dictionaries, rules, or heuristic patterns as noisy labelers).
- Active learning, where the model asks humans to label the most informative or ambiguous examples.

The quality of these labels directly affects model performance. Noisy labels can sometimes be tolerated in large quantities, but systematic mislabeling (e.g., treating all mentions of "price cuts" as positive) will bias your models.

**Metadata and Catalog Labels**

Beyond model targets, you should assign semantic tags that describe each dataset:

- **Domain tags:** e.g., web-traffic, transactions, satellite, text-news.
- **Granularity tags:** e.g., daily-panel, event-level, tick-level.
- **Usage tags:** e.g., research-only, production-approved, restricted.

These metadata labels power your data catalog, making it easier for researchers to discover relevant datasets and understand their constraints.

## 3.8 A Dataset Lifecycle: From Raw Feed to Controlled Consumption

It is helpful to visualize the entire journey of a dataset inside your organization, from first ingestion to eventual use by models. Conceptually, the lifecycle includes:

- Raw ingestion.
- Quality checks and cleaning.
- Labeling and feature construction.
- Governance cataloging.
- Controlled consumption by researchers and production systems.
- Feedback from research and monitoring back to quality rules.

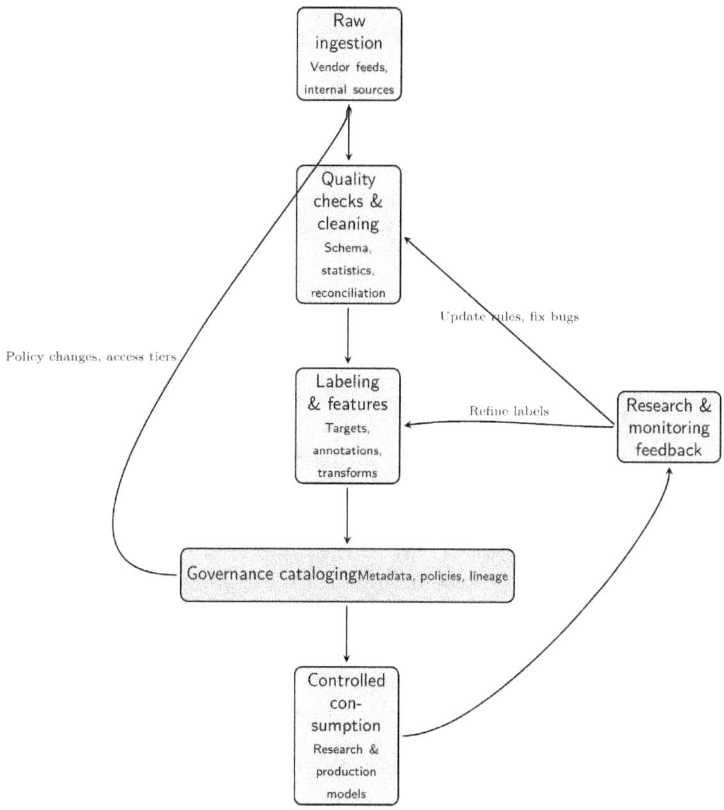
Raw ingestion
Vendor feeds, internal sources
Quality checks & cleaning
Schema, statistics, reconciliation
Labeling & features
Targets, annotations, transforms
Governance cataloging
Metadata, policies, lineage
Controlled consumption
Research & production models
Research & monitoring feedback
Update rules, fix bugs
Refine labels
Policy changes, access tiers

The following diagram encodes this lifecycle and highlights the feedback loops.

This lifecycle picture is not merely conceptual. It should guide how you structure your storage, pipelines, and documentation.

## 3.9 Governance: Ownership, Access, and Lineage

The final pillar is governance: ensuring that each dataset has clear owners, documented transformations, and controlled access. Governance connects directly back to the compliance and vendor-management topics from earlier sections, but here we focus on its internal technical expression.

**Assigning Data Owners**

Every dataset should have at least two clearly identified owners:

- A **business owner**, typically a lead researcher or portfolio manager, who is responsible for justifying why the dataset exists and how it contributes to strategies.
- A **technical owner**, typically a data engineer or platform team member, who is responsible for ingestion, quality checks, and operational reliability.

For particularly sensitive datasets, you may also specify a **compliance contact** who tracks constraints and participates in periodic reviews.

Owners are responsible for:

- Keeping documentation and metadata up to date.
- Responding to incidents (e.g., detected data errors, outages).
- Approving significant schema or methodology changes.

**Access Control and Views**

To respect compliance restrictions and minimize accidental misuse, access to data should follow the principle of least privilege.

Practical patterns include:

- **Role-based access control (RBAC):** Roles such as altdata-engineer, researcher, production-pipeline are mapped to specific datasets or tiers (e.g., raw vs. curated).
- **Project-scoped views:** Instead of giving researchers direct access to raw tables, create curated views that expose only approved fields, aggregations, and histories.
- **Temporal access policies:** For example, allow access to full history for research, but restrict real-time updates for interns or external collaborators.

Access changes (grants and revocations) should be logged so that you can answer who had access to what and when—essential in any investigation or audit.

### Lineage and Transformation Tracking

Lineage answers two fundamental questions:

- *Upstream:* Where did this dataset come from? Which raw tables and external vendors feed into it?
- *Downstream:* Which models, reports, and other datasets depend on it?

In practice, you can implement lineage via:

- Metadata in your data catalog that records upstream sources and key transformation steps.
- Automated integration with your pipeline orchestrator (e.g., DAGs that explicitly encode inputs and outputs).
- Experiment-tracking tools that log which dataset versions and features were used in each backtest or model training run.

Lineage is not only useful for debugging. It also supports:

- **Impact analysis:** If a vendor changes methodology, you can see which models must be re-evaluated.
- **Regulatory inquiries:** You can demonstrate how a trading decision traces back to particular data and transformations.

### Embedding Governance in Everyday Workflows

Governance must not be a separate, manual process that people bypass when busy. Instead, it should be embedded into the tools and workflows researchers already use.

Examples:

- When a new dataset is ingested, the onboarding job automatically creates or updates a catalog entry with owners, schemas, and quality checks.
- When a researcher creates a new feature table, a template prompts them for description, target use, and dependencies.
- When a production model is deployed, its configuration includes references to specific dataset versions and policies, enabling future reproducibility.

The ideal is that governance metadata is created as a byproduct of doing the work, rather than as a separate documentation exercise that people forget.

## 3.10 Why This Matters for Backtesting and Risk Control

From a modeling standpoint, good data quality, labeling, and governance have two major benefits.

**Reliable backtests.** Backtests are only as good as the data that feeds them. If you:

- Allow silent changes in coverage or schema,
- Misalign target labels with decision times,
- Or use poorly documented transformations,

then backtest performance can be inflated or misleading. High-quality, well-governed data reduces these risks and makes time-series cross-validation and other evaluation techniques more trustworthy.

**Robust production behavior.** In live trading, models need consistent inputs. Governance structures—quality checks, access control, lineage—act as guardrails that prevent sudden, unexplained shifts in features from going unnoticed. When something does change, you can quickly trace and remediate it.

Turning raw alternative data into alpha is not just a matter of clever models. It requires:

- **Data quality processes** that monitor completeness, accuracy, timeliness, consistency, and stability, supported by automated checks at ingestion and over time.
- **Thoughtful labeling**, both to construct proper supervised-learning targets and to semantically annotate text, events, and datasets in your catalog.
- **Strong governance**, with clear ownership, controlled access, and comprehensive lineage, so that every dataset is accountable and every model traceable.

With these pillars in place, your alternative data environment becomes a coherent research asset rather than a fragile collection of ad-hoc feeds. In the next section, we will examine specific alternative data domains—news and filings, web and social, sensor and location—and see how these quality, labeling, and governance principles play out in each, including their unique challenges and opportunities for finding alpha.

## 3.11 Alternative Data Domains: News, Web, and Sensor Signals

So far in this chapter we have built the foundations for using alternative data safely and effectively: compliance guardrails, disciplined vendor management, and internal processes for data quality, labeling, and governance. We now turn to the concrete *types* of alternative data you are likely to encounter, and how to connect them to tradable events in a statistically sound way.

This section surveys three major domains:

- News and corporate disclosures.
- Web and social signals.
- Sensor and transaction-type signals such as satellite imagery, location, and payment data.

For each, we will:

- Describe what the data actually looks like in practice.
- Explain how it can be aligned with specific trading decisions.
- Highlight the main sources of sampling error, bias, and noise that must be controlled for in research and production.

The goal is not to catalog every niche dataset, but to give you an intuitive mental model of how different domains behave and what caveats they carry.

### News, Filings, and Earnings Calls

News and corporate-disclosure data sits closest to the traditional information set used in fundamental and event-driven strategies, but at far greater scale. These sources are semi-structured text streams with clear links to issuers and events.

### What the Data Looks Like

Three common subtypes are:

**Real-time news wires.** Streams of short articles and headlines from financial and general-news providers, often tagged with:

- Timestamps (usually in UTC).
- One or more issuer identifiers (tickers, ISINs).
- Topics or categories (e.g., earnings, M&A, credit, macro).
- Source and language.

**Regulatory filings.** Periodic and ad-hoc reports—such as 10-Ks, 10-Qs, 8-Ks, annual reports, prospectuses—with:

- Official filing dates and times.
- Structured metadata (issuer, form type, period covered).
- Long-form text (management discussion, risk factors, footnotes).

**Earnings calls and corporate transcripts.** Audio and text records of management commentary, Q&A, and prepared statements, tagged with:

- Call start time and duration.
- Participants (management, analysts).
- Turn-level speaker labels and sections (prepared remarks vs. Q&A).

From an engineering standpoint, you are usually dealing with a sequence of text documents indexed by (timestamp, issuer) plus richer internal structure (paragraphs, sentences, speaker turns).

### Aligning with Tradable Events

For most systematic uses, you want to align these streams with specific trading events:

- **Earnings announcements:** Build features from pre-announcement news flow, language in filings, and tone in previous calls, then predict announcement-day or post-announcement returns.
- **Corporate actions and credit events:** Use news about downgrades, covenant issues, or regulatory scrutiny to predict spread moves.
- **Macro events:** Aggregate text about inflation, employment, or central banks to craft indicators that lead macroeconomic releases or risk sentiment.

Two timing issues are essential:

**Decision time vs. publication time.** You must respect the exact timestamp when the information became available. For example, if a filing is accepted by the regulator at 16:10 local time, and your strategy trades at the 16:00 close, that filing cannot influence today's close in a realistic backtest. It should instead be treated as available for trading at the next feasible decision time (e.g., tomorrow's open).

**Embargoes and revisions.** Some feeds, especially ratings, may be delivered to certain clients under embargo before public release, and filings can be corrected or restated. You must ensure that your backtests use the version and timestamp that matches your rights and actual access.

### Bias and Noise Considerations

Key pitfalls include:

**Coverage and survivorship bias.** Not all issuers receive equal news coverage. Large, controversial, or US-based firms may be over-represented relative to small, quiet, or emerging-market firms. If your strategy trains only on firms with rich news histories, it may not generalize to the full universe.

**Language and source bias.** News in different languages or from different outlets can systematically differ in tone and timing. If you only use English-language sources, you may overfit to markets and firms that communicate in English.

**Duplicate and syndicated content.** The same story can appear multiple times in slightly altered form. Deduplication (e.g., via hash-based similarity or clustering) is important to avoid overstating the intensity of an event.

Controlling these issues involves:

- Normalizing by baseline coverage (e.g., using sentiment relative to each issuer's typical news volume).
- Explicitly modeling the arrival intensity of news as part of the feature set.
- Carefully constructing training and test sets that mirror the cross-section and time periods you expect in production.

## Web and Social Data

Web and social signals promise a direct window into user attention, behavior, and sentiment. They also come with some of the most severe sampling and noise issues.

### What the Data Looks Like

Representative subtypes:

**Web-traffic and app-usage metrics.** Aggregated statistics such as:

- Daily visitors or sessions to a website or app.
- Time spent, pages per session, bounce rates.
- Install counts, active users, churn for mobile apps.

These often come from browser plugins, panel data, ISP logs, or SDKs embedded in apps, and are usually delivered as panel data keyed by (date, domain/app) with additional country or device segments.

**Search trends.** Aggregated counts or indices of how often users search for specific keywords. These are usually:

- Normalized indices rather than raw counts.
- Aggregated by region and time (daily/weekly).

- Subject to privacy-preserving noise and minimum-volume thresholds.

**Social media and user-generated text.** Streams of posts, comments, reviews, and ratings with:

- Timestamps, user IDs (often pseudonymous), and sometimes location.
- Text, emojis, and other media.
- Engagement metrics (likes, shares, replies).

These can be ingested through APIs, data resellers, or scraped content (subject to the compliance constraints discussed earlier).

**Entity Alignment and Tradable Events**

To use web and social data for trading, you must connect inherently messy online behavior to tradable instruments and events.

**Mapping entities.** For example:

- Map website domains and app names to listed companies (e.g., www.nike.com → NKE).
- Link product reviews or hashtags to brands or tickers (e.g., "#TSLA", "Tesla Model 3").
- Aggregate search queries containing a company or product name.

This mapping is error-prone. Many names are ambiguous (e.g., "Apple" the company vs. the fruit). Practical strategies include:

- Using curated mapping tables maintained by vendors.
- Building internal disambiguation models that use textual context and co-occurring terms.
- Maintaining confidence scores and excluding low-confidence matches from production signals.

**Aligning to trading horizons.** Examples:

- Short-horizon: sudden spikes in social chatter or search volume around a product issue may predict very short-term volatility or gaps.
- Medium-horizon: sustained increases in branded search activity or web traffic may forecast sales growth and thus earnings surprises.
- Long-horizon: shifts in review sentiment or brand perception might relate to multi-quarter performance and risk premia.

Here, you choose aggregation windows (e.g., 7-day moving average of search interest) and lags (e.g., using last week's activity to predict next month's returns) that match your strategy's rebalancing frequency.

**Sampling Bias, Bots, and Platform Regimes**

Web and social data are notorious for biases that can invalidate naive conclusions.

**Non-representative user bases.** A panel may overrepresent certain demographics, devices, or countries. Social-media platforms have their own demographic skews. If your model learns, for instance, that rising social buzz about a luxury brand is bullish, it may actually be picking up on the behavior of a narrow subset of high-engagement users.

**Bots and inauthentic activity.** Automated accounts, paid reviews, and coordinated campaigns can distort volume and sentiment metrics. Some platforms identify and remove such content over time, leading to revisions in historical data.

**Platform algorithm changes.** Changes in feed ranking, spam filters, or privacy defaults can abruptly alter what content is visible or collected, even if underlying user interest has not changed.

Mitigation strategies:

- Use vendor or internal filters to downweight suspected bot activity (e.g., accounts with extreme posting frequency or unusual network patterns).

- Work with long histories to estimate typical noise levels and detect structural breaks (e.g., using change-point detection on volume metrics).
- Normalize signals by platform-wide baselines—for example, using relative changes compared to sector-wide or market-wide activity, not absolute counts.

## Sensor, Location, and Transaction Signals

Sensor-based and transactional alternative data sources are particularly appealing because they measure physical or financial activity directly.

### What the Data Looks Like

Representative categories:

**Satellite imagery.** Images of the earth's surface taken at varying resolutions and revisit frequencies. In trading contexts, applications include:

- Counting cars in retail parking lots.
- Measuring shadows on oil-storage tanks to infer volume.
- Observing construction progress at large industrial sites.

The raw data consists of image tiles tagged with geospatial coordinates, timestamps, and sensor metadata (e.g., spectral bands, cloud cover).

**Geolocation pings.** Time-stamped latitude/longitude points from mobile devices, Wi-Fi, or beacons, delivered as:

- Device-level trajectories (often pseudonymized).
- Aggregated counts of visits or dwell time at specific locations (stores, malls, factories).

**Aggregated payment and transaction data.** Anonymized or aggregated spending metrics, such as:

- Daily card spend at merchants or merchant categories.
- Ticket sizes, transaction counts, or growth rates.
- Segment-level breakdowns (e.g., region, card type), subject to privacy constraints.

These are usually structured as panel data keyed by (date, entity), where the entity could be a store, merchant, postal code, or brand.

**From Physical Signals to Trading Variables**

The central modeling task is to convert raw physical or transactional measurements into features that connect to earnings, margins, or macro variables.

Examples:

**Store-visit and sales proxies.**

- Use visit counts or spending at a retailer's stores to estimate quarter-to-date sales, then infer the likelihood of an earnings beat or miss.
- Aggregate visits by region and compare to the firm's known store footprint to assess geographic performance.

**Production and logistics.**

- Track ship arrivals/departures or port congestion to infer supply-chain disruptions that may affect exporters and importers.
- Analyze nighttime lights or factory-activity proxies in industrial regions to infer production cycles.

**Commodity and capacity utilization.**

- Use satellite-based tank measurements to estimate oil inventories, then trade calendar spreads or related equities.
- Monitor utilization of key infrastructure (e.g., airports, toll roads) as macro indicators.

In all these cases, you must calibrate the lag between observed activity and reported financial outcomes, and decide whether you are targeting short-term price reactions (event-driven trades) or longer-term factor exposures.

**Coverage, Sparsity, and Privacy-Driven Noise**

Sensor and transaction data bring distinctive challenges:

**Sparse and irregular sampling.** Satellites may not pass over a given location daily; images can be obscured by clouds. Device data can be patchy in rural areas or certain countries. Card data may cover only specific issuers or card types.

This leads to:

- Uneven time-series coverage across entities and regions.
- Measurement error that depends on geography and demographics.

**Selection and panel drift.** The underlying panel (devices, cards, merchants) can change over time as users churn, apps change, or banks join/leave partnerships. If uncorrected, this can produce spurious trends.

**Privacy-driven aggregation and noise.** To comply with privacy laws, vendors often:

- Suppress low-count cells (e.g., not reporting store-level metrics if visits are below a threshold).
- Add noise to aggregated counts (differential privacy).
- Coarsen spatial or temporal resolution.

These mechanisms complicate the mapping from observed numbers to true activity.

To manage these issues:

- Use statistical techniques that explicitly model measurement error and sampling processes (e.g., hierarchical models that borrow strength across entities).

- Track panel composition over time—e.g., effective sample sizes per store, region, or merchant category—and adjust or normalize accordingly.
- Restrict production models to regimes and segments where coverage and noise properties are reasonably stable.

## Cross-Cutting Issues: Bias, Regime Change, and Robust Backtesting

Although each domain has its own quirks, several cross-cutting concerns recur.

### Survivorship and Look-Ahead Bias

In all domains, beware of building datasets retrospectively with knowledge you would not have had in real time. Examples:

- Filtering to firms that are currently listed and then backfilling their alternative-data history, ignoring delisted firms (survivorship bias).
- Using revised, cleaned, or augmented versions of vendor data in historical backtests, when in reality those corrections came later (look-ahead).

The cure is to:

- Use point-in-time snapshots or versioned histories when available.
- Simulate data availability (e.g., release delays, missed files) in backtests, based on actual vendor performance logs or realistic assumptions.

### Regime Changes and Non-Stationarity

Alternative data sources are embedded in complex socio-technical systems: platforms, devices, laws, and user habits all evolve.

Examples:

- A major privacy regulation leads to opt-out prompts, reducing panel coverage.
- A social-media platform changes its algorithm, altering what gets posted and engaged with.
- Smartphone adoption stalls or saturates in key demographics.

These changes can alter the meaning and predictive power of signals over time. Robust research therefore requires:

- Monitoring signal behavior (e.g., correlation with fundamentals or returns) across sub-periods.
- Stress-testing models across different regimes, not just global averages.
- Being prepared to retire or re-engineer signals whose data-generating processes have shifted.

### Combining Domains and Controlling for Confounds

Often, the strongest models arise from combining multiple domains—for example, news sentiment with card transactions and web traffic. When doing so, you must be careful to distinguish:

- **Unique information:** features that add incremental explanatory or predictive power.
- **Redundant proxies:** highly correlated signals that reflect the same underlying driver (e.g., buzz and search volume for the same event).

From a methodological standpoint:

- Control for basic risk factors, sector and size effects, and conventional variables before attributing alpha to alternative features.
- Use out-of-sample and out-of-time tests that mimic real deployment, including realistic feature-availability constraints.

Alternative data is not a monolith. News and filings, web and social streams, and sensor and transaction signals each offer distinct windows into corporate and macroeconomic reality:

- **News and filings** are tightly linked to formal corporate events, with relatively clean issuer mappings but complex timing and duplication issues.
- **Web and social data** illuminate attention and sentiment but suffer from strong platform, demographic, and bot-driven biases.
- **Sensor, location, and transaction data** provide concrete measures of physical and financial activity, yet are constrained by coverage, sparsity, and privacy mechanisms.

In all domains, the essential tasks are the same: align signals to well-defined trading decisions; understand and correct for sampling, bias, and noise; and embed these datasets into the quality, labeling, and governance framework established earlier in the chapter. With that foundation, the next section will show how to turn these heterogeneous inputs into coherent, time-aligned features and research pipelines that support scalable, reproducible model development.

## 3.12 Feature Engineering and Research Pipelines

Up to this point, we have focused on *what* data you may use (compliance), *where* to get it (vendor management), *how* to keep it clean (quality), and *how* to describe and govern it (labeling and cataloging). We now turn to the part most quants instinctively care about:

> *How do we turn heterogeneous alternative data into robust time-series features and build research pipelines that are scalable, reproducible, and production-ready?*

In many organizations, this is where discipline erodes: researchers download raw CSVs, write one-off scripts, and train models directly from ad-hoc tables. The result is fragile: backtests cannot be reproduced, features behave inconsistently across notebooks, and promoting a signal to production requires rewriting everything.

This section aims to replace that ad-hoc approach with a structured *research factory*. We will:

- Clarify the goals and constraints of feature engineering for time-series trading.
- Present a high-level architecture for research pipelines that turns vendor feeds into standardized feature tables.
- Discuss common transformations—rolling statistics, decay functions, surprise measures, and cross-sectional ranks—and how to avoid leakage.
- Explain how to separate research and production pipelines while sharing core components.
- Introduce experiment tracking as a first-class requirement for reproducible research.

## From Raw Events to Time-Aligned Features

Alternative data feeds are heterogeneous at the surface—text, events, images, pings—but the downstream models you build generally expect something simpler: time-indexed features keyed by assets and decision times.

## The Target Shape: Panel of Features

For most equity or macro strategies, your goal is to construct a panel:

$$X_{i,t} = \left(x_{i,t}^{(1)}, x_{i,t}^{(2)}, \ldots, x_{i,t}^{(K)}\right)$$

where:

- $i$ indexes assets (e.g., tickers).

- $t$ indexes decision times (e.g., daily bars, weekly rebalancing dates).
- $x_{i,t}^{(k)}$ is the $k$-th feature available at decision time $t$ for asset $i$.

You may also include lags (e.g., $x_{i,t-1}$, $x_{i,t-5}$) and aggregate cross-sectional or sector-level features, but the key is that all features are aligned on a common $(i, t)$ grid that matches your backtesting and trading calendar.

## Heterogeneous Raw Inputs

Alternative data arrives in many forms:

- **Event streams:** news articles, tweets, filings, transactions, visits—each with a timestamp and associated entity.
- **Irregular measurements:** satellite overpasses, survey responses, daily but with gaps.
- **Panel metrics:** pre-aggregated daily indices of web traffic, card spend, or app usage.
- **Text and embeddings:** textual documents or their vector representations.

The main engineering challenge is to *aggregate and align* these inputs so that, at each decision time $t$, you can query "what information was available for asset $i$?" in a way that is both accurate and computationally efficient.

## A High-Level Architecture for Research Pipelines

Before diving into specific transformations, it is useful to lay out the architecture that connects raw vendor feeds to features, models, and evaluations. Conceptually, the pipeline has several layers:

- Ingestion and raw storage.

- ETL / normalization and quality filters.
- Curated feature stores.
- Experiment tracking and model training.

The following diagram provides a high-level view.

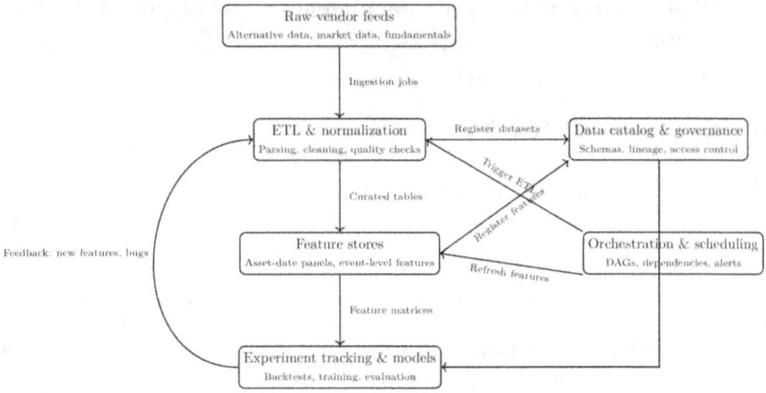


This architecture emphasizes a few key principles:

- **Separation of concerns:** Ingestion and ETL logic is centralized and reusable; researchers mostly consume from feature stores.
- **Standardized interfaces:** Feature tables have well-defined schemas (e.g., keys, timestamps, horizons), making it easy to plug them into models.
- **Governance integration:** The data catalog and orchestrator are integrated, ensuring lineage and quality checks are part of the pipeline, not afterthoughts.

## Time-Series Feature Engineering: Core Patterns

With the architecture in place, we can focus on how to construct useful features from the raw and curated tables. We will use simple notation:

let $s_{i,\tau}$ be a raw signal (e.g., web traffic, sentiment score, visit count) for asset $i$ at time $\tau$. Our goal is to produce features $x_{i,t}$ at decision times $t$.

## Aggregating Over Time Windows

Many alternative signals are high-frequency relative to your trading horizon (e.g., intraday events for daily strategies). A basic pattern is to aggregate over a lookback window:

$$x_{i,t}^{\text{sum}(L)} = \sum_{\tau \in (t-L,\, t]} s_{i,\tau}, \qquad x_{i,t}^{\text{mean}(L)} = \frac{1}{L} \sum_{\tau \in (t-L,\, t]} s_{i,\tau}.$$

For example:

- Count of news articles about firm $i$ in the last 5 days.
- Average daily card spend at a retailer in the last 30 days.
- Total number of store visits in the past 2 weeks.

The window length $L$ should reflect both the microstructure of the signal and your strategy's horizon. Shorter windows emphasize recent events; longer windows smooth noise but risk diluting rapidly changing information.

## Decay and Exponential Weighting

Events closer to decision time are often more informative than older ones. Instead of simple averages, use exponentially weighted sums:

$$x_{i,t}^{\text{exp}} = \sum_{\tau \le t} \lambda^{t-\tau} s_{i,\tau}, \quad 0 < \lambda < 1,$$

where $\lambda$ controls the effective memory. This is particularly natural for:

- Sentiment scores from news or social media (recent tone matters more).

- Engagement metrics (recent spikes may be more predictive than long-past popularity).

In implementation, exponential updates are efficient to maintain incrementally as new data arrives.

## Surprise Measures and Baselines

Raw levels are often less informative than *surprises*—deviations from expected or typical patterns. A generic construction is:

$$\text{surprise}_{i,t} = \frac{s_{i,t} - \mu_{i,t}^{\text{baseline}}}{\sigma_{i,t}^{\text{baseline}}},$$

where $\mu_{i,t}^{\text{baseline}}$ and $\sigma_{i,t}^{\text{baseline}}$ are rolling estimates of the mean and volatility of $s$ for asset $i$.

Examples:

- Abnormal web traffic: visits today relative to the last 60 days.
- Abnormal card spend: current week's spend relative to the same week-of-year across prior years (to respect seasonality).
- Abnormal news volume: today's article count relative to typical coverage for that firm.

Surprise measures help control for persistent cross-sectional differences (e.g., large firms always have more traffic and more news) and focus attention on changes.

## Cross-Sectional Ranks and Neutralization

Many strategies operate on cross-sectional relationships at a given time: you go long assets with high features and short those with low features. Rather than feeding raw values into the model, you can transform features into cross-sectional ranks or z-scores:

$$\tilde{x}_{i,t} = \frac{x_{i,t} - \mu_t}{\sigma_t},$$

where $\mu_t$ and $\sigma_t$ are the cross-sectional mean and standard deviation across assets at time $t$.

Alternately, use ranks:

$$\text{rank}_{i,t} = \frac{1}{N_t} \sum_j \mathbf{1}\{x_{j,t} \leq x_{i,t}\},$$

where $N_t$ is the number of assets at time $t$. Ranks are robust to outliers and non-linear scales.

You can also neutralize features with respect to known risk factors (e.g., sector, size) by regressing $x_{i,t}$ on these controls cross-sectionally and using residuals as features. This helps isolate the *alternative* component of the signal.

## Handling Irregular Timestamps and Missingness

Alternative data is rarely as regular as daily OHLC price bars. You must consciously deal with irregularity and gaps.

## Event Alignment

For event-level data (e.g., individual transactions, news articles), you need to assign each event to the appropriate decision time:

- For a daily close-to-close strategy, you might assign all events in $(t - 1 \text{ day}, t]$ to feature time $t$.
- For intraday strategies, define decision intervals (e.g., every 5 minutes) and bucket events accordingly.

When doing this, respect market hours and vendor delays: an article released after market close belongs to the next trading day's decision set.

## Imputation and Missing Data

You will encounter missing observations:

- Panel gaps where a vendor had an outage or changed coverage.
- Persistent zeros where the underlying activity truly is absent.

Naively filling gaps (e.g., forward-filling) can inject artificial persistence and lead to overconfident models. Strategies include:

- Use separate "missingness" indicators (binary flags) as features, allowing the model to learn that absence of data is itself informative or a sign of vendor issues.
- Restrict features to entities and periods with sufficient coverage, and mark others as missing (letting the model or downstream logic handle them).
- For truly continuous processes (e.g., daily indices) with occasional missing days, use conservative interpolation (e.g., local linear), but treat such cases with caution in backtesting.

## Avoiding Feature Leakage

Feature leakage occurs when features implicitly contain information from the future relative to the decision time. Alternative data pipelines are particularly vulnerable because:

- Vendor data may be backfilled or corrected later.
- Aggregation windows are easy to define incorrectly (e.g., including same-day close prices when predicting same-day returns).
- Aligning to calendars and time zones is non-trivial.

To avoid leakage:

- Always define feature-time explicitly as "information known (or knowable) as of time $t$ under production constraints".

- Simulate vendor delays and corrections: do not assume that backfilled history was available in real time.
- In code, prefer using lag operators that enforce strict inequalities (e.g., only include data with timestamps *strictly less than* the decision time).

Testing for leakage—for example, by running trivial models that achieve implausibly high performance or by deliberately shuffling labels in time—should be part of your standard research hygiene.

## Research vs. Production Pipelines

A common source of fragility is having completely separate pipelines for research and production. This leads to subtle differences in feature definitions and bugs that only appear after deployment. The remedy is not to merge everything into one system, but to *share core components* while allowing appropriate flexibility.

## Shared Core: ETL and Feature Definitions

Both research and production should:

- Use the same ETL code to parse and normalize raw feeds.
- Use the same feature-definition code (e.g., library of transformations that define each $x_{i,t}$).
- Refer to versioned datasets and feature tables via the same catalog.

In practice, this means building a library or package for feature engineering that is imported in both notebook-style research code and production pipelines.

## Differences: Schedules and Robustness

Research-specific differences include:

- Ability to join experimental datasets and run heavy computations.
- Flexible backtest windows, hyperparameter sweeps, and cross-validation schemes.

Production-specific differences include:

- Rigorous scheduling and orchestration (e.g., DAGs that ensure dependencies are met before trading).
- Strong monitoring, alerting, and fallbacks when features fail or are delayed.

The interface between the two is typically the *feature store*: in research, you can compute features on arbitrary histories; in production, you regularly refresh only the features required by active models.

## Experiment Tracking and Reproducibility

In a serious research program, you will run hundreds or thousands of experiments: different feature sets, architectures, training windows, and hyperparameters. Without disciplined tracking, you will lose the ability to understand why a particular model worked and to reproduce its results on demand.

## What to Log

At minimum, for each experiment you should log:

- Identifiers and versions of datasets and feature tables used.
- Model architecture and hyperparameters.
- Training, validation, and test period definitions.
- Objective and evaluation metrics (e.g., information ratio, drawdown statistics).

- Code or configuration version (e.g., Git commit).

This information can be stored in a centralized experiment-tracking system, or a well-structured database, but in either case it must be queryable and linked back to the data catalog.

## Benefits for Risk and Compliance

Experiment tracking is not just for scientists; it supports:

- **Model risk management:** You can reconstruct how a production model was developed and validated, and what alternatives were considered.
- **Regulatory defensibility:** If questioned, you can demonstrate that your strategy was based on systematic, documented research rather than cherry-picking.
- **Operational robustness:** When a vendor changes methodology, you can quickly identify all experiments and models that depend on the affected features.

## Storage Formats, Partitioning, and Scalability

Finally, some practical notes on making the machinery scale.

## Columnar Formats and Feature Stores

For large panel datasets, columnar storage formats (e.g., Parquet) and feature-store abstractions provide:

- Efficient I/O when you only need a subset of features or time ranges.
- Schema evolution with backward compatibility.
- Integration with distributed processing frameworks.

Feature stores typically expose APIs to read features for specific $(i, t)$ sets (e.g., the current universe on a given date) and to write back new derived features.

## Partitioning Schemes

Partitioning tables by date (and optionally asset buckets) helps:

- Prune irrelevant partitions during queries (e.g., only last year of data).
- Parallelize processing across time or cross-sectional shards.

However, over-partitioning (too many tiny files) can degrade performance; you must balance granularity against overhead.

## Scheduling and Orchestration

Modern orchestrators (Airflow-style DAGs, cloud-native schedulers) help you:

- Define dependencies between ingestion, ETL, feature computation, and model updates.
- Implement retries, failure alerts, and SLAs (e.g., features must be ready by 09:00).
- Visualize and audit runs over time.

These tools transform your research pipelines from a handful of brittle cron jobs into an observable, debuggable system.

Feature engineering and research pipelines are the bridge between raw alternative data and tradable signals. The key ideas in this section are:

- **Time alignment:** All features must be expressed on a common asset-time grid that reflects real information availability.

- **Robust transformations:** Use aggregations, decays, surprises, and cross-sectional standardizations to extract signal while controlling for noise and scale.
- **Leakage control:** Design windows and lags carefully, and simulate vendor behavior, so that backtests do not peek into the future.
- **Architected pipelines:** Separate ingestion, ETL, feature stores, and experiments, but share core definitions and integrate governance.
- **Reproducibility:** Treat experiment tracking and dataset versioning as non-negotiable, not optional extras.

With these tools, your alternative-data platform becomes a disciplined research factory: new feeds can be plugged in, transformed, and evaluated systematically, and promising signals can move from notebook to production with minimal friction and maximal transparency.

# Chapter 4

# NLP Foundations for Financial Text

*Markets move on words long before they move on prices. In this chapter, we turn earnings calls, macro speeches, research notes, and social chatter into structured, tradeable information. You'll learn how to clean and tokenize messy financial text, represent language as vectors, adapt transformer models to your domain, and extract entities, events, and sentiment that can be wired directly into your alpha pipeline.*

## 4.1 Text Preprocessing and Tokenization

In the previous chapter we treated text as an abstract information source: news, filings, and transcripts can move prices, and our objective is to convert those narratives into quantitative signals that a model—and ultimately a portfolio—can consume. In this section we take the first concrete step: turning messy raw documents into stable sequences of tokens.

For numeric time series you rarely worry about whether 1.23 was scraped as 1.23 or 1,23; the vendor takes care of it. With financial text you *are* the vendor. If you change the way you clean or tokenize a 10-K, all your downstream features can change. That means you must design the text pipeline with the same care you apply to return calculations, risk models, or backtest configuration.

Our goals are:

- Preserve symbols and identifiers that carry financial meaning (tickers, ISINs, CUSIPs, credit ratings).
- Handle numbers in a principled way, so that magnitudes, percentages, and ratios are represented consistently.
- Treat domain-specific phrases (*"credit default swap"*, *"free cash flow"*, *"non-GAAP"*) as stable model inputs rather than arbitrary word fragments.
- Produce a *versioned*, reproducible pipeline so that any change is explicit and auditable from a backtesting perspective.

We will gradually build a pipeline that starts with raw 10-Ks, news articles, and transcripts and ends with model-ready token sequences.

## From Raw Documents to Clean Text

Financial documents arrive in many formats: HTML web pages, PDF filings, plain-text news feeds, and partially structured transcript formats. They also arrive with encoding quirks, boilerplate, and layout artifacts. The first stage of the pipeline is to normalize these into a clean, consistent textual representation.

## Document ingestion and decoding

At ingestion, your tasks are:

- **Detect and fix character encodings.** Many legacy filings and emails use encodings such as ISO-8859-1, Windows-1252, or mixed encodings. Normalize all documents to UTF-8 and replace non-printable characters with safe placeholders or by deletion.

- **Strip irrelevant markup.** From HTML, you may want to preserve headings, paragraph breaks, lists, and tables but remove navigation menus, ads, and JavaScript. From PDFs, you want text content and layout hints, but not page headers/footers repeated on every page.

- **Track provenance.** Attach metadata: document type (10-K, 8-K, earnings call transcript, news), issuer, source, and timestamps (publication time, filing time). This is essential for avoiding look-ahead bias later and for linking text back to securities.

At this stage you still keep a relatively rich structure: paragraph breaks, table boundaries, and section headings are helpful for later processing such as sentence segmentation and context-aware feature extraction.

## Cleaning and boilerplate control

The next step is to remove noise without destroying signal. Financial text includes large chunks of repeated or low-information content:

- Standard risk disclosures that barely change year to year.
- Legal boilerplate in press releases.
- Repeated copyright and safe harbor statements.

A naïve model trained on such text will overfit to boilerplate rather than to incremental information. Practical techniques include:

- **Boilerplate dictionaries.** Maintain lists of known boilerplate segments (e.g., paragraph-level strings) and strip or down-weight them. You can identify candidates by high document frequency but near-identical content across issuers or years.

- **Duplicate detection.** Within a document, remove exact duplicate paragraphs or lines, which frequently appear across PDFs and transcripts as repeated headers or disclaimers.

- **Section-based filtering.** For some tasks you may choose to ignore entire sections (e.g., *"Forward-Looking Statements"* sections for certain sentiment tasks) or at least tag them so a model can treat them differently.

The key principle is to treat cleaning as *domain-aware*. You are not simply deleting all frequent text; you are selectively suppressing content that is *known* to be non-informative for your target tasks.

## Character normalization and punctuation

After gross cleaning, you normalize characters and punctuation:

- Map curly quotation marks to straight quotes, normalize dashes (em-dash, en-dash) to simple hyphens, and standardize bullet characters.

- Canonicalize whitespace: collapse repeated spaces, convert non-breaking spaces, and decide how to handle line breaks (e.g., joining lines within a paragraph).

- Normalize Unicode variants of the same symbol (e.g., Greek letters in formulas, special percent signs) to a single representation.

From a modeling perspective, this step reduces spurious sparsity: you do not want separate tokens for “risk” and "risk", or for various dash characters.

## Sentence Segmentation and Structured Layout

Most modern NLP models operate at the level of sentences or segments rather than entire documents. Long filings can run to tens of thousands of tokens, so you must break them into manageable units while preserving enough context.

## Sentence segmentation in noisy financial text

Standard sentence splitters use simple heuristics: periods followed by spaces and capital letters usually mark sentence boundaries. Financial text violates these assumptions:

- Ticker symbols (e.g., BRK.B), abbreviations (Inc., Ltd., Co.), and initials create many false sentence boundaries.
- Tables and bullet lists may omit terminal punctuation entirely.
- Transcripts include speaker tags, interruptions, and asides.

A robust sentence splitter for finance should:

- Use domain-specific abbreviation lists to avoid splitting after Inc., Corp., Mr., etc.
- Treat common ticker patterns ([A-Z]{1,5}[A-Z]) as single tokens and *not* as sentence breaks.
- Handle bullet lists by treating each bullet as a separate segment even without final punctuation.
- Recognize transcript speaker patterns (e.g., Operator:, Analyst:, John Smith - CFO) as segment boundaries.

These details matter because many tasks—sentiment labeling, guidance detection, event extraction—operate at the sentence or clause level. If you segment poorly, your labels and features will be noisy.

## Tables, lists, and mixed-layout content

Filings contain both narrative and tabular data. For example, a 10-K may have a revenue table and then explanatory text immediately below it. There are three common strategies:

- **Text-only mode.** Drop tables entirely and focus on narrative. This is reasonable for initial language modeling but discards explicit numeric detail.

- **Inline placeholders.** Replace tables with structured placeholders like <TABLE_REVENUE> and preserve the accompanying caption and nearby text. This acknowledges the presence of numeric content without exploding token counts.

- **Hybrid extraction.** Parse tables separately into numeric arrays (used as traditional features) while keeping the surrounding text for language features. This is attractive for multi-modal models that combine text and fundamentals.

Whichever you choose, you must be consistent across your dataset; otherwise, backtests will silently compare apples and oranges when your pipeline changes.

## Designing Tokenization for Financial Text

With reasonably clean text and sensible segmentation, we can turn to the core question: *how do we break text into tokens?* Tokenization is the bridge between raw strings and numerical representations. Poor tokenization can destroy exactly the symbols and phrases that carry alpha.

## What is a token?

Conceptually, a token is an atomic unit for your model. Different tokenization schemes define "atomic" differently:

- **Whitespace or rule-based tokens:** roughly align with words or punctuation.

- **Subword tokens:** learned units that may be whole words (risk) or fragments (re, ##structur, ##ing).

- **Character or byte tokens:** individual characters or bytes.

We will focus on options that are practical for finance: rule-based tokens, and subword tokenization methods such as Byte-Pair Encoding (BPE), WordPiece, and unigram models (e.g., sentencepiece).

## Rule-based tokenization: strengths and limits

A simple rule-based tokenizer might:

- Split on whitespace.
- Separate punctuation from words (e.g., risk. becomes risk, .).
- Treat numbers as individual tokens.

For many classical models (bag-of-words, TF–IDF, simple n-grams), this is adequate and easy to interpret. In finance, however, you need additional rules:

- **Protect tickers and identifiers.** You want AAPL, BRK.B, US0378331005 (ISIN), or 037833100 (CUSIP) to appear as single tokens. That may require regex patterns that suppress splitting on interior dots or digits.
- **Handle rating symbols.** Credit ratings such as BBB+ or Aa3 should be preserved as units, not split into "BBB" and "+" or "Aa" and "3".
- **Normalize casing carefully.** Lowercasing everything (a common NLP practice) would collapse tickers (A vs a) and abbreviations (EPS vs eps). In finance, casing often carries information. A compromise is to keep original case but maintain a parallel lowercase form for matching.

Rule-based tokenizers are transparent and fast. They are often your first choice for prototyping and for models where interpretability is paramount. Their main limitations are vocabulary growth (every new variant is a new token) and poor handling of rare or noisy words.

## Subword tokenization: BPE, WordPiece, and unigram models

Modern transformer models almost universally use subword tokenization. The idea is simple: rather than treating each word as atomic, you learn a vocabulary of frequently occurring character sequences (subwords). Rare words are composed of multiple subwords.

For example, a generic BPE tokenizer might segment:

```
"deleveraging" -> "del", "##ever", "##aging"
"micro-hedge" -> "micro", "-", "hedge"
```

This has three important consequences:

- The vocabulary can be relatively small (e.g., 30k tokens) while still covering many word forms.
- Any new word can be represented as a sequence of existing subwords (no true out-of-vocabulary tokens).
- Frequent morphemes (prefixes, suffixes) and domain fragments are captured as reusable units.

However, off-the-shelf subword tokenizers trained on general web text do not know that "EBITDA" or "CDS" should be single atomic units and that BRK.B is a ticker, not the word "BRK" followed by a period and "B". If you simply plug financial text into a generic tokenizer, it may:

- Split tickers into unnatural pieces, diluting their semantics.
- Merge numbers and punctuation in unhelpful ways (e.g., 10-K into 10, -, K, losing the fact that this is a specific filing type).
- Break multi-word financial phrases into fragments that are hard to interpret or aggregate.

To address this, you have two main levers:

- **Custom vocabulary.** Train or extend a tokenizer on an in-domain corpus (filings, news, transcripts). Ensure that common tickers, rating symbols, filing types, and financial abbreviations appear as whole tokens. Most tokenizer training tools let you seed the vocabulary with a list of required tokens.

- **Special tokens.** Reserve special tokens for structured entities such as <TICKER_AAPL>, <RATING_BBB+>, <MACRO_-FED>. You can map raw text to these during preprocessing, then rely on the model to learn distinct embeddings for each.

In practice, customizing the tokenizer may yield larger gains in financial NLP than marginally increasing model size.

## Preserving and Normalizing Numbers

Numbers are central to financial text: revenues, growth rates, leverage ratios, loss reserves, guidance ranges. Yet many generic NLP pipelines either ignore numeric detail or treat every distinct number as a separate token, leading to huge vocabularies and poor generalization.

You must make explicit design choices about *when* to normalize numbers and *how* to encode their values.

## Numeric placeholders vs raw values

Consider two sentences:

```
Revenue grew 15% year-over-year.
Revenue grew 17% year-over-year.
```

If you treat 15 and 17 as separate tokens, the model will rarely see each and may struggle to generalize. A common alternative is to map all numbers in a certain context to a placeholder:

```
Revenue grew <PCT> year-over-year.
```

Now the model learns that *"revenue grew <PCT>"* is generally positive, without overfitting to the exact number. But this suppresses useful magnitude information: a 2% growth and a 50% growth are qualitatively different.

A reasonable compromise is context-dependent:

- **Tables and dense numeric zones.** For numeric columns in tables (e.g., revenue in dollars, headcount, assets), you often handle the numbers *outside* the language model, as structured features. In text, you can use placeholders for these regions.

- **Narrative percentages and ratios.** For growth rates, margins, leverage ratios described in prose, you may want a coarse numeric encoding (e.g., negative, small positive, large positive). One simple approach is binning: replace numeric values with bucket tags such as <PCT_NEG>, <PCT_SMALL_POS>, <PCT_LARGE_POS>.
- **Key counts and thresholds.** Some raw values (e.g., *"downgraded to junk"*, *"breach of $1 billion"*) are qualitatively important. You can treat dollar thresholds and rating levels as special tokens or bins (<USD_1B_PLUS>).

For transformer models that can process token embeddings and separate numeric embeddings, more sophisticated schemes are possible: pass the normalized numeric value as an additional feature alongside the token sequence. But even in simpler pipelines, being explicit about numeric policy avoids silent inconsistencies.

## Formatting consistency

Whichever numeric strategy you adopt, enforce it consistently:

- Standardize decimal separators and thousands separators (e.g., 1,000.50 vs 1.000,50).
- Normalize percentages to a common format (e.g., map "15 percent", "15%", and "0.15" to a single numeric value and a consistent text form).
- Remove currency symbols or map them to separate tokens (e.g., $1 million → <CURR_USD>, 1, million).

This is analogous to normalizing price and return series before feeding them into a factor model: you want comparability across sources and time.

## Domain-Specific Phrases and Multi-Word Expressions

Many financially meaningful concepts are expressed as multi-word phrases: *"credit default swap"*, *"share repurchase program"*, *"going concern"*, *"material weakness"*. If your tokenizer splits all words independently, you may lose the fact that these words form specialized terms.

## Detecting collocations

One straightforward approach is to identify common collocations (frequent bigrams or trigrams) in your corpus and treat them as single tokens or named entities. For example:

- Compute bigram frequencies for all consecutive word pairs in your corpus.
- Filter by a statistical association measure (e.g., pointwise mutual information) to find pairs that co-occur far more often than chance.
- Among these, manually or semi-automatically select domain-relevant phrases and add them to your vocabulary (e.g., `credit_default_swap`).

Once identified, you can modify the tokenizer to merge these sequences into single tokens. This is conceptually similar to adding new factors to a risk model: you elevate certain patterns to first-class features.

## Balancing granularity and sparsity

There is a trade-off:

- If you merge too many phrases, your vocabulary becomes huge, and many tokens are rare, causing sparsity.
- If you merge too few, your model must infer phrases from individual words, which may be difficult for smaller or simpler models.

A practical strategy is to:

- Focus on phrases that either have strong domain meaning (*"non-GAAP"*, *"leveraged loan"*) or are strongly predictive in exploratory models.
- Version-control your phrase list; treat changes as configuration changes in your pipeline that require backtest re-runs.

With modern transformer models, explicit phrase merging is less crucial (they can learn phrase-level representations via attention), but it can still be highly useful for interpretable classical models and for aligning with human domain intuition.

## Custom Vocabularies and Special Tokens

By this point, we have:

- Cleaned, normalized text.
- Sentence-level segments.
- A tokenizer that knows something about tickers, numbers, and phrases.

The next design decision is the vocabulary: the set of tokens your models can see. For sparse models, this directly determines feature dimensionality. For neural models, it determines the rows in the embedding matrix.

## Vocabulary curation

Starting from all tokens in your corpus and simply discarding rare ones is rarely optimal. In finance, rare tokens can be important (e.g., specific product names or issuer-specific abbreviations), while some frequent tokens are low-value boilerplate (*"hereby"*, *"thereof"*).

Effective vocabulary curation involves:

- **Frequency thresholds** that differ by token type. You may retain rare tickers and identifiers but drop rare generic words.
- **Domain-specific stopwords.** Beyond generic stopwords ("the", "and"), include legal boilerplate terms that add little marginal information.
- **Task-aware pruning.** For a sector-specific model (e.g., financials only), you can drop terms that almost never appear in that sector.

When using subword models, vocabulary curation mainly happens during tokenizer training, but you can still blacklist or whitelist specific tokens.

## Special symbol tokens

Finally, special tokens are an important tool for injecting structure into text:

- <DOC_START>, <DOC_END>, <SENT_START>, <SENT_END> delimit segments.
- <TICKER> or <TICKER_AAPL> mark issuer mentions.
- <NUM>-style placeholders mark numeric content.
- <TABLE>, <FOOTNOTE>, <RISK_SECTION> indicate structural regions within filings.

These are analogous to flags or dummy variables in a regression: they do not carry textual content themselves but provide the model with positional and categorical signals.

## A Reproducible, Versioned Pipeline

Putting everything together, your text preprocessing and tokenization pipeline should be treated like any other critical research component: versioned, tested, and monitored.

Right after describing the high-level stages, it is helpful to visualize the flow.

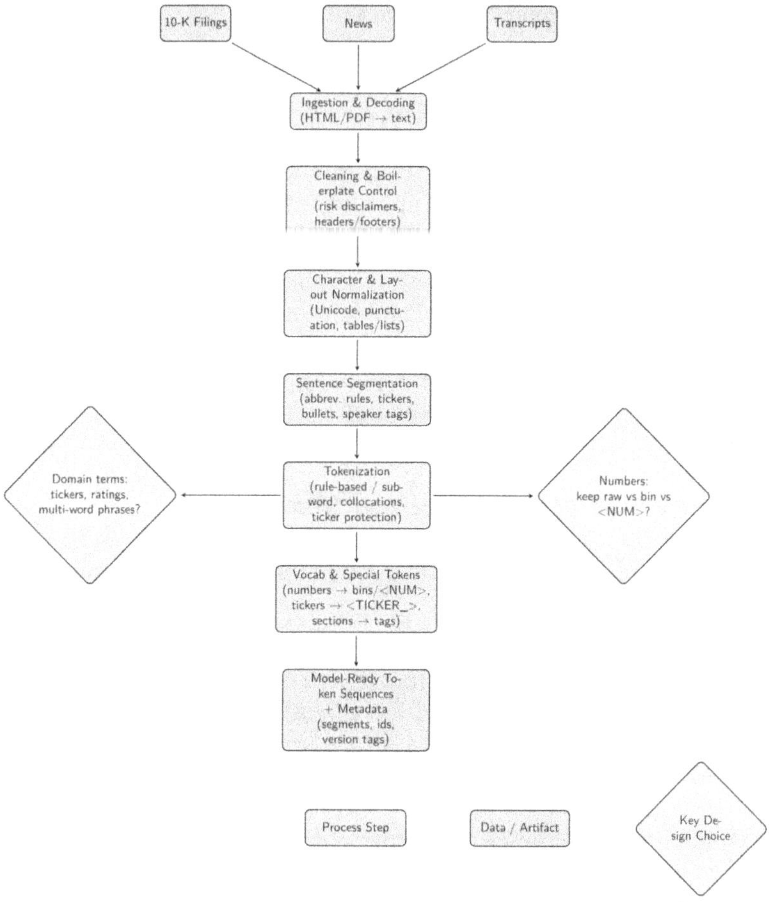


## Versioning and tests

Two practical disciplines make this pipeline usable in serious research:

- **Versioning.** Treat the preprocessing and tokenization configuration as a versioned artifact. For each experiment or production model, record the exact pipeline version (code commit, configuration file, tokenizer vocabulary hash). When you change any component—boilerplate dictionary, tokenizer rules, numeric binning—increment the version.

- **Regression tests.** Maintain a suite of canonical documents (e.g., a few representative 10-Ks, news articles, and transcripts) and expected tokenization outputs. When you update the pipeline, run regression tests to detect unintended changes (such as a ticker suddenly splitting into two tokens).

From a backtesting and bias-control perspective, this is crucial. Silent pipeline drift can create illusory alpha or hide real signal degradation. By making preprocessing explicit and reproducible, you align your NLP work with best practices you already apply in time-series modeling, cross-validation, and model evaluation.

## Latency and memory considerations

Finally, your design must be grounded in operational constraints:

- **Latency.** For intraday or real-time use, complex parsing or very large tokenizers may be too slow. You may need a simplified pipeline for live trading and a richer one for offline research.

- **Memory.** Tokenization choices influence sequence length (and therefore model memory footprint). Aggressive subword fragmentation increases the number of tokens per document, which can be costly. Merging domain phrases or using sensible segment lengths can mitigate this.

As with all engineering in quantitative finance, you balance fidelity against cost. A well-designed financial text preprocessing and tokenization pipeline appreciates the peculiarities of the domain—tickers, numbers, multi-word expressions—while remaining robust, reproducible, and resource-aware. This pipeline is the foundation on which all subsequent representations, embeddings, and models will rest.

## 4.2 Representations and Embeddings

In the previous section we built a robust preprocessing and tokenization pipeline for financial text. Conceptually, that pipeline converts a messy document like a 10-K or a news story into a clean sequence of tokens:

$$\text{“revenue grew 15\% year-over-year”} \longrightarrow [t_1, t_2, \ldots, t_n].$$

Tokens, however, are still symbolic objects: strings or discrete IDs. Trading models need *numbers*. This section explains how to turn sequences of tokens into numerical representations that capture useful financial meaning while remaining compatible with your modeling stack.

We will proceed in three stages:

- **Classical sparse representations:** bag-of-words, n-grams, and TF–IDF.
- **Static dense embeddings:** word2vec, GloVe, fastText.
- **Contextual embeddings:** transformer-based sentence and document representations.

At each stage we will tie the concepts back to concrete uses in factor construction, risk modeling, and alpha generation.

### From Tokens to Vectors: What Are We Trying to Capture?

Before diving into methods, it is worth clarifying the objective. When we map text to vectors, we want:

- **Semantic proximity:** texts with similar meaning (e.g., two downgrades of the same issuer) should be close in vector space.
- **Task-relevant structure:** distinctions that matter for the trading problem (e.g., positive versus negative guidance, idiosyncratic versus macro news) should be encoded in directions that models can exploit.

- **Compatibility with time-series tools:** the representations should plug into standard machinery: regressions, tree models, portfolio optimizers, and backtesting frameworks.

Think of a text representation as a very high-dimensional factor describing the document. Different methods correspond to different ways of engineering this factor.

## Bag-of-Words and N-Grams

The simplest representation is the *bag-of-words* (BoW). Suppose your tokenizer maps each document to a sequence of tokens drawn from a fixed vocabulary of size $V$:

$$\mathcal{V} = \{w_1, w_2, \dots, w_V\}.$$

The bag-of-words representation for a document $d$ is a vector

$$\mathbf{x}^{(d)} \in \mathbb{R}^V,$$

where $x_j^{(d)}$ is typically the count of how many times token $w_j$ appears in $d$.

For example, imagine a toy vocabulary:

$$\mathcal{V} = \{\text{“downgrade”}, \text{“upgrade”}, \text{“risk”}, \text{“AAPL”}\},$$

and the document:

```
"AAPL faces downgrade on increased risk."
```

If we ignore case and punctuation, the bag-of-words vector might look like:

$$\mathbf{x}^{(d)} = (1, 0, 1, 1),$$

corresponding to one “downgrade”, zero “upgrade”, one “risk”, and one “AAPL”.

**Properties of bag-of-words**

Bag-of-words has several important features:

- **Order-invariant.** It ignores word order. For many coarse tasks (e.g., is this document about a downgrade of AAPL?) the exact order is less critical than the presence of certain tokens.
- **High-dimensional and sparse.** In finance, vocabularies can easily reach tens or hundreds of thousands of tokens, but each document uses only a small fraction. Thus, $\mathbf{x}^{(d)}$ is mostly zeros. Sparse linear algebra tools exploit this structure efficiently.
- **Interpretable.** Each dimension corresponds to a token. Feature weights in a linear model are easy to explain: a positive coefficient on "downgrade" increases predicted negative sentiment, for example.

Because of its simplicity and interpretability, bag-of-words is still widely used in quantitative finance for:

- Classifying news or filings into broad topics (e.g., litigation, M&A, ratings actions).
- Building simple text-based sentiment indicators.
- Screening for specific risk terms or regulatory phrases.

### N-grams: capturing short phrases

Bag-of-words discards word order entirely. To reintroduce some local context, you can extend the vocabulary to include *n-grams*: sequences of $n$ consecutive tokens.

For example, in the sentence

```
"guidance was revised down sharply"
```

the bigrams (2-grams) are:

```
"guidance was", "was revised", "revised down", "down sharply"
```

and the trigrams (3-grams) include:

```
"guidance was revised", "was revised down", "revised down sharply"
```

In financial text, n-grams are particularly useful for domain phrases:

- "credit default swap"
- "material weakness"
- "share repurchase program"
- "going concern"

Including these as features allows models to distinguish between, say, "concern about growth" and the specific audit term "going concern".

The downside is combinatorial explosion: if your unigram vocabulary has size $V$, there are potentially $V^2$ bigrams and $V^3$ trigrams. In practice, you only keep n-grams that appear frequently enough to matter.

## Term Weighting: From Counts to TF–IDF

Raw counts treat all tokens equally. In practice, some tokens are far more informative than others. Words like "the" or "company" appear in almost every filing; their presence tells you little about what makes one document different from another.

A simple and effective refinement is *Term Frequency–Inverse Document Frequency* (TF–IDF). For a given term $t$ and document $d$, define:

- *Term Frequency (TF):* how often $t$ appears in $d$, often normalized by document length.
- *Inverse Document Frequency (IDF):* a measure of how rare $t$ is across the corpus. A common formula is:

  $$\mathrm{IDF}(t) = \log\left(\frac{N}{1 + n_t}\right),$$

  where $N$ is the total number of documents and $n_t$ is the number of documents containing $t$.

Then the TF–IDF weight is:

$$w_{t,d} = \mathrm{TF}(t, d) \cdot \mathrm{IDF}(t).$$

Intuitively:

- A term that appears frequently in a document but rarely elsewhere (e.g., a specific product name or unusual risk term) gets a high weight.
- A term that appears in nearly all documents (e.g., "company") has low IDF, and therefore low TF–IDF even if it appears often in a given document.

In financial applications, TF–IDF can:

- Highlight unusual disclosures or risk factors specific to an issuer or period.
- Down-weight common boilerplate and legal phrases.
- Provide richer document vectors for clustering and similarity search (e.g., finding past filings most similar to a new one).

Mathematically, TF–IDF yields the same data structure as bag-of-words (a sparse vector in $\mathbb{R}^V$), but with more informative values in each dimension.

**Dimensionality reduction for sparse text factors**

For many downstream models (especially those integrated with time-series factors) you might not want to carry around a 100,000-dimensional sparse vector. Two common strategies are:

- **Vocabulary restriction.** Keep only the top $K$ most informative tokens (e.g., by document frequency or mutual information with a target). In sector-specific models, $K$ can be quite small (hundreds to low thousands).
- **Projection to a lower-dimensional space.** Apply linear methods such as Singular Value Decomposition (SVD) or Principal Component Analysis (PCA) to the document–term matrix. The top components can be viewed as *text factors* capturing dominant themes (e.g., credit risk, growth optimism, regulatory scrutiny).

This mirrors standard practice in quantitative finance: reduce many raw signals to a smaller set of interpretable factors before feeding them into portfolio construction.

## Static Word Embeddings

Bag-of-words and TF–IDF treat each token as a distinct dimension with no notion of similarity: "rating" and "downgrade" are as far apart as "rating" and "banana". *Word embeddings* address this by representing each token as a dense, low-dimensional vector that captures semantic relationships.

### Intuition: meaning as geometry

The central idea is that words used in similar contexts should have similar vectors. Models such as word2vec and GloVe learn embeddings by solving prediction tasks on large text corpora. For instance, in the *skip-gram* variant of word2vec, the model learns to predict surrounding words given a center word. Training adjusts the embedding vectors so that words that occur in similar neighborhoods ("loan", "credit", "debt") end up close in vector space.

In a financial corpus, well-trained embeddings might exhibit patterns like:

- Vectors for ticker symbols of banks clustering together.
- Embeddings for "downgrade", "cut rating", "lowered outlook" lying in a similar region.
- Vector arithmetic capturing analogies:

$$\mathbf{v}(\text{“Fed”}) - \mathbf{v}(\text{“US”}) \approx \mathbf{v}(\text{“ECB”}) - \mathbf{v}(\text{“EU”}).$$

Each word $w$ gets a vector $\mathbf{e}_w \in \mathbb{R}^d$ with $d$ typically between 50 and 300.

### From word embeddings to document embeddings

To represent an entire document using static word embeddings, you can aggregate the vectors of its tokens. Common strategies include:

- **Simple averaging:**

$$\mathbf{z}^{(d)} = \frac{1}{|d|} \sum_{w \in d} \mathbf{e}_w.$$

- **TF–IDF-weighted averaging:** weight each word vector by its TF–IDF score in that document.
- **Concatenation of summary statistics:** combine mean, max, and min across each embedding dimension to capture more nuance.

These document embeddings are dense, low-dimensional vectors that can be used as features in any standard machine learning model: logistic regression for sentiment, random forests for event classification, or as inputs to time-series regressions for cross-sectional return prediction.

**Domain-specific static embeddings**

Generic pre-trained embeddings (trained on Wikipedia or web text) often perform poorly on financial language. They may fail to capture relationships like:

- The closeness of sector-specific tickers (e.g., airlines versus utilities).
- The special meaning of phrases like "non-GAAP" or "covenant-lite".

Training (or at least fine-tuning) embeddings on an in-domain corpus of filings, earnings calls, and financial news typically yields more meaningful geometry. Once trained, you can inspect nearest neighbors of key terms to sanity-check the learned structure—an important step in validating that the representation aligns with financial intuition.

## Contextual Embeddings and Transformers

Static embeddings have one major limitation: a word has the same vector regardless of context. In finance, context often flips meaning. Consider the word "charge":

- "recorded a one-time restructuring *charge* of $500 million" (negative).
- "no additional *charges* expected in 2025" (potentially positive or reassuring).

Contextual embeddings, typically derived from transformer models, solve this by assigning a different vector to the same word in different sentences.

**From tokens to contextual vectors**

Recall that a transformer encoder (which we will study in detail in the next section) processes a sequence of tokens and returns a sequence of hidden states:

$$[t_1, t_2, \ldots, t_n] \longrightarrow [\mathbf{h}_1, \mathbf{h}_2, \ldots, \mathbf{h}_n],$$

where each $\mathbf{h}_i \in \mathbb{R}^d$ is a *contextual embedding* for the $i$-th token, influenced by the entire sequence.

Practically, you often want a single vector for the whole sentence or document. Common choices include:

- Using the hidden state of a special $[\mathrm{CLS}]$ token (for BERT-like models).
- Averaging or pooling over token embeddings (possibly with attention weights).

The result is a dense vector $\mathbf{z}^{(d)}$ that captures both the words used and how they are used.

**Why contextual embeddings matter in finance**

Contextual embeddings are particularly powerful for subtle financial tasks:

- **Forward- vs backward-looking statements.** The difference between "expects to increase dividends" and "increased dividends last year" is purely temporal and relies on auxiliary words like "expects" and tense. Contextual models learn these patterns effectively.

- **Fine-grained sentiment.** Generic sentiment lexicons might flag "risk" or "loss" as negative, but in "risk has been reduced" or "losses narrowed" the overall sentiment is relatively positive. Contextual embeddings encode such nuances, improving classification performance.

- **Disentangling entities and events.** In a sentence mentioning multiple firms and events (e.g., supplier bankruptcies versus customer growth), self-attention mechanisms within the transformer help isolate which parts of the text relate to which entity.

In practice, you can view contextual embeddings as *high-quality, task-agnostic text features*. Downstream models (from simple linear layers to gradient-boosted trees) can then be trained on top of these features for specific alpha signals.

**Sentence- and document-level embeddings for factor construction**

Once you have contextual embeddings for sentences or documents, you can aggregate them over time and across sources to form text-based factors.

Examples include:

- **Issuer-level language factor:** for each firm $i$ and time $t$, average the contextual embeddings of all relevant texts in a lookback window (e.g., last quarter's filings and earnings calls), then project these vectors onto directions learned to predict future returns or fundamental changes.

- **Sector-level news sentiment factor:** embed all news stories about a sector in a given day, then aggregate (e.g., via a weighted average) to produce a daily sector-level signal that can be used alongside traditional risk factors.

- **Regime descriptors:** embed macroeconomic speeches and central bank statements. Clustering these vectors over time may reveal distinct language regimes (e.g., dovish versus hawkish periods) that you can align with asset return patterns.

From the perspective of time-series modeling, contextual embeddings provide a compact state representation of the textual information set at each date. You can then apply familiar tools such as rolling regressions, state-space models, or machine-learning forecasters on these state vectors.

## Choosing Between Sparse and Dense Representations

With several representation options at hand, how should you choose? The answer depends on your use case, data, and infrastructure.

**Interpretability vs expressiveness**

- **Sparse representations** (bag-of-words, TF–IDF, n-grams) are easy to interpret. Each dimension corresponds to a term, and model coefficients tell you exactly which words drive predictions. This can be important for model explainability, audit, and regulatory contexts.
- **Dense embeddings** (static or contextual) are typically more expressive: they capture nuanced semantics and generalize better across rare or unseen phrases. However, individual dimensions have no simple human interpretation.

In many trading shops, a hybrid approach is effective: use dense embeddings to generate powerful features, but also track a small set of interpretable sparse indicators for monitoring and sanity-checking.

**Computational and data considerations**

- **Data size.** For small labeled datasets (common in finance), pretrained contextual embeddings can be especially valuable: they inject knowledge learned from large corpora. Sparse models trained from scratch may overfit.
- **Latency and cost.** Computing transformer-based embeddings is more expensive than sparse TF–IDF. For real-time intraday trading, you might rely on pre-computed embeddings or simpler

representations; for overnight or slower strategies, the extra cost is often justified.

- **Storage and retrieval.** Sparse representations can be efficient for indexing and search (e.g., inverted indices). Dense embeddings are well suited for approximate nearest neighbor search in vector spaces, which can power similarity-based retrieval (e.g., find past events most similar to this news story).

### Alignment with downstream models

Finally, consider how the text features will integrate with other signals:

- For linear factor models and traditional risk toolchains, low- to medium-dimensional dense embeddings often plug in smoothly after standardization.
- For tree ensembles or non-linear models, both sparse (via feature hashing or careful feature selection) and dense inputs are viable; the choice often hinges on engineering constraints.
- For deep multi-modal models combining text with structured fundamentals or market data, contextual embeddings are typically the natural choice: they provide compact, differentiable inputs that can be trained end-to-end.

## Validating Representations in a Financial Context

Regardless of which representation you choose, you should validate that it behaves sensibly on financial data. Beyond generic NLP metrics, consider finance-specific checks:

- **Nearest neighbor sanity checks.** For key terms (e.g., tickers, "default", "margin expansion"), inspect their nearest neighbors in embedding space. Do they align with domain expectations?
- **Portfolio behavior.** Build simple long/short strategies using text features alone (e.g., a sentiment score or language factor) and test them using robust backtesting design: proper timestamp alignment, walk-forward or time-series cross-validation, and careful control for look-ahead bias.

- **Stability over time.** Track whether the mapping from text to representation is stable as your corpus grows or regimes change. For contextual models, monitor whether embeddings for benchmark phrases drift unexpectedly after model updates.

Think of this as the analog of validating a new risk factor: you are not only checking in-sample predictive power, but also the economic plausibility and robustness of the representation.

Text representations and embeddings form the quantitative interface between language and your trading models. Starting from the token sequences produced by your preprocessing pipeline, you can:

- Use bag-of-words, n-grams, and TF–IDF to build sparse, interpretable document vectors.
- Learn static embeddings that encode semantic similarity between tokens and produce compact document vectors via aggregation.
- Leverage contextual embeddings from transformers to capture fine-grained meaning in financial narratives, enabling sophisticated sentiment and event-driven signals.

In the next section we will open the black box behind contextual embeddings by examining the transformer architecture itself, and then show how to adapt these powerful models to financial data under realistic latency and cost constraints.

## 4.3 Transformers and Domain Fine-Tuning

So far we have turned raw financial documents into sequences of tokens and learned how to represent those tokens as numerical vectors, from simple bag-of-words to sophisticated contextual embeddings. In this section we open the "black box" that produces modern contextual embeddings: the transformer. We then show how to adapt large transformer-based language models to financial data and deploy them under realistic latency and cost constraints.

The perspective throughout will be that of a quantitative researcher: we want enough architectural understanding to make sound modeling and engineering choices, without drowning in implementation details.

## Why Transformers for Financial Text?

Traditional sequence models, such as recurrent neural networks (RNNs) and LSTMs, process text token by token in order. They struggle with very long sequences and have difficulty capturing dependencies between distant parts of a document. A 10-K filing or a long earnings call transcript, however, is full of long-range structure:

- A risk disclosed in one section may be quantified or mitigated several pages later.
- A statement in the Q&A may contradict or qualify prepared remarks at the beginning of the call.
- Guidance language often relies on context built up over multiple sentences.

Transformers address this by using *self-attention*: a mechanism that allows every token to directly "look at" (attend to) every other token in the sequence when forming its representation. This makes it much easier to capture patterns like "this negative phrase refers to the supplier, not to the issuer" or "this sentence modifies the earlier guidance statement."

## The Transformer Encoder: A High-Level View

We will focus on the *encoder* part of the transformer, which is the backbone of models like BERT that are commonly used for classification, retrieval, and feature extraction.

Starting point: a preprocessed, tokenized sentence or segment:

$$[t_1, t_2, \ldots, t_n].$$

The transformer encoder converts this into contextual embeddings:

$$[\mathbf{h}_1, \mathbf{h}_2, \ldots, \mathbf{h}_n],$$

where each $\mathbf{h}_i$ is a vector encoding token $t_i$ in its full context.

The main components are:

1. **Token embeddings:** look-up vectors for each token ID.
2. **Positional encodings:** signals indicating where each token sits in the sequence.
3. **Stacked encoder layers,** each containing:

- Multi-head self-attention.
- A position-wise feed-forward network (FFN).
- Residual connections and layer normalization for stability.

4. **Task-specific head:** a small neural network on top of the encoder outputs, tailored to your problem (e.g., classification, regression, span prediction).

Let us unpack these components intuitively.

## Embeddings and positional encodings

The first step is to convert tokens into vectors. For each token $t_i$ we obtain a token embedding $\mathbf{e}_i \in \mathbb{R}^d$ from an embedding matrix. But embeddings alone do not tell the model anything about order: the multiset $\{t_1, \ldots, t_n\}$ has no inherent sequence.

To encode order, we add a positional vector $\mathbf{p}_i$ to each embedding:

$$\mathbf{x}_i = \mathbf{e}_i + \mathbf{p}_i.$$

You can think of $\mathbf{p}_i$ as an offset that tells the model "this is the 5th token in the sentence" or "this token is near the beginning of the document." When the model attends over these $\mathbf{x}_i$ vectors, it can take position into account as well as content. In finance, this helps differentiate, for example, between an early high-level overview and a later detailed footnote.

## Self-attention: letting tokens look at each other

Given the input vectors $\mathbf{x}_1, \ldots, \mathbf{x}_n$, the self-attention mechanism computes a new representation for each token as a weighted average of all tokens in the sequence, where the weights reflect relevance.

For each token, we compute three internal vectors:

- A *query* vector $\mathbf{q}_i$ (what this token is asking about).
- A *key* vector $\mathbf{k}_j$ for each token $j$ (what this token offers as an answer).
- A *value* vector $\mathbf{v}_j$ (the information carried by that token).

The attention weight from token $i$ to token $j$ is roughly:

$$\alpha_{ij} \propto \exp(\mathbf{q}_i^\top \mathbf{k}_j),$$

normalized so that $\sum_j \alpha_{ij} = 1$. The new representation of token $i$ is:

$$\mathbf{z}_i = \sum_{j=1}^{n} \alpha_{ij} \mathbf{v}_j.$$

Intuitively, each token scans the entire sequence and decides which other tokens matter most to its representation. In an earnings call:

- The word "guidance" might attend strongly to nearby numbers and verbs like "raise" or "withdraw."
- "Litigation" might attend to tokens indicating magnitude, counterparties, and settlement status.

*Multi-head* attention runs several such attention mechanisms in parallel, each with its own projection of queries, keys, and values. Different heads can specialize in different patterns: one head might focus on syntactic structure (subject–verb relationships), another on named entities and numerical relations, and so on.

## Feed-forward networks and stacking layers

After self-attention, each token representation passes through a small fully connected network (applied independently at each position). This nonlinearity allows the model to combine attended information in complex ways—for example, to detect patterns like "negative adjective + guidance + future period."

A single encoder layer (self-attention plus feed-forward network) is powerful but limited. In practice, we *stack* many such layers (12, 24, or more). Each layer refines the representation:

- Lower layers capture local patterns and phrase-level structure.
- Higher layers encode more abstract semantics and task-relevant features.

Residual connections (adding the input of a sub-layer to its output) and layer normalization help stabilize training and allow gradients to flow through many layers, making deep transformers trainable.

## Encoder, decoder, and encoder–decoder variants

Transformers come in three main architectural flavors:

- **Encoder-only** (e.g., BERT, RoBERTa): excellent for understanding tasks such as classification, regression, retrieval, and extraction from existing text. These are often the natural choice for financial NLP factors.
- **Decoder-only** (e.g., GPT variants): generative models that predict the next token given previous ones. Useful for drafting commentary, question answering, and scenario generation.
- **Encoder–decoder** (e.g., T5): designed for sequence-to-sequence tasks, such as summarizing long filings or translating regulatory text between languages.

In practice, for most alpha-oriented applications (document-level sentiment, event detection, question answering over filings), encoder-only or encoder-like components of larger models are the workhorses for generating contextual embeddings.

## A Conceptual Block Diagram

To anchor these ideas, it is useful to view the transformer encoder as a data-processing pipeline from token IDs to task outputs.

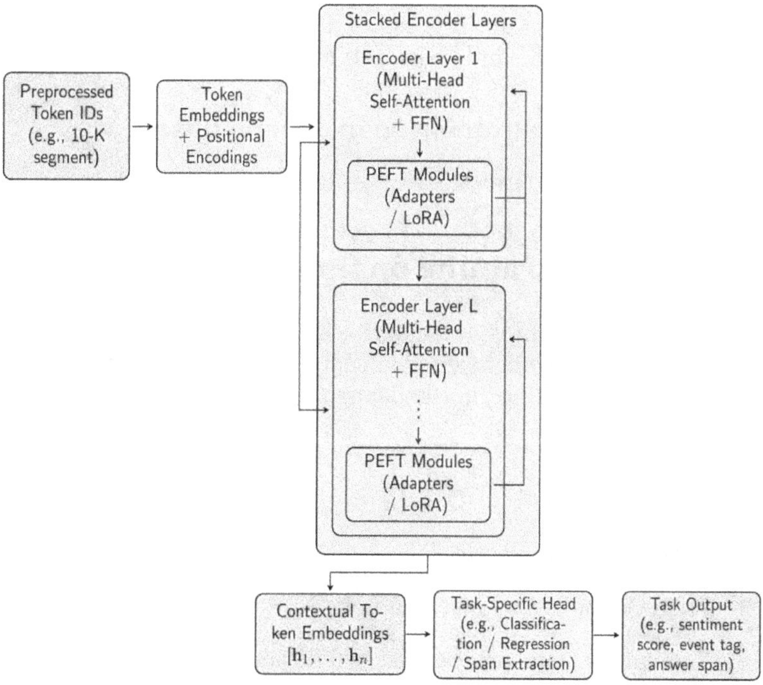


This diagram highlights where we can intervene when adapting a general-purpose model to financial tasks: in the embeddings (e.g., financial tokenization and vocab), in the encoder stack (via fine-tuning or PEFT), and in the task-specific head.

## Domain Adaptation: Making Transformers Speak Finance

Generic language models are trained on diverse web text, books, and encyclopedias. They know a little about many topics, including some finance. But they often misinterpret specialized terms (*"going concern"*, *"level 3 assets"*), mis-handle tickers and identifiers, or fail to capture subtle patterns of disclosure.

Domain adaptation is the process of aligning a generic transformer with financial language and tasks. It typically proceeds in two stages:

1. **Continued pretraining on in-domain text.**
2. **Task-specific fine-tuning on labeled financial data.**

## Continued pretraining on financial corpora

In continued pretraining, you start with a general model and keep training it on large unlabeled financial corpora using the same self-supervised objective (e.g., masked language modeling). Sources might include:

- SEC filings (10-K, 10-Q, 8-K).
- Earnings call transcripts.
- Financial news and research notes.
- Regulatory texts, prospectuses, and rating agency reports.

Objectives such as masked language modeling encourage the model to learn:

- Financial terminology and its usage.
- Typical structures of filings and announcements.

- Relationships between entities, instruments, and macro concepts.

The result is a *financially fluent* base model. Empirically, even a modest amount of continued pretraining can lead to substantial gains on downstream financial tasks, especially when labeled data are scarce.

## Task-specific fine-tuning

Once you have an in-domain base model, you adapt it to specific tasks relevant for trading or risk:

- Document or sentence-level sentiment (e.g., classify earnings call segments as positive, neutral, or negative).
- Event detection (e.g., detect guidance changes, credit events, regulatory actions).
- Question answering over filings (e.g., "What is the company's total long-term debt?" at a given date).
- Text regression (e.g., predict future earnings surprises from language).

Fine-tuning typically involves:

1. Adding a small task-specific head on top of the encoder (e.g., a linear layer over the [CLS] embedding for classification).
2. Training on labeled examples, updating the head parameters and usually some or all of the transformer parameters.

If your labeled dataset is large enough and you have sufficient compute, full fine-tuning (updating all parameters) can yield strong performance. However, in finance we often face the opposite: limited labeled data, strict latency/compute budgets, and the need to maintain multiple task variants. This is where parameter-efficient fine-tuning becomes attractive.

## Parameter-Efficient Fine-Tuning (PEFT)

PEFT methods adjust only a small fraction of the model parameters for each task, leaving the bulk of the base model frozen. This brings several benefits:

- Lower memory and compute requirements during training.
- Faster experimentation cycles.
- Easier deployment of many task-specific variants (e.g., different regions, sectors, or time horizons) sharing a single base model.
- Reduced risk of catastrophic forgetting of general language knowledge.

We highlight three main PEFT strategies.

## Adapters

Adapters add small bottleneck layers inside each transformer block. Concretely, for a hidden representation **h**, an adapter module applies:

$$\mathbf{h}' = \mathbf{h} + f_{adapter}(\mathbf{h}),$$

where $f_{adapter}$ is a small neural network with far fewer parameters than the original layer.

During fine-tuning:

- The original transformer weights remain frozen.
- Only adapter parameters (and the task head) are trained.

You can think of adapters as *task-specific correction layers* that gently bend the behavior of the base model toward your financial task. Different tasks can have different adapter sets, all plugged into the same underlying model.

## LoRA (Low-Rank Adaptation)

LoRA modifies the weight matrices in attention and/or feed-forward layers by adding low-rank updates. For a weight matrix $W$, LoRA parametrizes the update as:

$$\Delta W = AB,$$

where $A$ and $B$ are thin matrices (rank $r \ll$ dim). During fine-tuning:

- $W$ is fixed.
- $A$ and $B$ are trained.

This yields similar benefits to adapters but integrates more tightly with the existing architecture. In practice, LoRA is often memory efficient and easy to apply to large pre-trained models.

## Prompt and prefix tuning

Instead of modifying internal weights, *prompt tuning* and *prefix tuning* learn additional virtual tokens or prefixes that steer the model toward the task. For example, you might prepend a trainable sequence of vectors to the input embedding sequence. These extra parameters capture task-specific behavior but are small compared to the full model.

Prompt-based methods are especially useful when you view your task as "instruction plus text" (e.g., "Classify the sentiment of this earnings call excerpt:" followed by the text), and are common in decoder-only, generative setups. For encoder-based financial tasks, adapters and LoRA are currently more standard, but prompt methods are increasingly being explored.

## Latency, Context Window, and Cost Constraints

In real trading systems, transformers must operate under time and resource constraints that academic benchmarks often ignore. There are three main levers:

1. Context window management.
2. Model size and compression.
3. Online versus offline computation.

## Managing long documents with limited context

Transformers have a maximum context length (number of tokens) they can process at once, and attention cost scales at least quadratically with sequence length. Large filings or call transcripts may exceed this limit.

Common strategies include:

- **Sliding windows:** Break documents into overlapping chunks (e.g., 512 tokens with 128-token overlaps), run the model on each, and aggregate outputs (e.g., max or average over chunk-level scores).
- **Section-based segmentation:** Use structural cues (headings, sections like "Risk Factors" or "MD&A") to segment intelligently. Different sections may feed different task heads (e.g., risk-focused models versus growth-focused models).
- **Hierarchical models:** First embed sentences or paragraphs, then feed those embeddings into a second-level model (often a simpler transformer or recurrent network) that aggregates information. This spreads computation across levels and can be more scalable.

For many alpha strategies, you do not need to read the entire 200-page 10-K every time. A domain-aware segmentation can focus computation on historically informative sections.

## Model size, distillation, and quantization

Larger models are often more accurate but slower and more expensive. You can reduce model size and cost while keeping most of the performance:

- **Knowledge distillation:** Train a smaller "student" model to mimic the outputs of a larger "teacher" model. For example, use the teacher to label a large unlabeled corpus with soft predictions, then train the student on those predictions. The student can then serve as a production model with lower latency.
- **Quantization:** Represent model weights and activations with lower precision (e.g., 8-bit integers instead of 32-bit floats). This reduces memory and can speed up inference on hardware that supports low-precision arithmetic. For many applications, the loss in accuracy is small.
- **Layer pruning or early exiting:** Remove or skip some layers at inference time when the model is confident early. This is more experimental but can provide dynamic speed-ups.

From a portfolio construction perspective, it is often better to have a slightly less accurate model that runs reliably and cheaply in production than a marginally better model that is operationally fragile.

## Online vs offline computation and feature caching

Not every use of transformers must be real-time. Distinguish clearly between:

- **Offline feature generation:** Embedding large historical corpora, computing issuer-level or sector-level text factors, and updating them nightly or weekly. Here you can afford heavier models.
- **Online scoring:** Reacting to new news or filings arriving intraday. Here you may need a smaller or distilled model, or even a tiered system where a cheap filter screens events and a more expensive model is invoked only for high-impact candidates.

Caching embeddings is particularly effective: once you embed a static document (e.g., a past filing), you can reuse its vector representation across many strategies and experiments, just as you would reuse precomputed factor exposures.

## Experiment Tracking, Versioning, and Monitoring

As with preprocessing and tokenization, transformers and their fine-tuning workflows must be treated as versioned, auditable components of your research and production stack.

Key practices include:

- **Model versioning:** Assign clear version identifiers to base models, tokenizer/vocabulary configurations, PEFT modules, and task heads. A given backtest should specify exactly which versions it used.
- **Experiment tracking:** Log hyperparameters (learning rates, batch sizes, context lengths), training data ranges, and evaluation metrics. Time-series cross-validation is especially important to avoid look-ahead bias and to approximate live deployment conditions.
- **A/B testing:** When deploying a new model or fine-tuning update, run it in parallel with a baseline for a while, comparing not just predictive metrics but also portfolio-level impacts (turnover, drawdowns, factor exposures).
- **Monitoring for regime shifts:** Track input distributions (e.g., length, vocabulary), representation drift (e.g., embedding statistics), and output behavior (e.g., sentiment score distributions) over time. Sudden shifts may indicate model degradation due to regime change or data pipeline issues.

This brings transformer-based NLP into alignment with broader best practices in quantitative research and risk management.

Transformers provide the modern backbone for extracting meaning from financial text:

- Their self-attention architecture naturally captures long-range dependencies in complex documents like 10-Ks and earnings calls.
- Encoder-based models produce context-aware embeddings that are powerful inputs for downstream alpha models and risk tools.

- Domain adaptation—through continued pretraining and task-specific fine-tuning, often via parameter-efficient methods like adapters and LoRA—makes these models speak the specialized language of finance.
- Practical deployment requires careful management of context windows, model size, and computation, along with rigorous versioning, experiment tracking, and monitoring.

With these tools, you can move from generic language understanding to finance-specific models that encode the nuanced signals buried in textual disclosures, news, and commentary, all in a way that fits into a disciplined, production-grade trading research pipeline.

## 4.4 Information Extraction and Sentiment Analysis

The previous sections equipped us with three essential ingredients: a reliable preprocessing and tokenization pipeline, numerical representations of text (sparse and dense), and powerful transformer models adapted to financial language. We now bring these pieces together to answer a practical question:

*How do we convert free-form financial narratives into structured, time-stamped signals that a trading or risk model can actually use?*

In this section we will:

- Extract and normalize *entities* (issuers, instruments, products, geographies).
- Detect *events* (earnings surprises, guidance changes, downgrades, regulatory actions, M&A).
- Measure *sentiment* (how positive or negative the information is).
- Aggregate these into issuer- and portfolio-level features that fit naturally into a time-series and cross-sectional modeling framework.

Throughout, we keep a tight focus on data structures and decisions that matter for backtesting, risk control, and production deployment.

## From Text to Entities: Named Entity Recognition and Linking

Raw documents talk about many actors: firms, regulators, products, currencies, countries, counterparties, and individuals. The first step is to identify these mentions and link them to stable identifiers.

### Named entity recognition (NER)

*Named Entity Recognition* is the task of labeling spans of text with entity types. In financial NLP, typical categories include:

- **Organizations:** listed companies, subsidiaries, banks, funds.
- **People:** executives, analysts, regulators.
- **Financial instruments:** tickers, ISINs, CUSIPs, bond names, indices.
- **Products and services:** flagship products, business lines.
- **Locations:** countries, regions, cities relevant for exposure and risk.
- **Regulatory bodies:** SEC, DOJ, ECB, local regulators.

Modern NER models usually build on transformers: each token gets a contextual embedding, and a classifier predicts entity labels for tokens or spans (often using BIO tags such as B-ORG, I-ORG, O).

For example, given the sentence:

"Moody's downgraded ACME Corp.'s senior unsecured notes to Ba1."

a financial NER model might produce:

- "Moody's" → ORG_RATING_AGENCY
- "ACME Corp." → ORG_ISSUER

- "senior unsecured notes" → INSTRUMENT
- "Ba1" → RATING

The quality of NER has a direct impact on everything downstream: misattributing an event to the wrong issuer is analogous to misaligning price data to the wrong ticker.

**Entity normalization and ID mapping**

Entity mentions in text are messy:

- The same company may appear as “Apple Inc.”, “Apple”, “AAPL”, or “the company”.
- Instruments can be referenced by ticker, ISIN, CUSIP, or descriptive name.

*Entity linking* (or normalization) maps each textual mention to canonical identifiers:

- Issuer IDs: internal master IDs, PERMNO, LEI.
- Security IDs: ticker+exchange, ISIN, CUSIP, FIGI.
- Geography codes: ISO country or region codes.

This step often combines:

- Deterministic rules (e.g., patterns for tickers, ISIN formats).
- Lookups in reference databases (security master, issuer databases).
- Fuzzy matching using embeddings (to match slightly different product or entity names).

Good ID mapping transforms “ACME Corp.” in text into, say, an internal issuer ID ISSUER_12345. This is what allows you to line up textual events with time-series of prices, fundamentals, and holdings—a prerequisite for rigorous backtests and risk attribution.

### Coreference resolution

Humans freely use pronouns and shorthand: "the company", "it", "the bank", "they". *Coreference resolution* is the task of determining when different mentions refer to the same entity.

For example:

```
"ACME Corp. announced a share repurchase program. The company
expects the buyback to be accretive to EPS."
```

We want to know that "the company" and the implied subject of "expects" both refer to ACME Corp. In practice:

- Full-fledged coreference models can be heavy but useful, especially for long filings.
- Simpler heuristics can capture many patterns: nearest preceding organization in the same section, or enforcing that "the company" refers to the primary issuer of a filing.

Resolving coreference ensures that events and sentiments are attached to the correct entity even when the entity is not explicitly named.

## From Entities to Events

Entities by themselves are not yet informative: we know who is involved, but not what happened. *Event extraction* bridges this gap.

### Defining event schemas

An event schema specifies what you want to detect and how to represent it structurally. For trading and risk, common event types include:

- **Earnings:** earnings release, earnings surprise, revenue surprise.
- **Guidance:** guidance initiated, raised, lowered, withdrawn.
- **Credit events:** rating upgrade/downgrade, outlook change, default, restructuring.

- **Corporate actions:** M&A announcements, share buybacks, dividend changes, stock splits.
- **Regulatory and legal:** investigations, fines, settlements, enforcement actions.

Each event type has slots (attributes). For a rating downgrade, you might define:

- Issuer ID(s) and possibly instrument ID(s).
- Rating agency.
- Previous rating, new rating.
- Outlook (if present).
- Event time (usually publication time of the news or filing).

For guidance changes:

- Issuer ID.
- Metric (EPS, revenue, margin).
- Horizon (next quarter, full-year).
- Direction (raise, lower, withdraw).
- Magnitude or range if extractable.

Thinking in schemas forces clarity: you specify exactly what you want your model to output, paving the way for feature engineering and backtesting.

**Approaches to event detection**

There are three broad families of methods, often combined in practice.

**Pattern-based and rule-based methods.**

You can encode expert knowledge as patterns or rules:

- Regular expressions for rating actions (e.g., "downgraded to [A-Z]{1,3}[+-]?").
- Phrase patterns for guidance ("raised guidance", "cut its full-year EPS outlook", "withdrew its previously issued guidance").
- Keyword patterns for regulatory actions ("charged with", "entered into a settlement with the SEC").

Rule-based methods are transparent and often perform well on well-structured texts like press releases. Their drawbacks are brittleness (phrasing changes can break them) and limited coverage.

**Classical machine learning.**

You can treat event detection as a supervised classification problem at the sentence or paragraph level:

- Input: sentence embeddings (TF–IDF, static, or contextual) plus metadata (section, document type).
- Output: binary or multi-class label (e.g., NO_EVENT, GUIDANCE_UP, GUIDANCE_DOWN).

For structured attributes (e.g., previous vs new rating), you may combine classification with simple extraction rules or token-level models.

**Transformer-based extraction.**

Modern event extraction often uses transformer encoders directly:

- **Sequence classification** for event presence and type.
- **Token classification** to label event arguments (e.g., the span of text that contains the new rating).
- **Question answering** formulations such as: "What is the new rating?" or "What metric did the company change guidance for?"

Because transformers capture context well, they can distinguish between:

- Hypothetical events ("a downgrade could occur") and actual events ("was downgraded").
- Events about the issuer and those about peers or macro indices.

In practice, many production pipelines combine rules (to enforce consistency and precision) with transformer-based models (to cover linguistic variety and edge cases).

**Timestamping and de-duplication**

For use in time series models, every event must have a precise *effective timestamp*:

- For regulatory filings: the time the filing was made public on the regulator's system.
- For news: the publication or feed dissemination time you observed.
- For internal research or notes: a logged time when the information became available to your system.

You must also handle duplicates:

- The same event reported by multiple news wires.
- Updates or corrections to earlier stories.
- Multiple documents referring to the same corporate action.

De-duplication strategies include:

- Hashing normalized event attributes (issuer, type, key values) within a short time window.
- Clustering similar texts with embeddings and consolidating events.

Correct timestamping and de-duplication are critical to avoid look-ahead bias and artificially inflated signal strength.

## Measuring Sentiment in Financial Text

Events tell us *what* happened. Sentiment tells us *how positive or negative* the information is, from the market's perspective.

**Lexicon-based sentiment**

The simplest approach is to count positive and negative words using a finance-specific lexicon (e.g., lists of words labeled as positive, negative, uncertain, litigious).

For a given sentence or document $d$:

$$\text{Sentiment}(d) = \frac{N_{pos}(d) - N_{neg}(d)}{N_{pos}(d) + N_{neg}(d) + \epsilon},$$

where $N_{pos}$ and $N_{neg}$ are counts of positive and negative words and $\epsilon$ is a small constant to avoid division by zero.

Advantages:

- Transparent and easy to implement.
- No labeled training data required.

Drawbacks:

- Ignores context, negation, and domain-specific nuance ("losses narrowed" vs "losses widened").
- Treats all words equally, missing strength differences.

Lexicon scores can still be useful as baselines or as simple explanatory features alongside more sophisticated models.

**Supervised sentiment classifiers**

A more powerful approach is to learn sentiment from labeled examples. Typical design:

- **Input:** sentence or paragraph embeddings (often contextual) plus metadata (document type, section).

- **Output:** sentiment label (e.g., positive, neutral, negative) or a continuous score.

You can obtain labels by:

- Manual annotation by domain experts.
- Heuristics (e.g., short-term returns following news as a noisy sentiment proxy).
- Transfer learning from generic sentiment datasets with financial adaptation.

A transformer-based sentiment classifier may, for example, take an earnings call segment and output a probability of being positive. Because it uses contextual embeddings, it can recognize patterns like:

- "expects margins to expand" (positive).
- "expects margins to contract" (negative).
- "no material impact expected" (neutral or mildly positive).

### Document-level and issuer-level sentiment

While many models operate at the sentence or paragraph level, trading signals often need issuer-level or document-level sentiment:

- Aggregate sentence-level scores across a document (e.g., an earnings call) using averages or more sophisticated weighting (e.g., giving higher weight to management Q&A than to boilerplate).
- Aggregate across multiple documents and sources in a time window (e.g., all news about an issuer on a given day).

You might define an issuer-day sentiment feature:

$$S_{i,t} = \sum_{d \in \mathcal{D}_{i,t}} w_d \cdot s_d,$$

where:

- $\mathcal{D}_{i,t}$ is the set of documents about issuer $i$ on day $t$.
- $s_d$ is the model sentiment score for document $d$.
- $w_d$ are weights, e.g., based on source reliability or document recency.

This aggregated sentiment $S_{i,t}$ can then feed into cross-sectional return models, risk models, or scenario analysis.

## From Extracted Information to Trading Features

Entities, events, and sentiment scores are intermediate products. Trading models need well-defined features over time and across assets.

**Event-driven features with decay**

For an event type $k$ (e.g., negative guidance change), you can construct an event-driven signal:

$$E_{i,t}^{(k)} = \sum_{\tau \le t} \mathbf{1}\{\text{event of type } k \text{ for issuer } i \text{ at time } \tau\} \cdot \exp\left(-\frac{t-\tau}{\lambda_k}\right),$$

where $\lambda_k$ is a decay parameter controlling how quickly the impact of past events fades. This is analogous to how you might model the decaying effect of earnings surprises on returns.

If you have event sentiment as well, you can weight each event by its sentiment or severity.

**Textual risk and theme exposures**

By aggregating over extracted entities and events, you can build risk-like features:

- **Litigation exposure:** rolling count or decayed intensity of litigation-related events for each issuer or sector.
- **Regulatory pressure:** frequency and severity of regulatory actions or investigations tied to an issuer.

- **ESG themes:** counts of events or negative sentiment in categories like environmental incidents or governance controversies.

These can be treated as additional factors in risk models, or as conditioning variables in alpha models.

**Aligning with prices and fundamentals**

As with any alternative data, alignment with market and fundamental data is crucial:

- Use event timestamps to ensure information is only available to models after it becomes public.

- Aggregate features into the same time buckets as your return forecasts (daily, weekly, etc.).

- Where necessary, lag features appropriately to reflect realistic processing delays.

The result is a set of structured features $\mathbf{x}_{i,t}$ that sit alongside traditional signals (valuation ratios, momentum, analyst revisions) in your supervised learning or factor models.

## Putting It All Together: An End-to-End Pipeline

We can now summarize the full transformation from raw financial text to model-ready features.

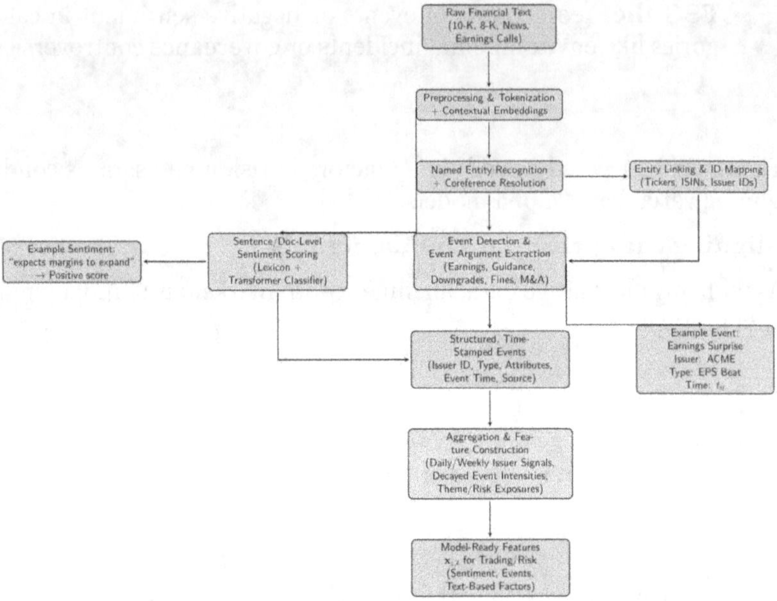


This pipeline emphasizes:

- **Structure:** entities and events with IDs and timestamps.
- **Context:** sentiment and embeddings capturing textual nuance.
- **Alignment:** features aligned with price and fundamental data in time and by issuer.

## Stress-Testing and Avoiding Overfitting

Because financial text is noisy and regimes change, it is easy to overfit extraction and sentiment models to particular news cycles or wording conventions.

To guard against this:

- **Use time-based splits** (walk-forward or rolling windows) for training and evaluation, not random splits that mix old and new documents.

- **Test across regimes:** pre-crisis, crisis, and post-crisis periods; bull and bear markets; quiet and volatile regimes.
- **Conduct ablation studies:** compare models using only sentiment, only event counts, and both, to understand incremental value.
- **Compare against simple baselines:** e.g., lexicon-only sentiment, naive event counts, or price-based signals. Advanced models should deliver clear and stable improvements.

As with any factor research, the goal is not just in-sample statistical significance but economic robustness and interpretability. A carefully built information extraction and sentiment pipeline can transform unstructured financial narratives into a disciplined set of signals that integrate naturally with your existing return, risk, and performance metrics.

# Chapter 5

# From Text to Tradable Signals

*Most NLP work in finance stalls at sentiment scores and topic labels that never quite make it into the trading stack. This chapter closes that gap. You'll learn how to bend general-purpose language models toward markets, turn textual surprises into measurable abnormal returns, and assemble evolving thematic baskets that actually rebalance with the news cycle-all while rigorously tying messy entities in text back to clean, tradable instruments. By the end, you won't just extract meaning from text; you'll engineer signals that can compete for capital.*

## 5.1 Financial Domain Adaptation and Sentiment Alpha

In previous sections we treated text as a rich but noisy observation of what market participants know, believe, and fear. We saw how large language models (LLMs) can map raw documents into embeddings and labels. In this section we tighten the focus: how do we turn *generic* language models into *financially adapted* models whose sentiment and stance scores line up with economically meaningful surprises, not just with linguistic mood?

The central idea is simple:

> A sentiment model is useful for trading only to the extent that its scores forecast risk-adjusted returns, conditional on what the market already knows.

This is a much stronger requirement than "agreeing with human judgments about positivity" in movie reviews or product feedback. Our task is to bridge the gap between linguistic sentiment and *return-relevant* sentiment.

## Generic Sentiment vs. Return-Relevant Sentiment

Off-the-shelf sentiment models are typically trained on domains such as:

- movie reviews (positive/negative),
- product reviews (1–5 stars),
- social-media posts about consumer brands.

They learn that words like "great", "love", "terrible", "disappointed" are strong signals of polarity. This works well for their native tasks. It fails systematically in finance.

## Why generic sentiment fails on financial text

Financial communication is:

- **Strategic**: managers choose words to manage investor expectations and legal risk;
- **Constrained**: disclosure norms and compliance rules limit extreme language;

- **Contextual**: the same phrase can be good or bad depending on the macro regime or prior expectations.

As a result, many phrases that sound positive to a generic model are actually negative, or at least less positive than they appear. Consider the following examples (all paraphrased for illustration):

- "We remain *cautiously optimistic* about the back half of the year."
- "We are taking steps to ensure *prudent capital discipline*."
- "The board has initiated a *strategic review* of strategic alternatives."

A generic sentiment model will typically mark these as positive. A financial model—and the market—often interprets them differently:

- **Cautiously optimistic** frequently means "less optimistic than before" or "visibility is deteriorating".
- **Prudent capital discipline** often appears when management is cutting capex, buybacks, or dividends—signaling weaker growth opportunities or balance sheet stress.
- **Strategic review** is sometimes code for "the business is underperforming and we are considering restructuring, a sale, or asset divestitures."

The key is that *returns are driven by* changes *in expectations*. A glossy sentiment score that misses the nuance of expectation revisions will not generate alpha.

## From linguistic mood to economic surprise

To be return-relevant, sentiment scores must:

- Reflect the text *relative to prior information* (guidance, consensus forecasts, prior tone).

- Capture subtle shifts in stance (e.g., "strong" → "solid" is negative).
- Recognize domain-specific polarity (e.g., "cost cutting" might be good in a crisis, bad at the top of the cycle).

Our adaptation process will therefore do two things:

- **Adapt the language model** so that its internal representations reflect financial language and conventions.
- **Align its outputs** (sentiment/stance scores) with realized returns, controlling for known risk factors.

## Domain Adaptation of Language Models for Finance

We start by reshaping the linguistic knowledge of a generic LLM to the financial domain. Three complementary strategies are particularly effective.

## Continual pretraining on financial corpora

Generic LLMs are pretrained on broad web and book corpora. They "know" a bit of finance, but this knowledge is diluted. We can *continually pretrain* them on large, unlabeled financial text to specialize their internal representations.

**Data sources.** Typical corpora include:

- 10-K, 10-Q, 20-F, 8-K, and MD&A sections;
- earnings-call transcripts (prepared remarks and Q&A);
- broker and independent research reports;
- press releases (corporate, regulatory, rating-agency);
- structured news headlines and stories;

- social media and forum posts (with compliance screening).

**Objective.** We reuse the original pretraining objective (e.g., masked language modeling). Intuitively, the model learns that:

- "liquidity", "covenant", "write-down", "impairment", "run-rate" are common;
- phrases like "material adverse impact" often co-occur with risk disclosures;
- the co-occurrence structure of firms, sectors, and macro terms is financial rather than generic.

This does *not* yet give us return labels. It builds a foundation: better token representations and contextual embeddings tuned to financial language, which we can then fine-tune for sentiment tasks.

## Supervised fine-tuning on financial sentiment datasets

To obtain sentiment labels that matter economically, we fine-tune on labeled financial text. Obtaining high-quality labels is non-trivial; three approaches are common.

**Human-annotated labels.** Analysts label sentences or paragraphs as:

- positive / neutral / negative,
- or more nuanced: good news / bad news / uncertainty / litigation / accounting irregularity.

Annotation guidelines explicitly capture domain-specific polarity. For example:

- "cautiously optimistic" $\rightarrow$ mildly negative relative to strong optimism;

- "strategic alternatives" $\rightarrow$ negative unless explicitly framed as opportunistic.

**Heuristic or distant labels.** When hand labels are scarce, we can exploit "silver-standard" labels:

- map rating changes (upgrade/downgrade) or guidance raises/-cuts to positive/negative labels for surrounding text;
- use large same-day abnormal returns (e.g. $|\text{AR}_t| > 5\%$) as proxies for strong good/bad news.

These labels are noisy but plentiful, allowing large-scale supervised fine-tuning.

**Fine-tuning objective.** We typically minimize a cross-entropy loss over sentiment classes, or a regression loss when predicting a continuous "news surprise" proxy. Because our model is already continually pretrained on financial text, it can learn relatively quickly that:

- minor wording changes in guidance paragraphs matter;
- volatility- or risk-related terms often precede negative moves;
- expansive growth language, when novel, often precedes positive reactions.

## Curated finance-specific lexicons as priors

Lexicons—lists of words/phrases with associated polarity or semantic category—provide useful priors and interpretability. Classic examples are domain-specific word lists for uncertainty, litigation, and negative tone in filings.

We can integrate lexicons in several ways:

- **Features**: include lexicon-based counts or scores as additional inputs to a classifier on top of LLM embeddings.
- **Regularization**: penalize models that deviate excessively from intuitive lexicon-based polarity.

- **Weak supervision**: assign preliminary labels from lexicons to bootstrap training data.

Lexicons help anchor the model's behavior on rare but critical phrases (e.g., "going concern", "material weakness", "covenant breach") that may be underrepresented in generic corpora.

## Subtle Polarity Shifts and Regime Dependence

Adaptation is not only about vocabulary; it is about *context and regime.*

## Subtle wording changes in corporate communication

Managers rarely announce "bad news" explicitly. Instead, they adjust tone:

- "We are seeing *robust* demand" → "We are seeing *solid* demand."
- "We expect *strong* growth" → "We expect *good* growth."
- "We are *on track* to meet guidance" → "We are *working hard* to meet guidance."

An adapted model learns to treat these shifts as negative relative to the prior quarter's language, even though each phrase, in isolation, sounds positive. One practical trick is to feed the model:

- the current period text,
- the prior period text (or summary),
- and ask it to output a *stance change* label or score.

This explicitly encourages the model to reason in terms of deltas, which are closer to returns.

## Sarcasm and informality in social feeds

In social media and forums, we face the opposite challenge: language is informal, often sarcastic, and sometimes outright ironic:

- “Great, another *brilliant* acquisition at the top of the cycle ...”
- “Love how they *prudently* wiped out common shareholders.”

Generic sentiment models misclassify these as positive. Two mitigations help:

- Include sarcastic and ironic examples in the fine-tuning set, labeled according to their economic message, not their literal wording.
- Use context windows that include reply chains or previous posts; sarcasm is often signaled by contrast with earlier content.

## Regime-dependent meaning

The economic meaning of language can flip across regimes. “Cost cutting” during a deep recession may be viewed as prudent and positive; the same during a boom may signal missed growth opportunities.

We can handle this by conditioning the sentiment model on regime indicators:

- macro variables (e.g., yield curve slope, credit spreads);
- volatility index levels;
- cross-sectional stress indicators (e.g., proportion of firms with negative earnings surprises).

Practically, we append regime features to the model’s input or to a downstream prediction head. The same sentence can then yield different economic sentiment scores under different regimes.

## Aligning Textual Features with Returns

Having adapted the language model, we now connect its outputs to realized returns. This is where the finance meets the NLP.

## Timestamping and mapping to securities

Every text item we score must be linked to:

- a canonical security or issuer (via entity linking; see later sections),
- a precise timestamp $t$ at which the information became available to the market.

We then construct features such as:

$$\begin{aligned} s_{i,t}^{(\text{sent})} &= \text{sentiment score for firm } i \text{ at time } t, \\ s_{i,t}^{(\text{unc})} &= \text{uncertainty or risk tone score}, \\ s_{i,t}^{(\Delta)} &= \text{change in stance vs. previous period}. \end{aligned}$$

If multiple documents appear in a short window, we can aggregate by weighted average (e.g., weighting by document length or source importance).

## Horizon-specific features

The impact of sentiment depends on the return horizon. Short, sharp news (e.g., an unexpected lawsuit) may affect intraday or 1–5 day returns; gradual tone shifts in MD&A may forecast 1–3 month drifts.

We therefore construct horizon-specific features, such as:

- intraday event returns: $r_{i,t}^{(0,1\text{d})}$,
- short-horizon: $r_{i,t}^{(1,5\text{d})}$,

- medium-horizon: $r_{i,t}^{(1,60\mathrm{d})}$.

For each horizon $h$, we can compute:

$$\mathrm{AR}_{i,t}^{(h)} = r_{i,t}^{(h)} - \hat{r}_{i,t}^{(h)},$$

where $\hat{r}_{i,t}^{(h)}$ is an expected return from a market or factor model, as discussed in return and risk fundamentals. Sentiment alpha is then about forecasting $\mathrm{AR}_{i,t}^{(h)}$ using $s_{i,t}$.

## Controlling for known risk factors

To isolate *true* information content, we must control for standard risk factors (size, value, momentum, quality, etc.). The simplest way is via cross-sectional regressions in each period:

$$\mathrm{AR}_{i,t}^{(h)} = \alpha_t + \beta_t s_{i,t} + \gamma_t^\top \mathbf{f}_{i,t} + \varepsilon_{i,t},$$

where $\mathbf{f}_{i,t}$ are firm characteristics. A statistically and economically significant $\beta_t$ averaged over time suggests incremental information in the sentiment scores.

## Backtesting Workflow for Sentiment Alpha

We now put the pieces together into a disciplined backtest.

## Avoiding look-ahead and survivorship bias

Two pitfalls are especially dangerous when working with textual data:

- **Look-ahead bias:** Using text or labels that were not yet available at time $t$ to predict returns starting at $t$. For example, using a corrected filing date instead of the original release date, or using future corporate actions in training.

- **Survivorship bias:** Restricting the universe to firms that survive to the end of the sample, thereby overstating performance.

We must ensure:

- Every text document's timestamp reflects when it became public.
- The entity master and ticker mapping are point-in-time.
- The universe includes delisted firms, and we use point-in-time index memberships where relevant.

## Constructing sentiment portfolios

A standard cross-sectional approach is:

- At each rebalancing date $t$, compute sentiment scores $s_{i,t}$ for all eligible firms $i$.
- Sort firms into deciles (or quantiles) based on $s_{i,t}$.
- Form equal-weighted (or value-weighted) portfolios $P_t^{(1)}, \ldots, P_t^{(10)}$.
- Compute forward returns over horizon $h$ for each portfolio.

We then examine:

- the average returns of each decile over time;
- the long-short spread $P^{(10)} - P^{(1)}$ (high vs. low sentiment);
- the information ratio and factor-adjusted alphas.

This "decile sort" gives an intuitive picture: if sentiment has predictive power, high-sentiment portfolios should outperform low-sentiment ones, after risk adjustment.

## Turnover and capacity

Sentiment signals often update with each new document. This can lead to high turnover, particularly at shorter horizons. We quantify:

$$\text{Turnover}_t = \frac{1}{2} \sum_i |w_{i,t} - w_{i,t-1}|,$$

where $w_{i,t}$ are portfolio weights. High turnover may:

- erode gross alpha via transaction costs;
- limit capacity due to market impact and liquidity constraints.

We thus evaluate net performance under realistic trading cost models and assess whether sentiment alpha survives at the scale we care about.

## Visualizing the Impact of Domain Adaptation

At this point we can compare two backtests:

- a portfolio strategy driven by generic sentiment scores;
- a strategy driven by financially adapted sentiment scores.

A clear way to illustrate the value of domain adaptation is to plot the cumulative returns of the respective long-short portfolios, along with confidence bands.

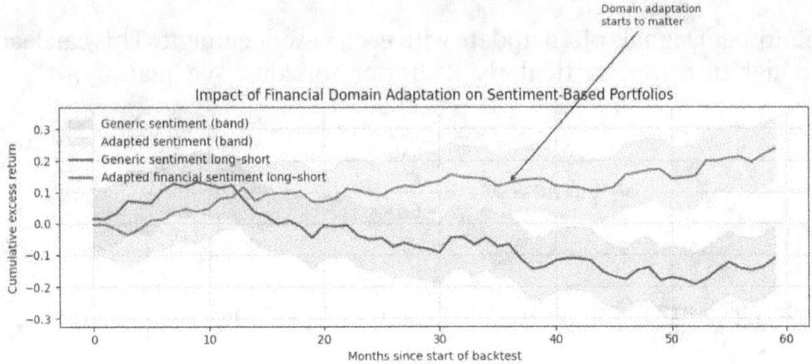


This figure encodes the narrative of this section: both generic and adapted sentiment models may show some relation to returns, but the adapted model, grounded in financial language and return alignment, delivers more stable and higher cumulative performance.

## Sentiment Drift and Evolving Corporate Language

An additional challenge is *sentiment drift*: the way firms communicate changes over time. Phrases that once signaled caution may become boilerplate; regulatory changes may introduce new disclosure templates; macro shocks (such as crises or pandemics) may shift the baseline tone.

If we freeze our sentiment model, its mapping from language to economic meaning may degrade. To mitigate this, we:

- periodically refresh continual pretraining with recent financial corpora;
- update supervised fine-tuning on more recent labeled examples;
- monitor performance decay via rolling backtests and recalibrate when necessary.

Importantly, all such updates must respect point-in-time constraints in backtests: for a given historical date, you may only use data available up to that date to train the model, otherwise you risk look-ahead contamination.

## Diagnosing Genuine Information vs. Overfitting

Finally, we must distinguish true information content from data-mining artifacts. Beyond standard backtesting diagnostics (Sharpe, drawdown, turnover), sentiment-specific checks include:

- **Monotonicity**: do returns increase roughly monotonically from low to high sentiment deciles?
- **Stability**: are coefficients on sentiment stable across subsamples (pre/post-crisis, bull/bear markets)?
- **Robustness**: does the signal survive when

- excluding microcaps and illiquid names,
- varying rebalancing frequency and holding period,
- changing the way we aggregate multiple documents per firm.

- **Economic interpretability**: can we explain performance by intuitive mechanisms (e.g., slower diffusion of textual information, investor underreaction to tone change) rather than by obscure model quirks?

If a sentiment model passes these tests, we upgrade it from a linguistic curiosity to a genuine alpha source. It becomes part of a broader signal library, to be combined with non-textual predictors under a coherent risk and capacity framework.

In summary, adapting generic language models to finance is not merely a matter of fine-tuning on a few labeled documents. It requires a careful combination of financial pretraining, supervised alignment with economically meaningful outcomes, regime awareness, rigorous backtesting, and continuous monitoring. Done well, domain-adapted sentiment and stance models can translate the messy, strategic language of financial actors into structured signals that earn their place in a modern quantitative trading toolkit.

## 5.2 Event Extraction and Event Studies

In the previous section we turned generic language models into finance-aware sentiment engines and connected their scores to cross-sectional returns. We treated text as a continuous stream of information, summarized by sentiment or stance. In this section we zoom in on *discrete* pieces of information: economically meaningful *events*.

Our goal is twofold:

1. Detect and structure economically relevant events from raw text.
2. Quantify their price impact using rigorous event-study methodology that respects market microstructure and multiple-testing risk.

This bridges the gap between "this news sounds bad" and "this kind of downgrade, when it appears in this type of text, typically moves the stock by $-3\%$ over the next trading day, net of market and factor effects."

### What Counts as an Event in Text?

An *event* is a discrete piece of new information that may change investors' beliefs about an asset's cash flows, risk, or discount rates. In textual data, typical examples include:

- **Earnings-related events**
- **Corporate actions and capital structure**
- **Regulatory and legal events**
- **Product and strategy events**
- **Analyst and rating events**

All of these appear in text: headlines, news articles, filings, press releases, and transcripts. Our task is to convert unstructured text into a structured panel of events with clear attributes:

- event type (e.g., guidance cut, downgrade, enforcement action),
- event polarity (good/bad/neutral for the asset),
- event intensity (how big or surprising it is),
- timestamp (when the information became public),
- linked asset(s) (tickers or issuers).

Once we have this structured panel, traditional event study tools from empirical finance can be applied.

## From Raw Text to Structured Events

Event extraction is the process of identifying and labeling snippets of text that correspond to events. There is a spectrum of approaches, from simple rules to fully generative models.

### Rule-based extraction

The simplest approach uses pattern templates and lexicons. For example:

- A rating change pattern:

  <BROKER> raises | cuts <TICKER> to <RATING>.

- A dividend change pattern:

  declares quarterly dividend of \$<AMOUNT> (vs \$<PRIOR>).

Implementation typically proceeds in two stages:

1. **Candidate generation**: identify sentences that contain key trigger words (e.g. "downgrade", "guidance", "dividend").
2. **Pattern matching**: apply regular expressions or finite-state machines to extract specific fields.

Rule-based extraction is transparent and precise for a narrow set of standard disclosures (e.g. broker ratings, dividend actions). It struggles with:

- paraphrases and non-standard phrasing,
- multi-sentence descriptions ("...as a result, we now expect ..."),
- ambiguous or figurative language.

### Supervised classification over candidate spans

A more flexible approach is to treat event detection as a supervised learning problem:

1. Segment documents into sentences or clauses.
2. For each segment and firm, construct a feature vector (e.g. LLM embedding, plus metadata such as section type and source).
3. Train a classifier to label each segment as one of:
    - no event,
    - event of type $k$ (e.g. guidance raise, guidance cut, legal settlement, downgrade).

Labels can come from:

- manual annotation by domain experts,
- heuristic labels aligned with structured data (e.g. match guidance changes recorded in a fundamentals database to nearby text describing them),
- distant supervision using large returns (e.g. segments around extreme abnormal returns are more likely to contain strong events).

Once trained, the classifier outputs both an event type and a confidence score. Downstream we can threshold by confidence or incorporate it as a measure of event reliability.

### Generative and few-shot prompting approaches

With large language models, we can use prompting to directly elicit structured events. For example:

```
prompt = """
You are a financial analyst. Extract all economically relevant events
from the following text. For each event, output:
- event_type (one of: guidance_raise, guidance_cut, downgrade, ...)
- polarity (positive, negative, neutral)
- intensity (low, medium, high)
- affected_tickers (list)

Text:
""" {news_article} """
"""
```

The model's output is then parsed as JSON. This has several advantages:

- It can generalize beyond explicitly seen templates.
- It can handle long-range dependencies (e.g. referring back to previous sentences).
- It can infer polarity and intensity from context.

However, generative extraction requires careful evaluation and guardrails:

- quality varies with prompt design and model version,
- hallucinated events must be filtered or penalized,
- consistency of schema over time must be monitored.

In practice, many production systems combine these approaches: rules for high-precision "easy" events, classifiers for broader coverage, and generative models for complex or rare cases.

## Event-Study Pipeline: From Text to Abnormal Returns

Once we have candidate events, we need to align them with prices and compute their impact. The core steps are:

1. raw text → extracted events,
2. events → clean timestamps and assets,
3. prices → expected and abnormal returns,
4. abnormal returns → statistical tests.

The following diagram summarizes this pipeline.

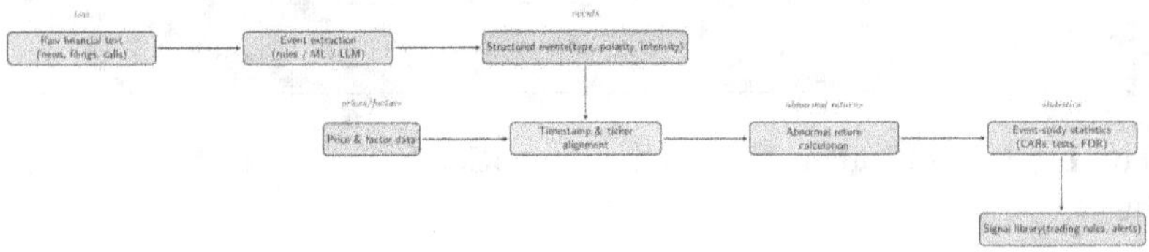


We now unpack each component, paying particular attention to market microstructure and multiple testing.

**Timestamping and market microstructure**

For each extracted event, we must decide *when* the market could first react to it. Key nuances include:

- **Publication vs. detection delay**. A news article may be timestamped at 10:03:17, but your data vendor may record it at 10:03:30. For intraday studies, these seconds matter.
- **Exchange vs. off-exchange hours**. If a press release crosses at 6:00am, the first chance to trade on most exchanges is at the open. For events released after the close, the primary reaction is at the next day's open.
- **Batching of text**. Long documents (e.g. 10-Ks) may be processed with some latency relative to their EDGAR filing time. You should use the earliest credible public timestamp, not the time your system finished parsing.

For event studies at daily frequency, a standard convention is:

- if the event timestamp is between the previous close and the current close, assign it to the current day;
- if the event arrives after the close, assign it to the next trading day.

For intraday studies, it is common to use *event time* measured in minutes or seconds relative to the event timestamp, and to restrict analysis to periods with sufficient depth and liquidity.

**Linking events to assets**

Each event must be associated with one or more traded instruments, typically via:

- entity recognition and linking (company, issuer),
- mapping to canonical tickers (with point-in-time awareness),
- handling multi-firm events (e.g. acquirer and target in M&A).

If an event affects multiple firms asymmetrically (e.g. a supplier's recall hurts downstream customers), you may represent it as several event-firm pairs, each with its own polarity and intensity.

## Estimation Windows, Event Windows, and Abnormal Returns

With event-firm pairs and clean timestamps, we can compute abnormal returns. The key concepts are:

- **Estimation window**: a pre-event period used to estimate a normal-return model.
- **Event window**: the period over which we measure the market's reaction.
- **Abnormal return (AR)**: realized return minus expected return.

- **Cumulative abnormal return (CAR)**: sum of ARs over an event window.

### Choosing estimation and event windows

Denote the event date (in trading days) by $\tau = 0$ for a given firm $i$. A classic design is:

- Estimation window: $\tau \in [-120, -21]$ (roughly $[-6, -1]$ months).
- Event windows:
  - short: $[0, 0]$ (same-day),
  - slightly wider: $[0, 1]$ (day of and day after),
  - pre-announcement: $[-1, -1]$ (possible leakage).

For intraday events, we might instead work in minutes relative to the event time, e.g. an estimation window of days at daily frequency and an event window of $[0, 60]$ minutes post-event, while controlling for intraday seasonality.

### Normal-return models

Let $R_{i,t}$ be the asset return (or log-return) for firm $i$ at time $t$, and $R_{m,t}$ a broad market index return. Common models for expected returns $\hat{R}_{i,t}$ include:

- **Market model**:

$$R_{i,t} = \alpha_i + \beta_i R_{m,t} + \varepsilon_{i,t},$$

  estimated over the firm's estimation window.

- **Factor model** (e.g. Fama-French style):

$$R_{i,t} = \alpha_i + \boldsymbol{\beta}_i^\top \mathbf{F}_t + \varepsilon_{i,t},$$

  where $\mathbf{F}_t$ contains size, value, momentum, etc.

- **Characteristic-based model**: expected returns as functions of firm characteristics (size, value, etc.), fit cross-sectionally.

Abnormal returns are then:

$$\mathrm{AR}_{i,t} = R_{i,t} - \hat{R}_{i,t}.$$

For an event window $\mathcal{T}$ (e.g. $\mathcal{T} = \{0, 1\}$), the cumulative abnormal return is:

$$\mathrm{CAR}_i(\mathcal{T}) = \sum_{t \in \mathcal{T}} \mathrm{AR}_{i,t}.$$

## Practical Complications: Clustering and Overlap

Real-world text rarely delivers one clean event per firm per month. Instead, we face:

- **Clustered events**: many firms experiencing the same type of event on the same day (e.g. sector-wide downgrades, regulatory sweeps).
- **Overlapping windows**: multiple events for the same firm whose event windows overlap (e.g. earnings release followed by a rating action).
- **Information trickle**: news that unfolds across multiple articles rather than a single discrete release.

### Clustered events across firms

When many firms share the same event date, abnormal returns may be cross-sectionally correlated, which affects standard error estimates. Solutions include:

- clustering standard errors by event date,
- using portfolio-level tests: form a portfolio of event firms and examine its CAR,
- simulation or bootstrap methods that respect cross-sectional dependence.

### Overlapping events within a firm

If firm $i$ has multiple events whose windows overlap, attributing CARs to individual events becomes ambiguous. Options include:

- restricting analysis to the first event in a given window,
- merging nearby events into a single composite event,
- modeling overlapping events jointly in a regression framework with multiple event dummies.

The choice depends on your research question. For trading signal design, it is often practical to treat closely spaced events as a single complex event and focus on the cumulative impact.

### Handling information trickle

Sometimes the market reacts to the first small article in a sequence, not the final "definitive" article. To avoid attributing the whole move to the last piece, you can:

- identify and group related articles into *news clusters* (e.g. by topic modeling or similarity of embeddings),
- treat the cluster's first article time as the canonical event time,
- assign attributes (e.g. intensity) based on all articles in the cluster.

## Controlling for Multiple Testing

In a modern NLP pipeline, we may consider dozens of event types, multiple polarities and intensities, and several event windows. If we test everything naïvely at the 5% significance level, many "significant" results will appear by chance.

Let $H_1, \ldots, H_m$ be $m$ null hypotheses (e.g. "no CAR for guidance raises over $[0, 1]$"). We compute corresponding $p$-values $p_1, \ldots, p_m$. Multiple-testing corrections help control:

- the **family-wise error rate** (FWER): probability of at least one false positive,
- the **false discovery rate** (FDR): expected proportion of false positives among rejected hypotheses.

**Bonferroni and Holm corrections**

The Bonferroni correction is simple and conservative:

- Use significance threshold $\alpha/m$ instead of $\alpha$.

The Holm step-down procedure is less conservative:

1. Sort $p$-values: $p_{(1)} \leq \cdots \leq p_{(m)}$.
2. For $k = 1, \ldots, m$, compare $p_{(k)}$ to $\alpha/(m - k + 1)$.
3. Reject $H_{(k)}$ until the first time $p_{(k)} > \alpha/(m - k + 1)$, then stop and accept all remaining hypotheses.

Both methods control FWER, making it unlikely that any false positive appears among your "discoveries", but at the cost of power when $m$ is large.

**False discovery rate (FDR) control**

In signal research, we often tolerate some false positives as long as most discoveries are real. FDR control (e.g. Benjamini-Hochberg) is more powerful:

1. Sort $p$-values: $p_{(1)} \leq \cdots \leq p_{(m)}$.
2. Find the largest $k$ such that
$$p_{(k)} \leq \frac{k}{m}\alpha.$$
3. Reject $H_{(1)}, \ldots, H_{(k)}$.

Under mild conditions, this controls the expected fraction of false rejections among all rejections at level $\alpha$. For an NLP-based event library with many candidate event types and windows, FDR control is usually the appropriate standard.

## From Event Studies to Trading Rules and Risk Overlays

Once we have validated that certain text-defined events systematically move prices, we can translate them into trading rules and risk tools.

### Building event-firm panels

We collect for each firm $i$ and calendar date $t$:

- indicators for event types (e.g. $\text{Downgrade}_{i,t}$, $\text{GuidanceCut}_{i,t}$),
- attributes (polarity, intensity, uncertainty in the language),
- corresponding abnormal returns over multiple horizons.

This panel can be used to:

- estimate cross-sectional models of future returns as functions of event dummies and attributes,
- design signal composites (e.g. combining event indicators with sentiment and fundamentals),
- study heterogeneity (e.g. do downgrades matter more for small caps?).

### Trading rules and alerts

Examples of trading rules derived from event studies include:

- go short firms experiencing a negative high-intensity regulatory event, hold for $h$ days;
- overweight firms with positive product-launch events that historically show underreaction;
- dynamically hedge portfolios around known high-impact event types (e.g. guidance cuts).

In many institutions, the first practical use of text-derived events is as alerts for human portfolio managers and risk managers, rather than as fully automated trading signals. Over time, as evidence accumulates, these can be elevated into systematic components of the signal library.

**Risk overlays and scenario analysis**

Event studies also inform risk management:

- estimate the typical CAR associated with certain negative event types (e.g. enforcement actions) and treat them as stress scenarios,
- simulate portfolios under shocks where all holdings experience adverse events of a given type,
- identify concentrations in event-exposed names (e.g. a portfolio heavily tilted to firms with high legal or regulatory event frequency).

These applications do not depend on the events being highly predictable ex ante; they exploit the *distribution* of event impacts to inform tail-risk management.

## Putting It All Together

This section has walked from raw text to tradable, statistically validated event signals:

1. Define economically meaningful event types and attributes.
2. Extract them from text via rules, supervised classifiers, or generative LLMs.
3. Carefully timestamp and link them to assets, respecting market microstructure.
4. Compute abnormal returns over well-chosen estimation and event windows.
5. Address practical complications: clustered events, overlapping windows, information trickle.

6. Correct for multiple testing when evaluating many event types and horizons.

7. Translate validated effects into trading rules, alerts, and risk overlays.

In combination with the sentiment and stance models from the previous section, event extraction and event studies give us a way to quantify how specific textual triggers move markets. The next step in the chapter will be to step back again and think more broadly about narratives: how clusters of related ideas in text form *themes*, and how we can build and trade dynamic thematic baskets that capture these evolving stories.

## 5.3 Topic Modeling and Thematic Baskets

The previous sections worked at the level of individual documents and discrete events. We asked questions like: *Is the tone of this earnings call negative?* or *Did this guidance cut move the stock?* In this section we zoom out.

Markets are also driven by *narratives* that unfold over quarters and years: "AI adoption", "energy transition", "supply chain reshoring", "regulatory tightening for big tech". These narratives cut across sectors and countries, and they rarely align neatly with standard factor models. Our task here is to:

- discover such themes from large corpora of financial text, and
- convert them into dynamic, tradable *thematic baskets* whose exposures we can monitor and manage over time.

This requires both good NLP and sound portfolio construction. We will proceed step by step, moving from classic topic models to modern embedding-based approaches, then from topics to firm-level scores, and finally to baskets and validation.

## Why Topics Matter for Trading

A topic, in the NLP sense, is a pattern in word usage. A theme, in the investing sense, is a coherent economic story that affects cash flows, risk, or discount rates for many securities at once.

Text is often the first place where new themes appear and where existing themes evolve. Consider:

- mentions of "electric vehicles", "battery technology", and "charging infrastructure" in earnings calls and filings,
- clusters of news about "supply chain disruptions", "port congestion", "semiconductor shortages";
- growing discussion of "carbon pricing", "emissions targets", "EU taxonomy" in regulatory and corporate texts.

If we can detect these patterns early and quantify how strongly each firm is exposed to them, we unlock several use cases:

- long-short thematic strategies (e.g. high vs. low exposure to "energy transition"),
- overlaying a broad portfolio with explicit thematic tilts,
- risk management and scenario analysis around theme-specific shocks.

## Limitations of Classic Topic Models in Finance

The traditional workhorse for topic modeling is Latent Dirichlet Allocation (LDA). It represents each document as a mixture of $K$ topics; each topic is a probability distribution over words. In practice, LDA has several drawbacks for financial applications.

**Instability over time**

LDA assumes that topics and their word distributions are *stationary*. In finance, language and narratives evolve:

- "Cloud" meant something different in 2005 than in 2025.
- New technologies, regulations, and business models introduce new vocabulary.
- Old themes fade away or merge with others.

If you run LDA on a long time span, topics may be hard to interpret and may mix several historical regimes. If you run it in rolling windows, topics drift and can be difficult to match across windows.

**Short texts and sparse word counts**

LDA works best with relatively long documents. Financial headlines and alerts are short—often under 15 tokens. In such cases, word-count vectors are extremely sparse; there is simply not enough information per document for LDA to produce stable, interpretable topics.

**Economic interpretability**

The most probable words in an LDA topic are often generic ("company", "quarter", "business", "market"). This makes it difficult to map topics to economically meaningful themes like "supply chain risk" or "regulatory tightening in fintech" without extensive manual curation.

These limitations motivate more modern, embedding-based approaches.

## Embedding-Based Topic Discovery

Modern language models can map sentences or documents into dense vectors (embeddings) in a high-dimensional space. Similar texts end up close together in this space, even if they do not share many explicit words. This is particularly useful for:

- capturing synonyms and paraphrases,
- handling short, noisy texts (e.g. headlines),
- representing context (e.g. "cloud" as a technology vs. weather).

**From documents to embeddings**

Given a corpus of documents $\{d_j\}_{j=1}^N$, we obtain embeddings $\mathbf{z}_j \in \mathbb{R}^p$ using a pretrained or domain-adapted language model:

$$\mathbf{z}_j = f_\theta(d_j),$$

where $f_\theta$ is the model's encoding function (e.g. the [CLS] token representation, or a sentence embedding). As discussed earlier in the chapter, domain adaptation (continual pretraining and fine-tuning on financial text) improves the quality of these embeddings for our purposes.

**Clustering embeddings into topics**

We can then discover topics by clustering these embeddings. Conceptually:

- Choose a clustering algorithm (e.g. $k$-means, hierarchical clustering, or density-based methods).
- Select a number of clusters $K$ (or a clustering resolution).
- Cluster the embeddings $\{\mathbf{z}_j\}$ into groups $\{C_1, \ldots, C_K\}$.

Each cluster $C_k$ contains documents that are semantically similar. We interpret cluster $k$ as a candidate topic. To understand it, we can:

- list the top-$n$ documents or headlines closest to the cluster centroid,
- compute the most distinctive words or phrases in the cluster,
- inspect which sectors and tickers dominate it.

Unlike LDA, this approach does not require word-count vectors or conjugate priors; the embeddings already encapsulate rich context.

**Guided topics with seed terms**

Purely unsupervised clustering may yield topics that are hard to map to economic ideas. To steer the model toward interpretable financial themes, we can use *seed terms*.

For example:

- "AI adoption" theme: {"artificial intelligence", "machine learning", "neural network", "LLM", "automation"}.
- "Supply chain risk" theme: {"shortage", "backlog", "capacity constraint", "logistics", "shipping delay"}.
- "Regulatory tightening" theme: {"compliance", "enforcement action", "fine", "consent decree", "capital requirement"}.

There are several ways to incorporate seeds:

- initialize cluster centroids using embeddings of seed phrases;
- bias clustering so that documents near seed embeddings are more likely to join a specific cluster;
- conduct a two-stage process: first cluster, then assign or merge clusters based on their similarity to seed sets.

This guided approach helps ensure that discovered topics line up with narratives an investment committee can understand and debate.

## From Topics to Firm-Theme Scores

Topics are patterns over documents; trading, however, happens at the level of securities. We therefore need to map topic intensities to firms.

**Document-level topic intensities**

Clustering provides a hard assignment of each document $d_j$ to a topic $k$. In practice, we often want *soft* assignments, reflecting the fact that a document may touch multiple themes.

Two common strategies:

- **Probabilistic classifier**: train a model to predict topic probabilities $P(\text{topic} = k \mid d_j)$ using cluster labels as pseudo-ground-truth; the model's softmax output gives soft intensities.

- **Similarity-based assignment**: compute cosine similarity between $\mathbf{z}_j$ and each topic centroid $\boldsymbol{\mu}_k$, and normalize:

$$w_{j,k} = \frac{\exp(\lambda \cdot \cos(\mathbf{z}_j, \boldsymbol{\mu}_k))}{\sum_{\ell=1}^{K} \exp(\lambda \cdot \cos(\mathbf{z}_j, \boldsymbol{\mu}_\ell))},$$

  where $\lambda$ controls how "peaked" the distribution is.

Here $w_{j,k}$ is the intensity of topic $k$ in document $j$.

**Aggregating to firm-theme scores**

Suppose document $j$ mentions firm $i$ (via entity linking, discussed later in the chapter). We can construct firm-theme scores by aggregating across documents:

$$S_{i,k,t} = \frac{\sum_{j \in \mathcal{D}_{i,t}} \omega_j \, w_{j,k}}{\sum_{j \in \mathcal{D}_{i,t}} \omega_j},$$

where:

- $\mathcal{D}_{i,t}$ is the set of documents mentioning firm $i$ in a given time window ending at $t$ (e.g. last month or last quarter),
- $\omega_j$ is a weight for document $j$ (e.g. 1, or based on source importance, recency within the window, or word count).

$S_{i,k,t}$ is then a normalized measure of firm $i$'s exposure to theme $k$ at time $t$.

**Correcting for coverage and volume bias**

Large firms naturally receive more coverage than small firms. If we simply count how often topics appear, we might mistake "being newsworthy" for "being thematic". To mitigate this, we can:

- work with *intensity shares* rather than raw counts (as in the normalized formula above),
- de-mean topic intensities at the firm level over a long history (focus on *changes* in thematic attention),

- scale scores by the total number of documents per firm to penalize cases where the theme appears only in a tiny fraction of coverage.

A simple yet effective tactic is to compute deviations from a firm-specific baseline:

$$\tilde{S}_{i,k,t} = S_{i,k,t} - \bar{S}_{i,k},$$

where $\bar{S}_{i,k}$ is the historical average of $S_{i,k,t}$ over a pre-specified period. This highlights firms whose exposure to theme $k$ is unusually high or low relative to their own past, rather than relative to absolute news volume.

## Constructing Dynamic Thematic Baskets

With firm-theme scores $\tilde{S}_{i,k,t}$ in hand, we can build and trade thematic baskets.

**Basic long-short construction**

For a given theme $k$ and rebalancing date $t$:

- Rank all eligible firms by $\tilde{S}_{i,k,t}$.
- Form a long portfolio $L_{k,t}$ of firms in the top quantile (e.g. top 20%), and a short portfolio $S_{k,t}$ of firms in the bottom quantile.
- Choose a weighting scheme:
  - equal weights within long and short legs;
  - or weights proportional to $\tilde{S}_{i,k,t}$ (capped to avoid concentration);
  - optionally neutralize sector or country exposures by constructing long and short legs sector-by-sector.
- Define the basket return over horizon $h$ as:

  $$R^{(h)}_{k,t} = R(L_{k,t}) - R(S_{k,t}),$$

  where $R(\cdot)$ denotes the portfolio return over $[t, t+h]$.

This long-short basket isolates the theme as much as possible: firms with unusually high exposure vs. those with unusually low exposure.

### Integrating with factor models

To avoid rediscovering known factors under a new label, we examine how the thematic basket loads on standard factors. Run a time-series regression:

$$R_{k,t}^{(h)} = \alpha_k + \boldsymbol{\beta}_k^\top \mathbf{F}_t + \varepsilon_{k,t},$$

where $\mathbf{F}_t$ includes market, size, value, momentum, quality, etc. A few interpretations:

- If $\boldsymbol{\beta}_k$ explains most of the variance and $\alpha_k$ is small, the theme may just be a repackaging of standard factors.
- If $\alpha_k$ is significant and economically meaningful, the theme adds incremental information beyond the factor set.
- The elements of $\boldsymbol{\beta}_k$ show which existing factors the theme most resembles (e.g. "energy transition" might load on value and growth in different regimes).

Even if a theme overlaps with known factors, making it explicit is still useful for communication and risk management.

### Turnover, liquidity, and capacity

Like sentiment signals, thematic scores $S_{i,k,t}$ evolve over time. Some themes are slow-moving (e.g. demographic shifts); others, such as "supply chain disruptions", can spike and subside quickly. Portfolio design must match this dynamic:

- choose rebalancing frequencies that reflect how fast the theme's cross-sectional pattern changes;
- monitor turnover and adjust thresholds to keep trading costs manageable;
- ensure minimum liquidity standards to avoid crowding into illiquid names.

A practical heuristic is to set minimum holding periods or rebalance only when a firm's rank changes by more than a threshold, smoothing out noise in the theme scores.

## Time-Varying Topics and Regime Shifts

So far we have treated topics as fixed clusters in embedding space. In practice, themes *evolve*. The vocabulary around "AI adoption" in 2015 (big data, predictive analytics) differs from 2025 (foundation models, copilots). We need methods that can track such evolution.

### Rolling windows and online clustering

One approach is to run the embedding-and-clustering pipeline in rolling time windows (e.g. 1-2 years):

- For each window, embed documents and cluster into topics.
- For each new set of topics, match them to previous ones using similarity of centroids and top documents.
- Track births (new topics), deaths (topics that disappear), and splits/merges.

This yields a time series of topic definitions, which can then be aligned into longer-lived themes. For example, several related short-lived topics may all be classified under a broader "AI adoption" umbrella.

### Dynamic topic models

More advanced approaches, such as dynamic topic models, explicitly model topic-word distributions as evolving over time. When combined with embeddings, one can:

- learn latent trajectories of themes in embedding space,
- capture gradual drifts and sudden shifts in narrative focus,
- maintain continuity of themes while allowing vocabulary and context to change.

From a trading perspective, the key is not the modeling detail but the ability to:

- detect when a theme is gaining or losing market attention,
- observe how the cross-section of firm exposures to the theme rotates,
- understand whether the economic meaning of the theme has changed (e.g. from speculative growth to regulated utility).

## Validating Thematic Baskets

Before committing capital, we must test whether our thematic baskets capture something economically meaningful, not just noise or existing factors.

**Linking themes to subsequent returns**

For each theme $k$, we can:

- examine the time series of basket returns $R_{k,t}^{(h)}$:
  - average return, volatility, Sharpe ratio,
  - drawdowns and regime dependence.
- analyze cross-sectional spreads:
  - do high-exposure firms outperform low-exposure firms when the theme gains attention?
  - is there underreaction (drift) or quick reversal?

It is also informative to stratify firms by theme exposure and examine their realized fundamentals: earnings growth, capex, margins. If a theme is economically meaningful, highly exposed firms should show patterns consistent with the story (e.g. higher R&D for "AI adoption").

**Checking against macro and factor surprises**

Many themes are closely tied to macro variables or policy. For example:

- "Energy transition" baskets might respond to carbon-price shocks or climate policy announcements.
- "Regulatory tightening" baskets might move with changes in enforcement tone or legislation.

Event-study methodology (from the previous section) can be reused:

- treat key macro or policy announcements as events,
- measure abnormal returns of thematic baskets around these dates,
- test whether the responses are consistent with the narrative.

Similarly, regressing basket returns on macro surprises (e.g. inflation, growth, rate decisions) can reveal whether a theme is just a proxy for macro exposure.

**Ensuring themes are not just rebranded factors**

As noted earlier, many intuitive stories correspond to familiar factors ("quality growth", "value turnaround"). To avoid self-deception:

- always evaluate factor-adjusted performance;
- examine how much of the theme's cross-sectional variation is explained by basic characteristics (size, value, momentum);
- stress-test the theme by re-estimating it on subsets of the text corpus (e.g. only filings vs. only news) and checking for consistency.

If the theme survives these tests with a clear economic interpretation and some incremental explanatory or predictive power, it deserves a place in the signal library.

## An Illustrative Example: Energy Transition

To make the abstract pipeline concrete, consider an "energy transition" theme.

- **Define seeds**: phrases like “renewable energy”, “solar farm”, “wind capacity”, “EV charging”, “carbon neutrality”, “scope 3 emissions”.
- **Collect text**: filings, earnings calls, and news mentioning these or related concepts.
- **Embed and cluster**: obtain document embeddings and cluster to find subtopics (e.g. “utility-scale renewables”, “EV infrastructure”, “oil & gas decarbonization”).
- **Map to firms**: via entity linking, aggregate soft topic intensities to firm-theme scores and normalize by firm.
- **Build baskets**: construct long-short portfolios of firms with unusually high vs. low energy-transition exposure.
- **Validate**:
  - examine basket performance around policy events (e.g. climate legislation),
  - check factor-adjusted alphas and macro sensitivities,
  - assess how exposures line up with sector knowledge (e.g. utilities, industrials, autos).

Through this lens, the theme is not just a marketing label or ETF ticker; it is a quantitatively defined, text-grounded narrative whose exposures and performance can be rigorously studied.

In this section we extended our toolkit from document-level sentiment and discrete events to broader narratives captured via topic modeling:

- We saw why classic topic models are often inadequate for financial text and how embedding-based clustering overcomes many limitations.
- We introduced guided topics, using seed terms to steer discovered topics toward interpretable economic themes.
- We mapped document-level topic intensities to firm-theme scores, adjusting for coverage bias and focusing on deviations from firm-specific baselines.

- We showed how to construct, trade, and validate dynamic thematic baskets, ensuring they add value beyond traditional factors and link sensibly to macro and policy shocks.
- We discussed time-varying topics and regime shifts, highlighting the importance of tracking how narratives and vocabularies evolve.

Together with domain-adapted sentiment and structured event signals, thematic baskets complete the picture: from the microscopic (sentences, events) to the macroscopic (narratives). The remaining piece is to connect all of this text-derived information robustly to tradable objects—which is the job of entity linking and knowledge graphs in the next section.

## 5.4 Entity Linking to Tickers and Knowledge Graphs

Up to this point, we have treated text at three different levels:

- sentence and document sentiment;
- discrete events with measurable price impact;
- medium- to long-horizon themes captured via topic modeling.

In every case, there was an implicit assumption: we knew *which* asset the text referred to. In practice, this is the most fragile step. News and filings talk about companies, brands, products, business units, counterparties, and sectors in ways that are often ambiguous. Trading systems, by contrast, operate on *tickers* and *instruments*.

This section focuses on the bridge between the two:

- mapping messy entity mentions in text to clean, point-in-time tickers and issuers (entity linking), and
- using a financial knowledge graph to consolidate these links into coherent, tradable signals.

Without this bridge, even the best NLP pipeline cannot reliably turn text into positions.

## The Challenges of Entity Resolution in Finance

Entity resolution, or entity linking, is the task of taking a mention like “Apple” or “the bank” and resolving it to a canonical identifier: an issuer ID, a ticker, an ISIN, a legal entity. Finance adds several sources of complexity.

**Ticker collisions and exchange differences**

Ticker symbols are not globally unique. For example:

- the same 3-4 letter code can be used on different exchanges for entirely unrelated firms;
- ADRs and local listings may share names but differ in ticker format;
- over-the-counter instruments may use internal codes not visible in public feeds.

A purely string-based match from text to ticker is therefore dangerous. We need context: exchange, region, sector, and co-mentions.

**Name changes, mergers, and corporate actions**

Corporate identities are not static:

- companies merge, spin off divisions, or rebrand;
- legal entities may change while the commercial brand remains the same;
- tickers can change following corporate restructurings.

A news article from 2012 mentioning “Google” refers to an entity that now sits within a different legal and ticker structure (Alphabet). A point-in-time aware mapping is essential to avoid look-ahead bias and mis-aggregation of history.

**Ambiguous references to units, brands, and products**

Text often refers to:

- brands (e.g. “iPhone”, “YouTube”),
- business lines (“the investment bank”, “the cloud division”),
- subsidiaries and joint ventures (“XYZ Bank Polska”),

without naming the listed parent. Economic exposure may reside primarily at the parent or be shared across multiple entities. A robust system must understand these hierarchies.

**Cross-asset and counterparty relationships**

Events affecting one entity can have implications for others:

- a supplier’s factory shutdown affects downstream customers;
- a sovereign downgrade affects banks holding its bonds;
- a regulatory change in one jurisdiction may affect multinationals with significant exposure there.

Capturing these linkages requires more than a flat table of names and tickers; it calls for a structured representation of relationships—a knowledge graph.

# A Modern Entity-Linking Pipeline

A practical entity-linking system typically contains four steps:

- named entity recognition (NER),
- candidate generation,
- candidate ranking,

- calibration and quality control.

We describe each step in turn.

**Named entity recognition (NER)**

The first step is to locate mentions of entities in text. NER models tag spans as ORG, PERSON, GPE (geo-political entity), and so on. For finance, we often extend the label set to distinguish:

- ISSUER: publicly traded corporations or bond issuers,
- INSTRUMENT: specific securities (bonds, structured notes),
- BRAND/PRODUCT: commercial names that may map to issuers,
- COUNTERPARTY: significant business partners.

Domain-adapted NER models, trained on filings, news, and research reports, markedly outperform generic models at detecting financial entities and reducing spurious tags.

**Candidate generation**

Once we have a mention span (e.g. “Apple”, “XYZ Bank Polska”), we search for plausible canonical entities. Candidate sources include:

- security master and issuer databases (with names, aliases, and historical names),
- exchange and regulatory registries,
- internal mapping tables maintained by operations teams.

Candidate generation often uses fuzzy matching on:

- normalized names (case-insensitive, punctuation stripped),
- abbreviations and acronyms (“JPM”, “BofA”),
- language-specific variants (“Banco Santander” vs. “Santander Bank”),

- brand-to-parent mappings (e.g. mapping "YouTube" to Alphabet).

The output is a set of candidate entities $\{e_1, \ldots, e_M\}$ for each mention, along with rough match scores.

**Candidate ranking using context**

Candidate ranking chooses the best entity (or entities) from the candidate set, using both textual and structured context.

**Textual context.** We embed the surrounding text (sentence or paragraph) and compare it to profiles of candidate entities:

- sector-specific words ("handset", "semiconductor") align with tech hardware;
- region-specific clues ("Tokyo", "yen", "JGB") align with Japanese entities;
- co-mentions (other companies or tickers) suggest sectors or regions.

The ranking model might take as input:

- mention string features (exact match, edit distance),
- contextual embedding similarity,
- sector, country, and exchange compatibility.

and output a probability that each candidate is the correct link.

**Structured constraints.** We can impose additional constraints from structured data:

- if the document is tagged as "US equities", favor US-listed tickers;
- if the sector or index is known, prune candidates from incompatible sectors;
- if the mention appears alongside a known ticker (e.g. "AAPL"), pair it with the corresponding issuer.

These constraints reduce the probability of implausible matches, especially in short, ambiguous texts.

**Calibration and quality control**

Finally, we calibrate the model's confidence scores and set thresholds for:

- **high-confidence links**: used directly in production (e.g. confidence $> 0.9$),
- **medium-confidence links**: flagged for downstream dampening or human review,
- **unresolved mentions**: either ignored or used for exploratory analysis without direct trading.

Periodic manual audits, with spot-checking of linked entities in random document samples, are essential to ensure drift or schema changes have not degraded performance.

# Introducing the Financial Knowledge Graph

Entity linking gives us a mapping from mentions to canonical issuers and instruments. But many important relationships are *indirect*: suppliers, customers, subsidiaries, sectors, and so on. This motivates a more general structure: a *financial knowledge graph*.

A knowledge graph is a set of nodes and edges:

- nodes represent entities: issuers, tickers, subsidiaries, sectors, indices, instruments, counterparties, geographies;
- edges represent relationships: "is parent of", "is subsidiary of", "supplies", "is in sector", "holds bond of", etc.

In our context, the knowledge graph serves three main purposes:

- provide a canonical backbone on which to aggregate text-derived signals,
- propagate signals along economically meaningful paths,
- enforce point-in-time consistency and avoid look-ahead bias.

**Typical node and edge types**

Common node types include:

- **Issuer**: legal entities that issue equity or debt.
- **Ticker/Instrument**: specific tradable securities.
- **Subsidiary / Business unit**: operating entities within a group.
- **Sector / Industry**: classification nodes (GICS, NAICS, etc.).
- **Counterparty**: customers, suppliers, joint ventures.
- **Country / Region**: geo-entities relevant for exposure.

Common edge types include:

- **Ownership**: parent–subsidiary relationships, with ownership percentages.
- **Listing**: links between issuers and their tickers on different exchanges.
- **Classification**: issuer–sector, issuer–country.
- **Economic links**: supplier–customer, lender–borrower, lessor–lessee.

Text-derived signals—sentiment, events, themes—are then attached to relevant nodes and propagated as needed.

# Projecting Text-Derived Signals onto the Graph

Assume we have already:

- extracted sentiment scores, event tags, and thematic intensities at the document level;
- linked document mentions to specific nodes in the graph (e.g. subsidiaries, brands, counterparties).

The next step is to project this information onto issuers and tickers for trading.

**Direct aggregation at the issuer level**

When mentions are already resolved to issuer nodes (e.g. "XYZ Corp"), aggregation is straightforward:

$$\text{Signal}_{issuer,i,t} = \sum_{j \in \mathcal{D}_{i,t}} \omega_j \cdot \text{Signal}_j,$$

where:

- $\mathcal{D}_{i,t}$ is the set of documents mentioning issuer $i$ over a window ending at $t$,
- $\omega_j$ are weights (e.g. based on source, recency, or coverage),
- $\text{Signal}_j$ may be a sentiment score, event intensity, or theme score.

These issuer-level signals then feed directly into equity or credit models via the issuer–ticker edges.

**Rolling up subsidiary and brand signals**

Often, text refers to subsidiaries or brands rather than the listed parent. We then need to roll signals up along parent–subsidiary and brand–issuer edges.

Suppose subsidiary $s$ is 100% owned by issuer $i$. A simple roll-up is:

$$\text{Signal}_{issuer,i,t} \mathrel{+}= \lambda_{s\to i} \cdot \text{Signal}_{sub,s,t},$$

where $\lambda_{s\to i}$ is a weight reflecting ownership share and materiality. For partial ownership and complex structures, we can generalize this to:

$$\text{Signal}_{issuer,i,t} = \sum_{s\in\mathcal{S}(i)} w_{i,s} \cdot \text{Signal}_{sub,s,t},$$

with $\sum_s w_{i,s} \leq 1$. Choices for $w_{i,s}$ can incorporate:

- ownership percentage,
- revenue share,
- region or sector focus.

Brand nodes can be treated similarly, using metadata about which brands materially contribute to which issuers.

**Propagating along economic links**

The knowledge graph also allows us to propagate shocks along economic relationships. For example:

- A negative event at a key supplier might lead to a risk signal for its major customers.
- A regulatory action against a bank in one country could signal risk to foreign banks with large exposures there.

Formally, if there is a supplier–customer edge from node $u$ (supplier) to node $v$ (customer), with weight $w_{u\to v}$ (e.g. fraction of $v$'s cost of goods sold), we can define:

$$\text{Signal}^{(indirect)}_{v,t} = \sum_{u\in\mathcal{N}(v)} w_{u\to v} \cdot \text{Signal}^{(direct)}_{u,t},$$

where $\mathcal{N}(v)$ are neighbors (suppliers) of $v$. This indirect signal can be used as:

- an additional explanatory variable in risk models,
- a source of cross-asset strategies (e.g. trading customers based on supplier news).

Care must be taken to cap propagation depth and avoid creating noisy, high-order chains that have little economic meaning.

## Point-in-Time Graph Versions and Bias Control

Just as price and fundamentals data must be point-in-time, the knowledge graph itself must respect historical reality. Two types of bias can otherwise appear:

- **Look-ahead bias**: using relationships or ownership structures that were only known after date $t$ to interpret text at or before $t$.
- **Survivorship bias**: only including nodes and edges for entities that survive until the end of your backtest.

To avoid this, we maintain *versioned* graphs:

- each edge has an effective start and end date (e.g. ownership from date $a$ to $b$),
- each node has a lifecycle (creation, delisting, merger),
- each mapping from issuer to ticker is time-stamped.

When processing a document dated $t$, we query the graph "as of" $t$:

- which issuers existed?
- what were their subsidiaries and brands?
- which tickers represented them?

This ensures that our text-to-signal mapping is consistent with what an investor could have known at that time.

## Knowledge Graph as a Signal Integration Backbone

By now, the role of the knowledge graph should be clear: it is the *backbone* that integrates multiple NLP outputs into a coherent, tradable view.

At a high level, the flow is:

- Raw text is processed into sentiment, events, and themes.
- Mentions are linked to graph nodes via the entity-linking pipeline.
- Signals are aggregated and propagated along graph edges to issuers and tickers.
- Portfolio holdings, also mapped to the graph, receive an overlay of signal exposures.

The following diagram summarizes this architecture.

This picture emphasizes two ideas:

- text-derived signals attach first to graph nodes (issuer, subsidiary, sector, etc.), not directly to tickers;
- portfolio holdings obtain signals by traversing the graph from tickers to related nodes and aggregating their signals.

## Improving Signal Quality with Graph-Aware Aggregation

Using a knowledge graph for aggregation does more than just tidy up mappings; it can materially improve signal quality.

**More accurate exposure calculations**

By correctly rolling up subsidiary and brand information and accounting for cross-listings, we avoid:

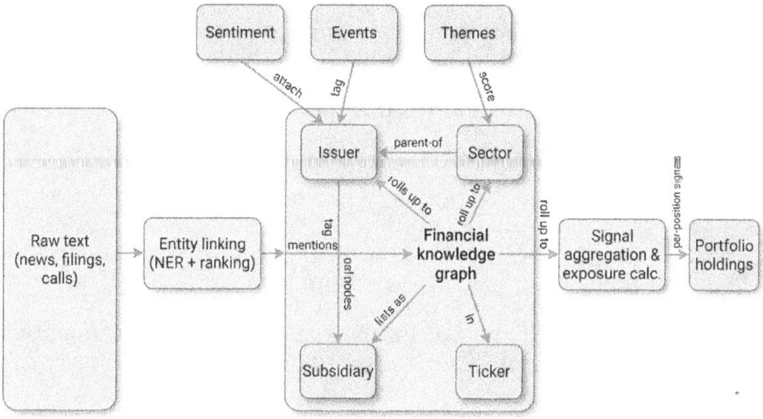


- undercounting exposures (missing key subsidiaries),
- double-counting (counting the same news at both issuer and subsidiary without adjustment),
- misattribution (assigning supplier shocks to the wrong customers or regions).

This leads to more reliable per-position exposures to sentiment, events, and themes.

**Better risk clustering and diversification**

Graph structure can also inform risk models. For example:

- clustering firms by graph distance (e.g. in supplier networks) may reveal non-obvious risk clusters;
- sectors with dense cross-ownership or shared counterparties may be more tightly coupled than sector codes alone suggest.

Incorporating this information can improve portfolio construction, stress testing, and scenario design.

**Cross-asset strategies via textual relationships**

Finally, the graph opens the door to cross-asset strategies informed by text:

- trading equity or CDS of firms based on negative textual signals about their major customers or suppliers;
- trading sector ETFs based on aggregated signals from constituent issuers;
- using sovereign-related news to adjust exposures to banks and corporates with high country risk via graph edges.

In each case, the knowledge graph provides the map that connects the textual signal's origin to the instruments we can actually trade.

Entity linking and knowledge graphs are easy to overlook because they do not produce flashy charts or models. Yet they are foundational:

- entity linking turns messy mentions in text into clean, point-in-time issuers and tickers;
- a financial knowledge graph encodes relationships among issuers, subsidiaries, sectors, counterparties, and instruments;
- together, they form the backbone on which sentiment, event, and theme signals are projected, aggregated, and propagated to portfolio holdings.

Without this infrastructure, NLP-derived signals will be noisy, biased, and hard to trust. With it, we can translate complex textual information into robust, tradable views that integrate smoothly with the rest of the quantitative investment stack.

# Chapter 6

# Machine Learning and Model Validation

*Most quant models look spectacular in backtests-and quietly bleed capital in production. This chapter shows you how to turn clever features into battle-tested alpha by treating markets as they are: non-stationary, adversarial, and data-snooping prone. You'll learn how to design supervised and deep models specifically for financial returns, validate them with walk-forward, leakage-aware procedures, and dissect their behavior with explainability and causal tools so that what survives your lab actually stands a chance in the wild.*

## 6.1 Supervised Learning for Alpha Signals

In the previous chapter we focused on how to turn raw market and alternative data into a structured feature matrix: lagged returns and volatilities, valuation ratios, order-book statistics, and text-derived sentiment scores. We now take the next step: using *supervised learning* to map those engineered features into forecasts of future returns that can drive trading decisions.

At a high level, supervised learning answers the question:

Given what I know now (features), what is the best guess of what will happen next (fu

Formally, we assume that at time $t$ we observe a vector of features

$$x_{i,t} \in \mathbb{R}^p,$$

for asset $i$ (or the market as a whole), and we want to predict a *label* or *target* $y_{i,t}$ that represents an economically meaningful outcome over some horizon, for example:

- next-day log return: $y_{i,t} = r_{i,t+1}$,
- 5-day cumulative return: $y_{i,t} = \sum_{k=1}^{5} r_{i,t+k}$,
- probability that the asset will outperform the cross-sectional median over the next month,
- a risk-adjusted score such as future return divided by realized volatility over the horizon.

Supervised learning chooses a function $f(\cdot)$ such that

$$\hat{y}_{i,t} = f(x_{i,t})$$

is a good approximation to the actual future outcome $y_{i,t}$. In a trading context, $\hat{y}_{i,t}$ is our *alpha signal*: a forecast we can convert into portfolio weights.

## From Features to Alpha: The Basic Mapping

It is useful to think of the end-to-end process as a pipeline:

$$\text{Raw data} \rightarrow \text{Features } x \rightarrow \text{Model } f \rightarrow \text{Alpha } \hat{y} \rightarrow \text{Portfolio.}$$

The feature engineering stage, covered earlier, compresses complex information into a manageable numeric representation. The supervised model $f$ then learns how different patterns in $x$ relate to future returns. Finally, the portfolio construction layer (treated in later chapters) transforms alpha scores into positions under risk and cost constraints.

Right after this conceptual mapping, it is helpful to visualize the flow.

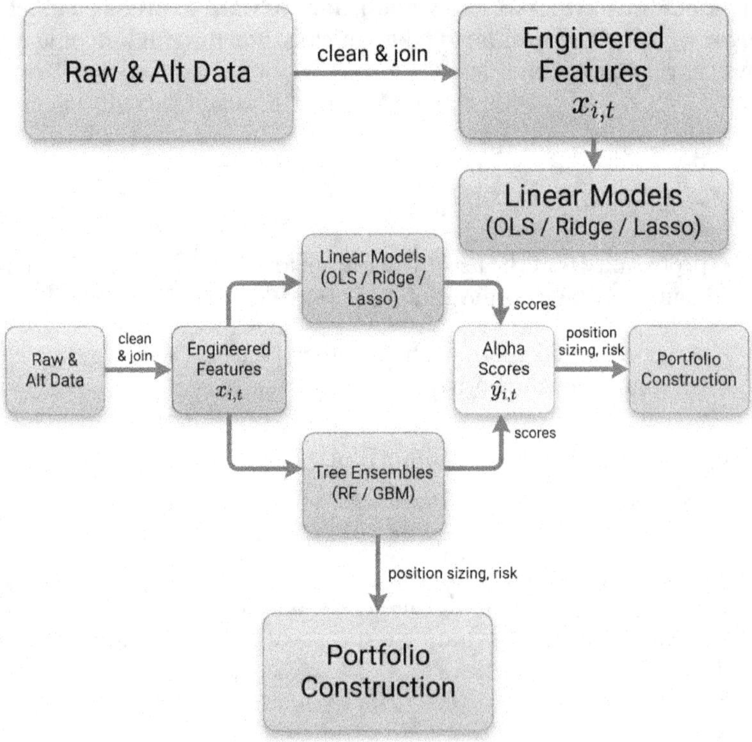


In the rest of this section we make this pipeline precise. We will:

- Define prediction targets appropriate for trading and explain why label design matters.

- Introduce linear models (OLS, ridge, lasso, elastic net) as transparent baselines.
- Discuss tree-based ensembles (random forests, gradient boosting) as powerful non-linear learners for tabular financial data.
- Show how to set up the data for cross-sectional vs. purely temporal prediction tasks.

## Designing Prediction Targets for Trading

The starting point of supervised learning is the pair $(x_{i,t}, y_{i,t})$. The choice of $y_{i,t}$ is not merely technical; it encodes your trading objective.

### Horizon and Overlapping Returns

Suppose we trade daily but care about a 5-day horizon. A natural label is the 5-day log return:

$$y_{i,t}^{(5)} = \log\left(\frac{P_{i,t+5}}{P_{i,t}}\right) = r_{i,t+1} + \cdots + r_{i,t+5}.$$

If we construct this label for every day $t$, adjacent labels share most of their underlying returns (overlap). This creates dependencies in the data that will matter for model validation and risk estimation (discussed in the next section of the chapter). For now, it is enough to be aware that:

- shorter horizons (e.g. 1-day) provide more samples but tend to be noisier,
- longer horizons smooth out noise but reduce the number of independent training examples.

The horizon should match both your holding period and your transaction cost structure. Intraday strategies might predict 5-minute returns; slow value strategies may target quarterly or annual excess returns.

### Regression vs. Classification Targets

You can frame return prediction as either regression or classification:

- **Regression:** predict a continuous number, e.g. $y_{i,t} = r_{i,t+1}$. The model directly estimates the magnitude and sign of future returns.
- **Classification:** predict a discrete label, such as

$$y_{i,t} = \begin{cases} 1, & \text{if } r_{i,t+1} > 0 \\ 0, & \text{otherwise,} \end{cases}$$

  or a multi-class label indicating which return bucket (e.g. bottom 30%, middle 40%, top 30%) the asset falls into.

Classification targets typically simplify the task and allow direct estimation of probabilities, such as $\mathbb{P}(r_{i,t+1} > 0 \mid x_{i,t})$. Regression targets retain more information, which can be valuable when sizing positions according to signal strength. Many practitioners start with regression and later post-process predictions into ranks or buckets for portfolio construction.

### Risk-Adjusted Targets

Raw returns treat all risk the same. But trading capital is limited, and risk constraints matter. You can incorporate risk awareness directly into the label, for example:

$$y_{i,t} = \frac{\sum_{k=1}^{H} r_{i,t+k}}{\sqrt{\sum_{k=1}^{H} (r_{i,t+k} - \bar{r}_{i,t})^2 + \varepsilon}},$$

a horizon-$H$ Sharpe-like ratio using realized volatility in the denominator. Predicting such a risk-adjusted quantity pushes the model to favor smoother payoffs, even if raw returns are slightly lower. This comes at the cost of more complex noise properties in the target. In practice, it is often easier to predict returns and impose risk targeting at the portfolio level, but understanding this alternative is conceptually useful.

## Linear Models: Transparent Workhorses

With labels defined, we can choose a model class. Linear models are the natural starting point: they are simple, fast, and interpretable.

**Ordinary Least Squares (OLS)**

In the basic linear regression model we assume:

$$y_{i,t} = \beta_0 + \beta^\top x_{i,t} + \varepsilon_{i,t},$$

where $\beta \in \mathbb{R}^p$ are coefficients and $\varepsilon_{i,t}$ is noise. The OLS estimator chooses $\hat{\beta}$ to minimize the mean squared error (MSE):

$$\hat{\beta} = \arg\min_{\beta} \sum_{(i,t)\in\mathcal{D}_{train}} (y_{i,t} - \beta_0 - \beta^\top x_{i,t})^2.$$

The fitted model outputs an alpha prediction

$$\hat{y}_{i,t} = \hat{\beta}_0 + \hat{\beta}^\top x_{i,t}.$$

The interpretation is straightforward: each feature contributes additively to the forecast, and each coefficient $\hat{\beta}_j$ is the marginal effect of a one-unit change in feature $j$, holding others fixed.

This transparency is particularly appealing when:

- you want factor-style signals (e.g. value, quality, sentiment) with linear exposures,
- you need to explain the model to a risk committee,
- you are building a low-turnover strategy whose edge may be modest but stable.

The downside is that OLS can overfit when there are many correlated features, and it cannot capture non-linear interactions.

**Regularized Linear Models: Ridge, Lasso, Elastic Net**

In real trading datasets, you will often have hundreds or thousands of features, some noisy or redundant. Regularization combats overfitting by shrinking or selecting coefficients.

**Ridge Regression.** Ridge adds an $\ell_2$ penalty to the OLS objective:

$$\hat{\beta}^{ridge} = \arg\min_{\beta} \sum (y_{i,t} - \beta_0 - \beta^\top x_{i,t})^2 + \lambda \|\beta\|_2^2.$$

The hyperparameter $\lambda \geq 0$ controls the strength of shrinkage: higher $\lambda$ pushes coefficients toward zero but rarely sets them *exactly* to zero. Ridge is useful when:

- many features are moderately informative,
- multicollinearity is strong (e.g. overlapping return lags, related sentiment scores),
- you want more stable coefficients across time.

**Lasso.** Lasso adds an $\ell_1$ penalty:

$$\hat{\beta}^{lasso} = \arg\min_{\beta} \sum (y_{i,t} - \beta_0 - \beta^\top x_{i,t})^2 + \lambda \|\beta\|_1.$$

The $\ell_1$ norm encourages sparsity: many coefficients become exactly zero. Lasso is attractive when:

- you suspect that only a subset of features is truly useful,
- you want automatic feature selection,
- interpretability (few active features) is important.

**Elastic Net.** Elastic net combines both penalties:

$$\hat{\beta}^{EN} = \arg\min_{\beta} \sum (y_{i,t} - \beta_0 - \beta^\top x_{i,t})^2 + \lambda_1 \|\beta\|_1 + \lambda_2 \|\beta\|_2^2.$$

This often works well when features are grouped or highly correlated, providing a compromise between ridge's stability and lasso's sparsity.

### When Linear Models Are Enough

Despite the excitement around more complex models, linear predictors remain competitive for many alpha problems, especially when:

- the signal-to-noise ratio is low and you prefer to avoid overfitting,
- your features already encode non-linear transformations (e.g. squared terms, interactions, regime indicators),
- latency and implementation simplicity matter (e.g. running in real-time on basic infrastructure).

As a rule of thumb, it is wise to benchmark any new sophisticated model against a strong regularized linear baseline. If you cannot beat that baseline after honest validation, your problem might not be rich enough to warrant extra complexity.

## Tree Ensembles: Non-Linear Powerhouses

Linear models assume that the effect of each feature is additive and constant. In practice, financial relationships are often non-linear and interaction-heavy: a positive sentiment surprise may matter more when valuation is cheap and volatility is low, for example.

Tree-based models, especially in ensemble form, excel at capturing such patterns in tabular data.

### Decision Trees in a Nutshell

A single decision tree partitions the feature space into regions by recursively splitting on feature values:

- At each node, the algorithm chooses a feature and split threshold (e.g. $\text{sentiment\_score} \geq 0.3$) that best separates the data with respect to the prediction target.
- The process continues until stopping criteria are met (minimum samples per leaf, maximum depth, etc.).
- Each leaf node predicts a constant value (for regression, the average $y$ in the leaf; for classification, class probabilities).

Trees are flexible and can model complex decision boundaries, but single deep trees overfit easily.

### Random Forests

Random forests mitigate overfitting by averaging many decorrelated trees:

- Each tree is trained on a bootstrap sample of the data.
- At each split, the algorithm considers a random subset of features.
- The final prediction is the average (regression) or majority vote (classification) across trees.

For return prediction, random forests can capture non-linearities and interactions without heavy feature engineering. They handle mixed data types and are relatively insensitive to feature scaling.

However, they can still overfit noisy returns if trees are excessively deep or if the forest is not properly regularized (e.g. via limiting depth or minimum samples per leaf). Moreover, prediction latency may become an issue for very large forests in high-frequency settings.

**Gradient-Boosted Trees**

Gradient boosting builds an ensemble sequentially:

- Start with a simple model (often a constant).
- At each iteration, fit a new shallow tree to the residual errors of the current ensemble.
- Add this tree to the ensemble with a small learning rate.

Popular implementations such as XGBoost, LightGBM, and CatBoost are widely used in quantitative finance for tabular alpha modeling. Their strengths include:

- strong performance on heterogeneous, sparse, and noisy features,
- fine-grained regularization controls (tree depth, learning rate, subsampling),
- automatic handling of many non-linearities and feature interactions.

Their weaknesses echo those of other powerful learners:

- risk of overfitting, especially when tuning hyperparameters aggressively on limited history,
- reduced interpretability compared with linear models (though tools such as SHAP mitigate this),
- potentially higher computational cost in training and sometimes in inference.

In practice, gradient-boosted trees are often the default "workhorse" for return prediction from tabular market and alternative data, provided you use careful time-series aware validation (next section of the chapter).

## Cross-Sectional vs. Temporal Prediction Setups

So far we have treated $(i, t)$ as a generic index. In trading, the way you arrange these indices fundamentally shapes the learning problem. There are two overarching perspectives:

- **Cross-sectional prediction:** For a given time $t$, you predict the *relative* performance of different assets.
- **Temporal (time-series) prediction:** For a given asset $i$, you predict its own future performance over time.

Most real-world models mix elements of both (panel data), but it helps to keep the two extremes conceptually separate.

### Cross-Sectional Learning

In cross-sectional learning, the basic unit is an *asset–time* pair, and you are interested in how assets compare *at the same time.*

For example, at each month-end $t$:

- $x_{i,t}$ contains firm-specific features (valuation, quality, sentiment, liquidity),

- $y_{i,t}$ is the stock's excess return over the next month relative to a benchmark.

You stack all assets and times into a single training set:

$$\mathcal{D} = \{(x_{i,t}, y_{i,t}) : i = 1, \dots, N_t; t \in \mathcal{T}\}.$$

Your model, linear or tree-based, learns patterns such as:

- cheap, high-quality, positive-sentiment stocks tend to outperform,
- small, illiquid stocks require stronger signals to justify trades.

At prediction time, for a given date $t^\star$, you feed in all $x_{i,t^\star}$, obtain predicted alphas $\hat{y}_{i,t^\star}$, and then construct a long–short portfolio based on ranks or thresholds.

Key characteristics of cross-sectional setups:

- the model focuses on *relative* performance (who beats whom),
- cross-sectional dependence matters for validation and portfolio construction,
- scaling features cross-sectionally (e.g. z-scoring by date) is common to stabilize distributions.

### Temporal (Time-Series) Learning

In a pure time-series setup, you consider one asset or aggregated index at a time. The training examples are successive time steps:

$$\mathcal{D}_i = \{(x_{i,t}, y_{i,t}) : t \in \mathcal{T}_i\}.$$

For instance, for an intraday strategy on a futures contract:

- $x_t$ might include recent order-book imbalances, short-horizon realized volatility, and microprice signals,

- $y_t$ is the 1-minute ahead return.

You can fit a separate model per instrument, or pool across instruments while keeping time order central to the validation scheme.

Key characteristics of temporal setups:

- emphasis on *absolute* direction and magnitude over time,
- strong autocorrelation and regime changes,
- feature scaling is often done over rolling windows in time.

Time-series models fit naturally into walk-forward evaluation frameworks, which we discuss in detail in the next section of this chapter.

**Panel Data: The Practical Middle Ground**

Most equity and multi-asset alpha models use *panel data*: many assets over many times. You can think of this as a 3D cube with axes (asset, feature, time). How you turn this cube into a 2D matrix for your model depends on your emphasis:

- Treat each (asset, time) pair as an independent row and let the model implicitly learn both cross-sectional and temporal structure.
- Explicitly engineer temporal features (lags, moving averages, regime indicators) so that a cross-sectional learner sees time history "baked in" to each row.
- For deep learning (covered later in the chapter), treat each asset's time history as a sequence and use sequence models.

Regardless of the exact setup, always respect temporal order: features at time $t$ must only use information available up to $t$, and labels must refer strictly to the future $(t+1, t+2, \dots)$. Violating this rule yields *look-ahead bias*, an error that can completely invalidate a strategy.

### From Predictions to Trading Decisions

While portfolio construction is treated in later chapters, it is helpful to close this section by briefly connecting model outputs to trades.

Once you have a trained supervised model $f$ and a feature snapshot $x_{i,t}$, you obtain predictions $\hat{y}_{i,t} = f(x_{i,t})$. In practice, you typically:

- convert $\hat{y}_{i,t}$ into a *rank* or *score* (e.g. cross-sectional z-score),
- map scores into desired positions subject to risk limits (e.g. max weight per asset, sector neutrality),
- account for transaction costs and market impact when deciding how aggressively to act on new signals,
- monitor realized performance and model drift over time.

The key conceptual point is that supervised learning provides a disciplined way to turn noisy, high-dimensional information into a one-dimensional "alpha" per asset and time. The sophistication of the model (linear vs. trees vs. deep networks) matters less than the integrity of the overall pipeline: label design, validation, risk management, and operational robustness.

In the next section, we turn to one of the most subtle parts of this pipeline: building validation schemes and hyperparameter tuning procedures that respect time, avoid information leakage, and yield realistic estimates of out-of-sample performance.

## 6.2 Time-Series Cross-Validation and Hyperparameter Tuning

In the previous section we treated supervised learning as a mapping from engineered features to future returns. We implicitly assumed that if a model fits historical data well, it will produce useful alpha out of sample. In practice, this assumption only holds if the model has been validated in a way that respects the structure of financial time series.

Financial data are not i.i.d. samples from a stable distribution. They exhibit strong time ordering, overlapping horizons, regime shifts, and cross-sectional dependence between assets. Naively shuffling observations and using standard $k$-fold cross-validation (CV) can produce impressive backtest metrics that vanish as soon as real money is deployed.

In this section we build a *leakage-aware* validation framework. Our goals are:

- obtain realistic estimates of future performance,
- select hyperparameters that generalize across regimes,
- reduce the risk of overfitting through data snooping.

We will:

- identify common sources of leakage and bias in trading backtests,
- replace naive $k$-fold CV with walk-forward schemes that respect time,
- introduce *purging* and *embargoes* to handle overlapping labels and event windows,
- discuss practical hyperparameter search strategies under limited, autocorrelated data,
- connect validation choices with research governance and experiment logging.

## Why Standard $k$-Fold Cross-Validation Fails for Trading

Classical $k$-fold CV assumes that the data are *exchangeable*: you can randomly permute samples without breaking underlying structure. In a typical machine learning task (e.g. image classification), this is a reasonable approximation. In trading, it is not.

Consider a simple example. You built a daily cross-sectional model that predicts next-day stock returns using features that include trailing 5-day returns and a sentiment score. You collect all $(x_{i,t}, y_{i,t})$ pairs into a dataset and apply random 5-fold CV:

- randomly split all observations into five folds,
- train on four folds, validate on the fifth,
- rotate which fold is the validation set.

This procedure mixes data from the future and the past in every fold. Several things go wrong:

- **Temporal leakage.** A validation observation at date $t$ may be predicted using a model trained on observations from dates $> t$. In reality, you cannot train on the future.
- **Overlapping labels.** If your labels use multi-day horizons (e.g. 5-day forward returns), then an observation at date $t$ and another at date $t + 1$ share many of the same underlying returns. If one goes to the training set and the other to validation, information leaks.
- **Cross-sectional dependence.** Even if you hold time fixed, assets are not independent. If stock A and stock B are in the same sector and react similarly to news, assigning one to train and the other to validation at the same date can create subtle leakage.

The net effect is that your CV scores are *too optimistic*. Because information about future conditions leaks into the training set, the model is implicitly "told" about the validation period. You might believe you have discovered a high-Sharpe, low-drawdown strategy, when in reality you have simply overfit historical noise.

## Walk-Forward and Rolling-Window Evaluation

The first step toward leakage-aware validation is to respect time ordering. The guiding principle is simple:

*You must only use the past to predict the future.*

Two closely related evaluation mindsets follow from this:

- **Walk-forward (expanding window):** start training from an initial period, then evaluate on the next period; expand the training set forward in time and repeat.
- **Rolling window:** similar, but keep the training window length fixed and roll both its start and end forward.

Formally, suppose your sample runs from $T_0$ to $T_{max}$. In a walk-forward scheme, you define ordered train–test splits:

$$
\begin{aligned}
\text{Split 1:} &\quad \text{Train } [T_0, T_1], \quad \text{Test } (T_1, T_2], \\
\text{Split 2:} &\quad \text{Train } [T_0, T_2], \quad \text{Test } (T_2, T_3], \\
&\vdots \\
\text{Split K:} &\quad \text{Train } [T_0, T_K], \quad \text{Test } (T_K, T_{K+1}],
\end{aligned}
$$

with $T_{K+1} \leq T_{max}$. In each split you fit the model on the training interval and record performance on the next test interval. Concatenating all test intervals yields a sequence of pseudo-out-of-sample predictions that mimic how the strategy would have evolved over time.

A rolling window variant fixes the length of the training window, say $L$, and for split $k$ trains on $[T_k - L, T_k]$ and tests on $(T_k, T_{k+1}]$. This is useful when you want the model to focus on recent regimes and avoid overweighting very old data.

Walk-forward evaluation addresses the most blatant temporal leakage, but it is not enough when labels overlap. For that, we need purging and embargoes.

## Purged and Embargoed Time-Series Splits

Returns-based labels often use multi-period horizons or event windows. For example:

- horizon-$H$ returns: $y_{i,t} = \sum_{k=1}^{H} r_{i,t+k}$,
- post-news performance over a 10-day window,
- post-earnings drift over the next month.

In all these cases, the label for time $t$ depends on events over $(t, t + H]$. If you include an observation with label window $(t, t + H]$ in the training set, and another whose label window $(s, s+H]$ overlaps with it in the validation set, the two labels share information. This can create leakage even when time ordering is respected at the level of $t$ and $s$.

## Purging Around Test Periods

*Purging* addresses this by removing from the training set any observation whose label window overlaps with the test period. Intuitively, you remove polluted training examples that "see" into the test window through their labels.

Suppose your test period for a given split is from $T_{test,start}$ to $T_{test,end}$, and your label horizon is $H$. Any training observation with reference time $t$ such that

$$(t, t + H] \cap [T_{test,start}, T_{test,end}] \neq \emptyset$$

is excluded from the training set for this split. This ensures that:

- no label in the training set uses returns from the test period,
- training labels are based entirely on returns before the test window.

Purging shrinks the effective size of the training set, especially for long horizons, but reduces optimistic bias.

## Embargoes After Test Periods

Purging eliminates overlap between training labels and the test *interval*, but it does not address the fact that market conditions may evolve smoothly over time. To reduce the chance of the model indirectly learning about the test period by training on points immediately after it, we can add an *embargo*.

An embargo is a buffer of time after the test period during which observations are excluded from the training set. If the embargo length is $E$, then for a test period $[T_{test,start}, T_{test,end}]$, we impose that training times $t$ must satisfy:

$$t \leq T_{test,start} - H \quad \text{or} \quad t \geq T_{test,end} + E.$$

In words:

- we already purged the training points whose label windows overlap with the test period,
- we additionally skip training examples immediately after the test window, up to $E$ time units into the future.

The embargo length should be chosen based on the typical duration of your events or the decay of serial dependence. For intraday strategies, $E$ might be minutes; for monthly strategies, it might be months.

## Visualizing Naive vs. Purged–Embargoed Splits

It is helpful to visualize the difference between naive $k$-fold splits and purged, embargoed walk-forward splits on a time axis.

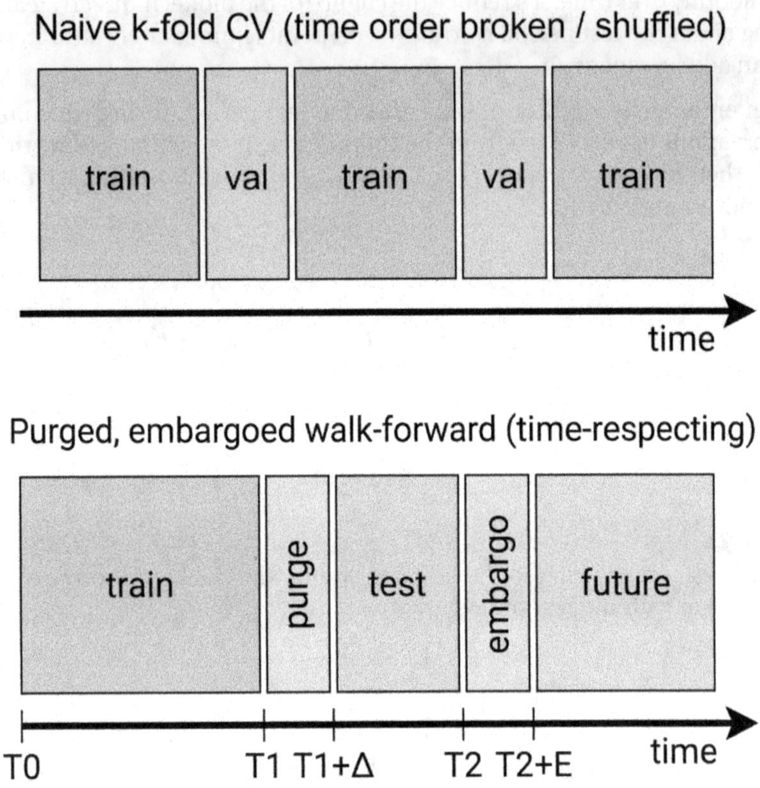


This figure reinforces the core idea: in a time-series CV for trading, the validation (test) band is surrounded by zones that are excluded from training to prevent information leakage.

## Evaluation Metrics Aligned with Trading Goals

Once you have proper time-series splits, you must decide what to measure. For trading, metrics should connect to economic performance, not just statistical accuracy.

Common choices include:

- **Information ratio (IR):** mean active return over its standard deviation, typically computed on the portfolio built from model scores across the validation period.
- **Sharpe ratio:** mean excess return over volatility, if you are directly simulating the trading strategy.
- **Hit rate:** fraction of times the direction of return is predicted correctly; useful but incomplete, as it ignores magnitude and risk.
- **Drawdown-aware metrics:** maximum drawdown, Calmar ratio, or other downside risk measures.

A common and robust practice is:

- Use the model to generate predictions on each validation fold.
- Translate predictions into a simple, fixed set of portfolio rules (e.g. long top decile, short bottom decile, volatility-scaled weights, no leverage optimization).
- Compute risk and return metrics on these validation portfolios.

This embeds model evaluation in a consistent trading protocol, reducing the risk of accidentally tuning hyperparameters to a metric that does not map cleanly to your final use case.

## Hyperparameter Tuning Under Time Dependence

With leakage-aware splits and meaningful metrics in place, we can address *hyperparameter tuning*. Hyperparameters control model complexity and behavior: regularization strengths in linear models, tree depth and learning rate in gradient boosting, number of estimators in random forests, and so on.

Tuning hyperparameters on time-series data faces two challenges:

- the effective sample size is smaller than the raw number of observations because of autocorrelation and overlapping labels,

- repeated experimentation increases the risk of *hyperparameter fishing*, where you implicitly search until you find a configuration that overfits noise.

## Grid Search and Random Search

The simplest tuning strategies are:

- **Grid search:** define a discrete grid of hyperparameter values (e.g. $\lambda \in \{0.01, 0.1, 1, 10\}$, tree depth $\in \{3, 5, 7\}$), evaluate all combinations using your purged walk-forward CV, choose the best.
- **Random search:** sample hyperparameter combinations at random from specified ranges or distributions, evaluate each, and keep the best.

Random search is often more efficient when only a subset of hyperparameters matter a lot: you avoid wasting effort on unimportant dimensions and can explore a broader space with the same budget.

In both cases, the procedure is:

- Fix a set of time-series CV splits (purged and embargoed).
- For each hyperparameter configuration:
  - Fit the model on the training part of each split.
  - Evaluate on the validation part using trading-aligned metrics.
  - Aggregate performance across splits (e.g. mean IR).
- Select the configuration with the best aggregated validation performance.

Because each evaluation runs over multiple splits, computational cost can be substantial. This encourages the use of more sample-efficient search methods.

## Bayesian Optimization and Bandit-Style Search

Bayesian optimization treats the mapping from hyperparameters to validation performance as an unknown function to be learned. At a high level:

- you start with a few random hyperparameter evaluations,
- fit a surrogate model (e.g. Gaussian process or tree-based regressor) that predicts performance as a function of hyperparameters,
- iteratively choose new hyperparameters to evaluate by balancing *exploration* (trying regions where the surrogate is uncertain) and *exploitation* (focusing on promising areas),
- stop when your evaluation budget is exhausted or improvement plateaus.

Bandit-style approaches (e.g. successive halving, Hyperband) focus on allocating more resources to promising configurations and terminating poor ones early. This is particularly useful when models can be partially trained or when early performance is predictive of final performance.

In trading, where each full evaluation involves walk-forward backtests over years of data, these more sophisticated search strategies can save significant time while exploring a richer hyperparameter space.

## Avoiding Hyperparameter Fishing

Regardless of the search method, you must guard against "fishing" for a good backtest by:

- **Limiting the search budget.** Decide in advance how many configurations you will test and stick to it.
- **Using nested evaluation.** Reserve a final *hold-out* period that is not used during tuning. Once you commit to a single chosen configuration, evaluate it on this untouched period to estimate true out-of-sample performance.

- **Penalizing model complexity.** All else equal, prefer simpler models or those with stronger regularization; consider adding an explicit complexity penalty to the selection criterion.

A useful mental model is to treat hyperparameter search itself as a source of overfitting. The more configurations you try, the higher the chance that one will look good by luck on historical data. Conservative search and strict separation between tuning and final evaluation help mitigate this.

## Practical Guidelines and Research Governance

Finally, time-series CV and hyperparameter tuning must be embedded in a broader research process. A few practical guidelines:

## Logging Experiments

Always log:

- data versions and preprocessing choices (e.g. feature sets, label definitions, handling of missing values),
- model type and hyperparameters,
- definition of CV splits (dates, purging and embargo lengths),
- evaluation metrics and their values on each split,
- code versions or git commit hashes.

This enables you to reproduce results, understand why a particular configuration was chosen, and audit the research process later.

## Formalizing Model Selection

Before running large-scale tests, define a *model selection protocol*. For example:

- Specify the set of candidate models and hyperparameter ranges.
- Specify the number and type of time-series splits, including purging and embargo lengths.
- Choose a primary selection metric (e.g. average IR across splits) and secondary diagnostics (e.g. maximum drawdown, turnover).
- Allocate a tuning budget (number of configurations, time limit).
- Reserve a final hold-out period and commit to using it only once per model family.

Treat deviations from this protocol as serious events that require justification. This discipline reduces the likelihood that backtests are unintentionally optimized to noise.

## Interpreting Validation Results

Even with a careful setup, validation results must be interpreted with caution:

- **Stability across splits.** A model that performs well in some periods and poorly in others may be regime-sensitive. You might still trade it, but with smaller risk allocation and explicit regime detection.
- **Robustness to small changes.** Check how performance changes when you vary the training window length, purging horizon, or lookback features slightly. If results are extremely sensitive, the signal may be fragile.
- **Economic plausibility.** Strong validation metrics are more convincing when the signal has a reasonable economic story and aligns with known risk premia or behavioral effects.

Time-series cross-validation and hyperparameter tuning are not afterthoughts; they are integral to whether your model can be trusted with capital. A leakage-aware framework has three pillars:

- **Respect time and structure:** use walk-forward or rolling splits, never random shuffles.
- **Control leakage:** purge overlapping label windows and add embargoes around test periods.
- **Tune cautiously:** use structured search with limited budgets, trading-aligned metrics, and final hold-out periods.

With these tools, you can turn the supervised learning models from the previous section into strategies with validation trails that risk managers and investment committees can scrutinize and, ultimately, trust. The next section builds on this foundation to explore deep learning architectures for sequential financial data, where these validation principles become even more crucial due to higher model capacity and greater overfitting risk.

## 6.3 Deep Learning for Sequential Financial Data

In the previous sections we treated supervised learning on financial data primarily through the lens of linear models and tree ensembles, and we learned how to validate those models honestly using walk-forward, purged, and embargoed cross-validation. Those tools already give you a powerful toolkit for extracting alpha from tabular features such as lagged returns, valuation ratios, sentiment scores, and liquidity measures.

Deep learning enters the picture when the structure of the data itself becomes richer than what fixed, hand-crafted features can easily capture. Two aspects are especially relevant for this book:

- **Sequential structure:** prices, volumes, order books, and text all arrive as time-ordered streams, often at high frequency.
- **High dimensionality:** tick-level order books, multiple horizons, and large cross-sections of assets create inputs that are wide (many features at a time) and long (many time steps).

Deep models—convolutional neural networks (CNNs), recurrent networks (RNNs/LSTMs/GRUs), and transformers—are designed to exploit such structure. However, financial returns are noisy and datasets are often small relative to typical deep-learning use cases (e.g., image or language models). As a result, deep learning must *earn its keep* in trading: extra complexity is only justified when it extracts patterns that simpler models, properly engineered, cannot.

In this section we will:

- clarify when deep learning is likely to add value in markets,
- show how CNNs, RNNs, and transformers can be applied to sequential financial data,
- outline practical design patterns that combine market and NLP-based features,
- discuss the key trade-offs involving latency, overfitting, and interpretability.

## When Is Deep Learning Justified in Finance?

Before diving into architectures, it is worth asking: *When is a deep network appropriate at all?* Three conditions tend to support its use:

- **Rich sequential structure.** You are working with high-frequency price/volume traces, full order books, or long histories where patterns play out over varying time scales. Capturing local motifs (e.g., microstructure patterns) and long-range dependencies (e.g., regime shifts) simultaneously is difficult with simple lags and moving averages.
- **High-dimensional alternative data.** You rely on inputs such as text embeddings, image features, or graph-structured relationships across assets that are naturally handled by deep architectures.
- **Sufficient effective data.** After accounting for autocorrelation, overlapping horizons, and regime shifts, you still have

enough "effective" examples to train a flexible model without immediate catastrophic overfitting.

If your dataset consists of a few thousand monthly observations of simple factors, deep learning is unlikely to outperform regularized linear models or boosted trees. Conversely, if you are modeling millisecond-level order book dynamics across many trading days, deep models designed for sequences may capture nuanced behaviors that fixed-window features miss.

## Representing Sequential Financial Data

Deep sequence models require inputs in a structured tensor form. A useful generic representation is:

$$X_{i,t} \in \mathbb{R}^{L \times C},$$

where:

- $i$ indexes an asset, instrument, or trading venue,
- $t$ indexes the prediction time,
- $L$ is the sequence length (number of past time steps you feed in),
- $C$ is the number of channels or features per time step.

For example, for a single stock at 1-minute resolution:

- $L = 60$: past 60 minutes,
- $C$ might include: open, high, low, close, volume, bid–ask spread, order-book imbalance, realized volatility over a short window, plus an NLP-derived news sentiment score at each minute (possibly carried forward from the last news event).

For panel data, you can either:

- train a shared model across assets by stacking examples $(i, t)$ with the same sequence shape $L \times C$, or
- treat the cross-section itself as another dimension (e.g. sequences of vectors indexed by both time and asset)—a perspective more natural for transformer-style models.

The key is to ensure that the sequence contains only information available up to time $t$. All future information must be strictly excluded to avoid look-ahead bias.

## Convolutional Networks for Temporal Motifs

Convolutional neural networks (CNNs) are best known from image recognition, but they can be applied in one dimension to time series. A 1D convolutional layer slides a set of filters across time to detect local temporal patterns.

### Intuition: Filters as Pattern Detectors

Consider an input sequence of mid-price changes and volumes over the last $L$ time steps. A 1D CNN learns filters of length $k$ (e.g., $k = 5$ or $k = 10$). Each filter is a small vector that, when convolved with the input, produces an activation that is high whenever a particular local pattern occurs.

In market terms, such filters might detect:

- short bursts of buying pressure (consecutive positive returns with high volume),
- sudden widening of bid–ask spreads,
- local volatility spikes or mean-reversion patches.

Stacking several convolutional layers with non-linearities allows the network to build hierarchical features: first detecting primitive patterns (e.g., small up-ticks), then combining them into more abstract motifs (e.g., three up-ticks in a row under light selling pressure).

### Applying 1D CNNs to Tick and Bar Data

A typical CNN-based alpha model for intraday data might look like:

- Input tensor $X_{i,t} \in \mathbb{R}^{L \times C}$ containing recent bar-level or tick-level features.
- Several layers of 1D convolutions across the $L$ dimension, with ReLU non-linearities and optional pooling (downsampling) to reduce sequence length.
- A global pooling operation (e.g. average or max over time) to aggregate information into a fixed-length vector.
- One or more fully connected layers that map this vector to an output: a predicted return over the next horizon or a probability that price will move up vs. down.

CNNs are attractive in trading because:

- they are relatively fast at inference, especially on GPUs,
- they naturally handle multiple channels (price, volume, microstructure features, text-based signals),
- their receptive field can be controlled via filter sizes and stacking depth, allowing you to focus on local patterns.

However, CNNs primarily capture local dependencies. To model very long-term interactions (e.g. relationships spanning hundreds or thousands of steps), you must either deepen the network substantially (which can hurt stability) or combine CNNs with other mechanisms, such as recurrent layers or attention.

## Recurrent Networks and LSTMs for Long-Term Dependencies

Recurrent neural networks (RNNs) were designed to model sequential dependencies by processing inputs one step at a time and maintaining a hidden state that summarizes the past.

### Vanilla RNNs and Their Limitations

In a basic RNN, at each time step $\tau$ you update a hidden state $h_\tau$:

$$h_\tau = g(W_x x_\tau + W_h h_{\tau-1} + b),$$

where $g$ is a non-linear activation (e.g. tanh), and $W_x, W_h, b$ are parameters. After processing the entire sequence, you use the final hidden state $h_L$ to make a prediction.

In finance, vanilla RNNs often struggle to learn long-range dependencies due to *vanishing* or *exploding* gradients during training. This is where LSTMs and GRUs come in.

### LSTMs and GRUs

Long Short-Term Memory (LSTM) networks and Gated Recurrent Units (GRUs) introduce gating mechanisms that control information flow through time. They maintain an internal memory cell that can keep information over longer horizons, learning when to remember, update, or forget.

Intuitively, an LSTM applied to a sequence of returns and macro indicators might learn to:

- remember that the asset entered a high-volatility regime several hours ago,
- slowly forget short-lived mean-reversion patterns,
- update its state sharply in response to a large news shock.

GRUs simplify the LSTM architecture while retaining many of its benefits. Both are widely used for sequence modeling in domains where long-term dependencies matter.

### Panel and Multi-Scale Designs

For panel data, a common pattern is:

- use a shared LSTM/GRU across all assets, treating each $(i, t)$ sequence as an independent example,
- optionally concatenate asset-specific static features (e.g. sector, size bucket) to the final hidden state before the output layer.

To capture multiple time scales (e.g. minutes, hours, days), you can:

- build separate sequences at different resolutions and process each with its own LSTM or CNN,
- concatenate their final representations before the final prediction layer.

This allows the model to simultaneously account for microstructural patterns (e.g. order flow over the last few seconds) and slower-moving context (e.g. intraday trend or overnight news).

## Transformers for Flexible Attention over Time and Assets

Transformers, originally developed for natural language processing, rely on self-attention mechanisms rather than recurrence or convolution. They have become state-of-the-art in many sequence tasks, and their flexibility makes them attractive for financial modeling as well.

### Self-Attention in a Nutshell

Given a sequence of input vectors $\{x_1, \ldots, x_L\}$, a self-attention layer computes, for each position $\tau$, a weighted combination of all positions:

$$z_\tau = \sum_{\kappa=1}^{L} \alpha_{\tau\kappa} V x_\kappa,$$

where the weights $\alpha_{\tau\kappa}$ are normalized attention scores that measure how relevant time $\kappa$ is to time $\tau$, and $V$ is a learned transformation. These scores are computed by comparing learned "query" and "key" projections of the inputs.

In market terms, a transformer can learn to:

- pay more attention to certain past events (e.g. large price jumps, major news releases),
- downweight routine noise,
- capture dependencies that span irregular intervals (e.g. linking a move today to one several days ago).

This is particularly appealing in financial sequences where important events can be sparse and not strictly aligned in fixed windows.

**Temporal and Cross-Sectional Attention**

Transformers can attend over:

- **Time only:** each asset is modeled independently; the sequence dimension is time, and self-attention captures temporal dependencies.
- **Time and assets:** flatten the panel so that positions in the sequence correspond to (asset, time) pairs. You then augment the inputs with positional encodings for both time and asset identity (or sector). Self-attention can then learn relationships both across time for a single asset and across assets at the same or different times.

The second approach opens the door to richer cross-sectional patterns, such as:

- learning that the response of a small-cap stock to an earnings surprise depends on how peers in its sector responded earlier in the season,
- modeling contagion or spillovers across markets (e.g. FX and equities).

However, it also dramatically increases computational cost, which can be problematic under strict intraday latency constraints.

**Practical Simplifications**

Full-scale transformers with many layers and heads, like those used in large language models, are rarely appropriate for trading data because:

- the effective dataset is relatively small,
- inference must often happen in milliseconds,
- interpretability requirements are higher.

Practical adaptations include:

- limiting the sequence length $L$ (e.g. last 60 or 120 steps),
- using a small number of attention heads and layers,
- combining transformers with convolutional or recurrent front-ends that first compress raw sequences.

These "lightweight" transformers can still exploit attention's flexibility while keeping complexity under control.

## Combining Market and NLP Features

In this book, textual and alternative data are central. Deep sequence models provide natural ways to integrate them with structured numerical features.

A common pattern is:

- Use a separate model (often a pretrained language model) to turn raw financial text—news, transcripts, social media—into dense vector embeddings at particular timestamps.
- Align these embeddings with your market data timeline (e.g. broadcast the latest news embedding forward until a new article arrives).
- Treat these embeddings as additional channels in your sequence input $X_{i,t}$.

For example, at each minute you might have:

$$x_\tau = \left[\text{price features}_\tau,\ \text{volume features}_\tau,\ \text{sentiment embedding}_\tau\right].$$

A CNN, LSTM, or transformer then learns how the interaction between order flow and news sentiment at different times predicts future returns. The deep model can, in principle, discover patterns such as:

- positive news that fails to move price immediately but leads to a drift over the next hour,
- negative tone during a low-liquidity period causing outsized price impact.

This integration is a key advantage of deep learning: it allows you to encode heterogeneous information sources into a unified, end-to-end trainable model.

## Managing Overfitting and Latency

The expressive power of deep models is a double-edged sword. Without careful controls, they will happily fit idiosyncratic noise in your historical dataset. The validation and tuning framework from the previous section becomes even more crucial.

### Regularization and Training Stability

Common regularization techniques include:

- **Weight decay (L2 regularization):** penalizes large weights in the loss function.
- **Dropout:** randomly zeros out units during training to encourage redundancy and robustness.
- **Early stopping:** monitors validation performance on purged, embargoed folds and stops training when performance stops improving.
- **Data augmentation:** for some data types, you can perturb inputs slightly (e.g. jittering timestamps within a small range) to improve robustness, though care is needed to avoid distorting actual trading conditions.

Additionally, financial returns are heavy-tailed and heteroskedastic. Loss functions that are more robust than plain mean squared error (e.g. Huber loss) or output transformations (e.g. predicting log-returns or standardized returns) can improve training stability.

### Latency and Deployment Constraints

Many deep models are trained offline on GPUs but must run in real time on CPU-bound trading systems. Latency constraints influence architecture choices:

- **Input size:** shorter sequences and fewer channels reduce compute and memory.
- **Model depth and width:** fewer layers and smaller hidden dimensions yield faster inference.
- **Precomputation:** heavy feature extraction (e.g. text embeddings, long-horizon aggregates) can often be precomputed in batch, so that the real-time model only needs to process a small incremental update.
- **Model compression:** techniques such as quantization (reduced-precision weights) or knowledge distillation (training a smaller "student" network to mimic a larger "teacher") can produce compact models with near-identical performance.

When latency is a hard constraint, it is often better to start from the simplest model that meets the constraint and gradually add complexity, measuring the marginal value of each addition in both performance and runtime.

## Interpretability and Diagnostics

Deep models are often seen as "black boxes." In a trading context, this is not acceptable: risk managers and regulators will demand some insight into what drives decisions.

Fortunately, many of the explainability tools discussed later in this chapter (e.g. SHAP values) apply equally to deep models. In addition, sequence models allow for more specialized diagnostics:

- **Saliency maps:** measure how sensitive the prediction is to perturbations at each time step or feature channel; highlight which parts of the recent sequence the model relied on.

- **Attention weights:** in transformers, visualize attention patterns over time and across assets; identify which events or assets strongly influenced a prediction.

- **Hidden state analysis:** for RNNs/LSTMs, track how hidden states evolve through different regimes; cluster hidden states to see if the model organizes experiences into interpretable modes (e.g. trending vs. mean-reverting).

These tools not only help with governance but also with research: understanding what the model has learned can suggest new features, reveal unintended leakage, or uncover regime dependencies.

Deep learning offers powerful tools for modeling sequential financial data, especially when you have:

- rich intraday or tick-level records,

- high-dimensional alternative data such as text-derived embeddings,

- the infrastructure and discipline to train and validate complex models honestly.

CNNs capture local temporal motifs efficiently, RNNs/LSTMs model longer-term dependencies via recurrent state, and transformers provide flexible attention over time and assets. Each architecture comes with trade-offs in expressiveness, latency, overfitting risk, and interpretability.

The key is to view deep learning not as a magic upgrade but as a modeling option whose value depends on the structure of your data, your trading horizon, and your operational constraints. When combined with leakage-aware validation and thoughtful deployment, deep sequence models can extract subtle patterns from market and NLP-derived signals, turning complex data streams into actionable alpha.

## 6.4 Explainability, Diagnostics, and Causal Inference

At this point in the chapter, you have a complete predictive pipeline: supervised learning models that map features to future returns, validation schemes that respect time and structure, and (potentially) deep architectures that exploit sequential data. The natural next question is not "How accurate is the model?" but rather:

> *Why should we trust this model with capital?*

Trust in a trading model has several dimensions:

- **Explainability:** Can we understand which features the model uses, and how, in a way that is coherent with economic reasoning and risk controls?
- **Diagnostics:** Does the model behave reasonably across time, assets, and regimes, or are there hidden failure modes and leakages?
- **Causality (or lack thereof):** Is the signal plausibly linked to underlying mechanisms, or is it just a statistical artefact of a particular backtest?

This section develops practical tools and a mindset for each dimension. The emphasis is not on formal philosophical debates, but on the concrete questions that arise when you present a model to an investment committee or risk manager.

### Prediction Quality vs. Economic Usefulness

A common pitfall is to equate good statistical performance with economic value. For instance, a classifier that predicts the sign of daily returns with 55% accuracy can be untradeable if its edge concentrates in illiquid names, disappears after costs, or coincides with large drawdowns.

Before diving into explanations and causal stories, we need to align on a basic principle:

> *A useful trading model must pass both statistical and economic tests.*

The statistical tests—out-of-sample information ratio, robustness across walk-forward splits, etc.—were the focus of prior sections. Economic tests, which you should keep in mind throughout this section, include:

- Does the model's performance survive realistic transaction costs and constraints?
- Are the exposures to known risk factors and sectors acceptable?
- Are drawdowns and tail risks consistent with the mandate?

Explainability and diagnostics form the bridge: they connect raw predictive performance to an economically grounded narrative about where the alpha comes from and where it is likely to fail.

## Opening the Black Box: Feature Importance and SHAP

Even relatively simple models (regularized regressions, gradient boosting) can be hard to interpret when they involve hundreds or thousands of features. For deep models, the opacity is even greater. Explainability methods aim to answer questions like:

- Which features are most important on average?
- For a particular prediction, what drove the model's decision?
- Do these drivers look stable across time and regimes?

### Global vs. Local Explanations

It is useful to distinguish between:

- **Global importance:** How much does each feature contribute to predictions *on average* across the dataset?
- **Local importance:** For a specific asset and date, how much did each feature push the prediction up or down relative to some baseline?

Global explanations help you understand the overall structure of the model (e.g., sentiment vs. valuation vs. momentum). Local explanations are critical for case studies: "Why did we go long this stock on this day?"

**SHAP: A Unified Framework**

SHAP (SHapley Additive exPlanations) is a popular framework that provides both global and local explanations, applicable to many model classes (tree ensembles, linear models, and neural networks via approximations).

At a high level, SHAP assigns to each feature $j$ and each example $n$ a value $\phi_{n,j}$ such that:

$$\hat{y}_n = \phi_{n,0} + \sum_{j=1}^{p} \phi_{n,j},$$

where $\hat{y}_n$ is the model's prediction for example $n$, $\phi_{n,0}$ is a baseline (e.g. average prediction), and $\phi_{n,j}$ measures how much feature $j$ contributed to moving the prediction away from the baseline. The key properties are:

- *Additivity:* local contributions sum to the prediction.
- *Consistency:* if a model's dependence on a feature increases, the SHAP value for that feature does not decrease.

In practice, you do not compute exact Shapley values (which are combinatorially expensive), but rely on efficient algorithms for certain model classes:

- TreeSHAP for tree ensembles,

- linear-time approximations for linear models,
- sampling-based methods for deep networks.

### Using SHAP in Cross-Sectional Models

For a cross-sectional equity model that predicts next-month returns, you can:

- Compute SHAP values $\phi_{i,t,j}$ for each asset $i$, date $t$, and feature $j$.
- Aggregate over assets and/or time to get global importance scores, e.g.
$$\text{Importance}_j = \mathbb{E}_{i,t}\left[|\phi_{i,t,j}|\right].$$
- Create SHAP summary plots (beeswarm plots) that show, for each feature, the distribution of contributions across the cross-section and their relationship to feature values.

These visualizations answer questions such as:

- Are text-derived sentiment features consistently among the top drivers of alpha?
- Does the model use extreme valuation ratios in an intuitive way (undervalued stocks contributing positive alpha, overvalued contributing negative)?
- Are there any surprisingly dominant technical features that might indicate leakage from the future (e.g., forward-looking variables accidentally included)?

At the local level, you can pick a specific stock and date and display a bar chart of SHAP values, showing which features pushed the model to a strong long or short recommendation.

## Residual Analysis for Trading Models

Explainability tells you *what* the model is using, but not necessarily *how well* it is behaving along dimensions that matter for trading. For that, classical residual analysis, adapted to financial data, is invaluable.

Let $y_{i,t}$ be your realized target (e.g., next-period return) and $\hat{y}_{i,t}$ the model prediction. Define the residual:

$$e_{i,t} = y_{i,t} - \hat{y}_{i,t}.$$

Studying the pattern of $e_{i,t}$ across time, assets, and conditions can reveal:

- remaining structure that the model has not captured,
- regimes where the model systematically underperforms,
- unintended factor exposures.

### Autocorrelation and Structure in Residuals

Ideally, residuals should look like noise: uncorrelated over time and across assets, with no obvious dependence on past information. In practice, you may find:

- **Serial correlation:** $e_{i,t}$ is correlated with $e_{i,t-1}$. This can indicate slow adaptation to regime changes or missing dynamics.
- **Cross-sectional structure:** residuals cluster by sector, size, or liquidity; perhaps the model is weak for small caps or emerging markets.
- **Dependence on features:** plotting residuals against key features might reveal nonlinearities or interactions not captured by the model.

If systematic patterns remain, you face a choice: augment the model (more features, different architecture) or accept that certain structure is unpredictable at your horizon and should not be exploited.

### Regime-Specific Performance

Regime analysis is particularly important in finance. You can slice residuals and performance metrics by:

- volatility regime (e.g., VIX quartiles),

- macro conditions (e.g., expansion vs. recession),
- market state (bull vs. bear, crisis vs. normal times),
- liquidity or turnover buckets.

For each slice, compute:

- average residual (bias),
- residual variance,
- information ratio or Sharpe of the associated trading strategy.

Consistent underperformance in certain regimes may not invalidate the model, but it should be part of the documented narrative: "The signal is designed for normal-to-low-volatility regimes and is expected to weaken or invert in crisis environments." This guides both allocation decisions and risk overlays (e.g., dynamic de-risking when entering historically hostile regimes).

**Unintended Factor and Style Exposures**

Even if your model is built on alternative data (e.g., NLP sentiment), its trades may load on familiar risk factors (value, momentum, size, quality, etc.). To diagnose these exposures:

- Construct the realized portfolio generated by your model over time (using the validation protocol from earlier sections).
- Run a time-series regression of the portfolio's returns on standard factor returns, e.g.

$$r_t^{portfolio} = \alpha + \sum_k \beta_k f_{k,t} + \varepsilon_t.$$

- Inspect the estimated $\beta_k$ and their stability across time.

If your "novel" alpha is largely explained by existing factors, you may still trade it, but you should:

- acknowledge that part of the return is factor exposure rather than pure alpha,
- ensure that any factor tilts are consistent with client mandates and risk limits,
- avoid double-counting alpha across different strategies that share exposures.

## Detecting Leakage and Artefacts

One of the most valuable uses of explainability and diagnostics is to detect leakage: situations where future information has inadvertently entered your features, labels, or validation setup.

Look out for patterns such as:

- Features with implausibly high SHAP importance that are derived from variables only known with a delay (e.g., end-of-day close when predicting intraday returns, corporate actions known ex post).
- Residuals that are suspiciously small or performance that is uniformly strong across all regimes and assets—a sign that the model might be "cheating".
- Abrupt drops in performance when you change data sources, adjust timestamp alignment, or enforce stricter availability constraints.

Simple but effective checks include:

- **Sanity lags:** deliberately lag all features further back in time (e.g., by one extra day) and confirm that performance degrades reasonably. If it does not, you may still be leaking future information via some path.
- **Randomization tests:** shuffle or randomly reassign certain features or labels and verify that the model's performance collapses. Non-collapse suggests that your validation might be flawed.

- **Label permutation:** within narrow time windows, permute labels across assets; a genuine cross-sectional alpha model should lose most of its edge.

Treat leakage detection as an ongoing process, not a one-off task. Each time you modify features, labels, or data sources, re-run basic sanity checks.

## From Correlation to Causality: Pragmatic Causal Inference

Most trading models are built on correlations: patterns in historical data that appear to be predictive. However, investors and regulators are increasingly concerned with whether these patterns have a plausible causal underpinning. In practice, you rarely prove causality in the strict scientific sense, but you can move along a spectrum from "mere correlation" toward "causally plausible."

### Clarifying the Question

The first step is to clarify what causal question, if any, is relevant. For example:

- *Does a positive change in sentiment (as measured by our NLP model) cause, on average, an increase in future returns, controlling for other factors?*
- *Does our trading activity in illiquid names have a causal impact on prices (market impact)?*

In this chapter, we focus on the first kind: whether an input signal has a causal effect on returns, beyond confounding variables.

### Lag Structure and Placebo Tests

Simple but powerful causal sanity checks include:

- **Lag structure sanity:** If sentiment is truly predictive, its effect should be strongest when you place it before returns and should weaken (or vanish) as you shift it further into the past or into the future. Regressions or models that show strong "predictive power" of *future* sentiment on *past* returns are a red flag.

- **Placebo tests in time:** Test whether your signal predicts returns in periods where it should not. For example, if your factor is based on earnings announcements, it should not predict returns far before the announcement window.
- **Placebo labels:** Replace returns with outcomes that should be unrelated (e.g., future returns on unrelated assets, or artificially generated noise) and verify that the signal loses predictability.

These tests are not full causal identification strategies, but they help rule out obvious artefacts.

**Pseudo Out-of-Sample Experiments**

Another pragmatic tool is to treat new regimes or markets as "quasi-experiments." For instance:

- If your sentiment signal was developed on U.S. equities from 2010–2018, test it unchanged on European equities from 2019 onward.
- If a structural event occurs (e.g., regulatory change, change in trading hours), assess whether the alpha persists in the post-event period.

The more the signal survives such tests without retuning, the more likely it reflects a structural behaviour (e.g., underreaction to news) rather than a fragile correlation.

**When to Consider More Formal Causal Tools**

In some settings, especially around questions of market impact and policy evaluation, more formal causal inference tools are justified:

- instrumental variables (IV),
- difference-in-differences (DiD),
- regression discontinuity designs (RDD),

- propensity score matching.

These methods require careful design and domain expertise, and they are beyond the scope of this section. The important takeaway is that causal inference in trading is context-specific and cannot be automated away by generic machine-learning pipelines. You should escalate to more formal approaches when:

- regulatory or client requirements demand a causal story (e.g., ESG impact, market integrity),
- strategic decisions (e.g., large-scale execution changes) hinge on understanding interventions rather than passive prediction.

## Building a Coherent Model Narrative

Explainability, diagnostics, and causal reasoning ultimately serve one overarching purpose: to build a coherent, defensible narrative about your model. A well-documented narrative might address:

- **Mechanism:** Which behaviours or frictions is the model exploiting (e.g., underreaction to news, liquidity provision, overextrapolation)?
- **Key drivers:** Which features matter most, and are they stable across time and markets?
- **Regime dependence:** Under which market conditions does the model tend to work or fail?
- **Risk and factor profile:** What factor exposures does the strategy carry, intentionally or unintentionally?
- **Robustness checks:** What stress tests, placebo tests, and out-of-sample experiments has the model passed?

This narrative is not marketing spin; it is part of risk management. It provides the basis for:

- deciding position limits and capital allocation,

- setting expectations for performance and drawdowns,
- knowing when to intervene, recalibrate, or retire the model.

In summary, moving from "the model fits our backtest" to "we understand, monitor, and trust this model" requires a deliberate toolkit of explainability methods, diagnostic analyses, and causal sanity checks. With these in place, you can deploy complex ML and NLP-driven trading strategies with greater confidence that their observed performance reflects genuine, economically meaningful structure rather than accidental backtest artefacts.

# Chapter 7

# Strategy Evaluation, Portfolio Construction, and Production

*You don't earn P&L from clever NLP features or beautiful model metrics-you earn it from capital allocated to live, executable strategies that survive real markets. This chapter connects the lab to the trading floor: you'll learn how to design honest backtests, translate model scores into controlled risk, assemble multiple signals into coherent portfolios, and trade them through cost-aware execution pipelines, all under a governance framework that keeps your AI stack reliable when money is actually on the line.*

## 7.1 Backtesting Design and Bias Control

In the previous chapter we focused on turning raw alternative data and NLP outputs into predictive signals. The natural next question is: *do these signals actually make money once traded in the real world?* Backtesting is the laboratory where we try to answer that question before committing capital.

This section is about building backtests that are both honest and useful. Honest means they do not quietly cheat by using future information or ignoring costs. Useful means they resemble live trading closely enough that failures in the backtest are meaningful warnings, and successes are at least plausible.

We will proceed in four steps:

- Clarify what a *production-grade* backtest is, and how it differs from an exploratory research notebook.
- Identify the main families of bias that can inflate AI/NLP strategy performance.
- Show how to evaluate strategies with walk-forward and nested procedures that respect the information actually available at each point in time.
- Add realistic costs, constraints, and stress tests, and wrap everything in an auditable process.

## From Exploratory Notebooks to Production-Grade Backtests

Most strategies begin life in a notebook: a few lines of Python, a CSV of prices, and an attractive equity curve. That is the *ideation* phase. The risk is that the same lightweight, informal practices that are perfect for exploration are disastrous if you mistake them for serious evaluation.

A **production-grade backtest** has a different goal from a research notebook. Its goal is not to generate ideas but to answer a specific question:

> *If we had traded this strategy in the past, using only the information we realistically had at each time and facing realistic costs and constraints, what would have happened?*

To support that goal, a robust backtest architecture has several required properties.

**1. Data versioning and deterministic replay.**

You must be able to re-run the backtest six months later and reproduce the same results, bit for bit, from the same inputs. That implies:

- Versioned datasets (e.g., a specific snapshot of your news corpus as of a given date).
- Fixed random seeds for any stochastic components (e.g., model initialization, bootstrap sampling).
- Logged configuration: parameters, universe definitions, cost model assumptions, and so on.

If you cannot reproduce a backtest, you cannot debug it or trust it.

**2. Explicit event and trading calendars.**

Time is not just an index; it is a sequence of events:

- Market open and close times by venue.
- Known holidays and half days.
- Corporate actions (earnings announcements, splits, dividends).
- Publication times for alternative data (e.g., when a news article first appears on the wire).

A credible backtest uses an explicit calendar structure. For each decision time $t$ you know which markets are open, which instruments are tradable, and which pieces of information are already observable.

**3. Clear separation of stages.**

Even simple strategies conceptually pass through a pipeline:

- **Raw data ingestion**: prices, volumes, corporate actions, text, alternative data.
- **Feature and signal generation**: transforming raw data into model inputs and predictions.
- **Portfolio construction**: turning predictions into target positions.

- **Execution and cost modeling**: simulating fills and transaction costs.
- **Reporting**: computing performance and risk statistics.

Implementing these as separate, testable modules pays off when you want to change the cost model without touching the signal generation, or re-run the same signals through a different portfolio construction engine.

Right after introducing this conceptual pipeline, it is helpful to visualize it.

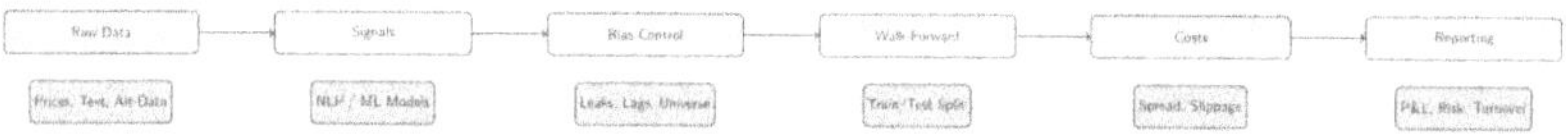


**4. Reproducible parameter sets.**

Machine learning strategies, especially NLP-driven ones, involve many hyperparameters: learning rates, regularization strengths, vocabulary choices, universe filters, and so forth. A production backtest stores these in a configuration file or database entry rather than scattering magic numbers through code. Backtest results are then tagged with a configuration identifier.

## Core Biases in AI and NLP Backtests

Biases are ways in which our simulated world quietly diverges from the real one. In trading, most important biases make the backtest *look better* than live trading would be. For AI and NLP strategies, three families of bias are particularly dangerous.

### Look-Ahead Bias: Using the Future by Accident

A backtest suffers from **look-ahead bias** if, at decision time $t$, it relies on data that were not actually known by $t$ in reality.

In classical quant strategies this happens, for example, by using end-of-day close prices to decide trades that supposedly occur at that same close. In NLP and alternative data strategies, there are more subtle pathways:

- **Revised fundamentals and macro data**. Economic series and company fundamentals are often revised after initial publication. If you use the latest, cleaned time series, you are implicitly giving the model revised information which traders did not have at the time.

- **Finalized transcripts vs. real-time information**. Earnings call transcripts may be released hours after the call and may be edited. But trades on the day often react to the live call, not the cleaned transcript.

- **Label leakage in supervised learning**. Suppose you label examples by whether a stock outperformed over the next 5 days and then let your model ingest text from the same 5-day window as features. The labels and features refer to overlapping time intervals, which can turn the model into a hindsight detector instead of a forecaster.

The antidote is to attach a *timestamp-of-availability* to every data item, not just a logical date. Your backtest must enforce the rule:

$$\text{At decision time } t, \text{ features may depend only on data with availability time } \leq$$

## Survivorship Bias: Only the Winners Survive

**Survivorship bias** arises when you backtest using only assets that currently exist, ignoring those that delisted, merged, or went bankrupt.

For an equity strategy, this usually means:

- Using a current security master (e.g., today's index constituents) for the historical universe.

- Ignoring delisted tickers in your historical price database.

This systematically removes some of the worst historical performers, often precisely those that a value or sentiment strategy might have traded. Performance appears artificially strong, and drawdowns look shallower than they would have been.

Avoiding survivorship bias requires *point-in-time universes*. For each day $t$, you determine which instruments were actually tradable on that day and use only those. Many institutional data vendors provide point-in-time index constituent histories and security masters for exactly this reason.

### Label Leakage and Target Alignment in Text Models

In supervised learning for alpha, you train a model to predict a target $y_t$ (for example, next-day return) from features $x_t$ (for example, sentiment scores or embeddings based on text).

Two alignment questions matter:

- What is the time interval covered by the text?
- When is the label period measured relative to that text?

A clean design might be:

- Features $x_t$ summarize all text published from the last close up to time $t$.
- Label $y_t$ is the return from $t$ to $t + \Delta$.

Common leakages include:

- Including text from the label period (for example, using news from $t$ to $t + 1$ to predict the return over the same window).
- Using rolling averages that extend beyond $t$ when computing sentiment features.
- Failing to handle late-arriving data (for example, vendor-stamped timestamps that differ from public release times).

To guard against these, make the alignment explicit in code and unit tests. For each training example, you should be able to answer: which exact documents are allowed in features, and what exact price path defines the label?

## Walk-Forward and Time-Series Evaluation Protocols

Once we trust our data alignment, we need to estimate how the strategy would perform out of sample. Classical $k$-fold cross-validation that randomly shuffles observations is inappropriate for time series, because it breaks temporal order and allows future observations to help fit past predictions.

Instead, we use **walk-forward** or **rolling** evaluation schemes.

### Simple Walk-Forward Backtest

In a simple walk-forward design:

- Choose an initial training window, for example from $T_0$ to $T_1$.
- Fit your model using data only from that window.
- Run the backtest over a subsequent test period $[T_1, T_2]$ without refitting.
- Optionally, roll the window forward: expand or slide the training period and repeat.

This mimics a manager who trains a model, then trades it for a while before retraining.

Two common patterns:

- **Expanding window**: Train on $[T_0, T_1]$, test on $(T_1, T_2]$; then train on $[T_0, T_2]$, test on $(T_2, T_3]$, and so on. The training set only grows.

- **Sliding window**: Train on $[T_0, T_1]$, test on $(T_1, T_2]$; then train on $[T_1, T_2]$, test on $(T_2, T_3]$, and so on. The training window length is fixed; older data are dropped.

The choice reflects your belief about stationarity. If you think older data remain informative, you might prefer an expanding window; if you suspect regime changes, a sliding window with more recent data might be better.

### Nested Cross-Validation for Hyperparameter Tuning

Hyperparameters (e.g., regularization strength, tree depth, or neural network architecture) are often tuned to maximize some performance metric. If you tune hyperparameters and evaluate performance on the same sample, you risk *overfitting the backtest itself.*

**Nested cross-validation** addresses this by separating:

- An outer loop that yields a sequence of test periods, strictly out of sample.
- An inner loop, run only within each outer training sample, where you tune hyperparameters using additional time-series splits.

Conceptually:

- For each outer split $k$:
  - Use data up to time $T_k$ as the outer training set; data from $(T_k, T_{k+1}]$ as the outer test set.
  - Within the outer training set, perform a walk-forward or rolling split to choose hyperparameters.
  - Refit the model on the full outer training set with the selected hyperparameters.
  - Generate predictions and a test-period backtest over $(T_k, T_{k+1}]$.
- Aggregate performance over all outer test periods.

This is more computationally intensive but gives a more realistic estimate of how the strategy will perform when both model and hyperparameters are selected based on past data only.

## Realistic Cost, Financing, and Constraint Modeling

A gross backtest that ignores costs is a useful filter: many ideas that do not work even before costs should be discarded. But any strategy that appears promising must be re-evaluated with a realistic model of frictions.

### Components of Transaction Costs

Total transaction costs have several components:

- **Explicit fees**: broker commissions, exchange fees, taxes.
- **Bid–ask spread**: if you cross the spread, you lose half the spread on each round trip, on average.
- **Slippage**: your execution price deviates from a benchmark (for example, mid-quote, arrival price, or VWAP) because markets move while you trade.
- **Market impact**: your own trading moves the market price against you, especially for large or illiquid orders.

In a backtest, we typically model these as functions of traded volume, volatility, and liquidity. A simple, conservative model might be:

$$\text{Cost}_t = c_{fixed} + c_{spread} \cdot |\Delta w_t| + c_{impact} \cdot \left(\frac{|\Delta w_t|}{\text{ADV}_t}\right)^{\alpha},$$

where $\Delta w_t$ is the change in portfolio weight in an asset at time $t$, $\text{ADV}_t$ is average daily volume, and $c_{fixed}$, $c_{spread}$, $c_{impact}$, $\alpha$ are calibrated constants.

### Financing, Shorting, and Other Frictions

Depending on the strategy, further frictions may be material:

- **Financing and funding rates**: for leveraged positions, you pay (or receive) a financing spread over a benchmark rate.
- **Borrow fees and recall risk**: for short positions, there may be borrow fees; in extreme cases, securities become hard-to-borrow or unavailable.
- **Position and exposure limits**: regulatory or internal risk constraints limit gross and net exposures, concentration in single names or sectors, and leverage.

The backtest should simulate how such constraints bind in practice. For instance, if adding a new position would violate a sector cap, the simulated portfolio construction step must either resize all positions or skip the trade.

## Stress Testing and Scenario Analysis

Even a carefully controlled, costed backtest is still a historical replay. It tells you how the strategy would have done in the specific sequence of events that actually occurred. But markets change, and histories are finite.

**Stress testing** asks: how fragile is this strategy to adverse but plausible changes in conditions?

Common stress test dimensions include:

- **Volatility spikes**: What happens if realized volatility doubles relative to history while correlations rise?
- **Liquidity droughts**: What if bid–ask spreads widen sharply and average daily volumes fall?
- **Regime breaks**: How does the strategy fare around crises (for example, 2008, 2020) or during prolonged bear markets?

In a backtest context, you can implement these by:

- Replaying specific historical episodes and examining drawdowns, turnover, and risk exposures.
- Perturbing your cost model (for example, multiplying spreads and impact coefficients by 2 or 3) and recomputing net performance.
- Perturbing model parameters within confidence intervals to see how sensitive performance is to modest shifts in behaviour.

The goal is not to eliminate all risk—that is impossible—but to identify which scenarios would be existentially dangerous and whether your risk management and capital allocation are compatible with that reality.

## Audit Trails and Interpretability of Results

Finally, credible backtesting is as much a *process* as a set of numerical outputs. When you present a strategy to an investment committee or risk manager, you should be able to answer:

- Exactly which data and versions were used.
- How the universe was defined and whether survivorship bias was controlled.
- How features and labels were aligned in time.
- What evaluation protocol was used (simple walk-forward, nested CV, etc.).
- Which cost and constraint assumptions were applied.
- How sensitive the results are to reasonable variations in these choices.

This implies logging and keeping:

- Configuration files for each backtest run.
- Code version identifiers (e.g., Git commit hashes).
- Links to data snapshots or checksums.
- Summaries of key performance and risk metrics, including distributions (not just point estimates).

NLP and alternative-data strategies add a further layer: model interpretability. For governance and regulatory reasons, you may need to explain, at least qualitatively, which types of inputs drive the model's decisions. While detailed explainability techniques are covered in later chapters, at the backtesting stage you should already monitor simple diagnostics:

- How often is the model trading around specific event types (for example, earnings vs. macro news)?
- Are there particular sectors or regions where the signal behaves very differently?
- Does performance concentrate in a narrow set of time periods?

Such checks help detect overfitting to quirks of the text corpus or data vendor rather than robust patterns in economic behaviour.

## Putting It All Together

A robust backtest for an AI trading strategy is not just a script that loops over dates and compounds returns. It is an engineered environment that:

- Starts from versioned, point-in-time data with realistic availability timestamps.
- Generates features and labels with rigorous temporal alignment.
- Controls for look-ahead, survivorship, and leakage biases.

- Evaluates performance with time-aware, often nested, walk-forward protocols.
- Incorporates realistic costs, financing, and constraints.
- Subjects the strategy to stress tests and documents all assumptions.

If this sounds demanding, that is because the default alternative—casual backtesting—consistently produces strategies that look brilliant on paper and disappointing in production. In the next section, we will build on this foundation and show how to translate AI model outputs into actual portfolio positions, with risk management frameworks that work hand in hand with the robust backtests you now know how to design.

## 7.2 Strategy Implementation and Risk Management

In the previous section we focused on how to backtest AI and NLP-driven strategies in a way that is honest about information, costs, and uncertainty. We now assume that you have such a backtest: you have a signal that appears to add value in realistic simulations. The next step is to turn that signal into *positions* and *trades* that fit within a coherent risk framework.

A common failure mode is to treat a model's outputs as oracles and translate them directly into large bets. This often works beautifully in backtests and catastrophically in production. The central idea of this section is that model outputs must be filtered through three layers:

- A **position mapping**: how we convert signals or return forecasts into desired positions.
- A **risk budget and volatility targeting** scheme: how much total risk the strategy is allowed to take and how that risk is allocated.

- A **regime-aware control system**: how exposure adjusts when markets move into stress regimes or when the model is clearly outside its comfort zone.

Together, these layers make the difference between an interesting model and a tradable strategy.

## From Signals to Positions

Most AI and NLP models output one of the following per asset and time step:

- A *score* $s_{i,t}$ (for example, a sentiment score or a predicted probability that returns will be positive).
- A *forecast return* $\hat{r}_{i,t}$ or *alpha* estimate.

The first design choice is: *what kind of portfolio are we trying to build?*

### Directional, Relative-Value, and Market-Neutral Implementations

For simplicity, suppose we are trading equities. Three common implementations are:

#### 1. Directional (long-only or long-biased).

You take net exposure to the market, often benchmarked to an index.

- **Long-only**: weights $w_{i,t} \geq 0$ and $\sum_i w_{i,t} = 1$. The model decides which names to overweight or underweight relative to a benchmark.
- **Long-biased**: you allow some shorting but maintain positive net exposure, for example $0 \leq \sum_i w_{i,t} \leq 1$.

NLP or alt-data signals often enter as *tilts* around a core portfolio, such as a benchmark index or factor portfolio. This stabilizes performance: the model is not responsible for explaining the entire equity risk premium.

**2. Relative-value (dollar-neutral with constraints).**

You structure the strategy to be roughly neutral to broad market moves, taking positions that are long some stocks and short others:

$$\sum_i w_{i,t} \approx 0, \quad \sum_i |w_{i,t}| = \text{target gross exposure.}$$

Text-based signals naturally fit this framework: you can go long stocks with strongly positive sentiment and short those with strongly negative sentiment, focusing on cross-sectional mispricings.

**3. Market-neutral or factor-neutral.**

You explicitly neutralize exposures to certain risk factors (for example, market beta, sectors, styles like value or momentum). Positions are chosen so that:

$$B^\top w_t \approx 0,$$

where $B$ is a matrix of factor loadings. This forces the portfolio's P&L to be driven mainly by the model's alpha rather than broad risk factors.

For AI and NLP signals, *neutral or near-neutral implementations are often safer*, because these signals can be noisy and regime-dependent. They tend to add incremental edge on top of risk factors rather than replacing them.

### A Simple Score-to-Weight Mapping

Regardless of the implementation type, we need a basic mapping from scores to desired positions. A common starting point is to standardize scores cross-sectionally and map them linearly to target weights.

Let $z_{i,t}$ be the standardized score of asset $i$ at time $t$:

$$z_{i,t} = \frac{s_{i,t} - \mu_t}{\sigma_t},$$

where $\mu_t$ and $\sigma_t$ are the cross-sectional mean and standard deviation of scores at time $t$. Then define preliminary, unscaled weights:

$$\tilde{w}_{i,t} = z_{i,t}.$$

We can impose basic constraints by rescaling:

- **Gross exposure constraint**: Set

$$w_{i,t} = \lambda_t \tilde{w}_{i,t}, \quad \text{with} \sum_i |w_{i,t}| = G_{target},$$

  where $G_{target}$ is the desired gross exposure and $\lambda_t$ is chosen accordingly.

- **Net exposure constraint**: If we want $\sum_i w_{i,t} = N_{target}$, we can subtract a constant from all $\tilde{w}_{i,t}$ before scaling.

In practice, more sophisticated portfolio construction (discussed in the next chapter) will sit on top of this basic mapping. For now, this provides an intuitive bridge between model scores and positions.

## Risk Budgets: How Much Risk Can the Strategy Take?

With a mapping from signals to positions, we now ask: *how large should the positions be?* The answer is not "as large as possible." Instead, we work backward from a risk budget.

### Defining a Risk Budget

A **risk budget** specifies how much variability in returns the strategy is allowed to contribute to the overall portfolio. At a basic level, this can be expressed as:

- A target annualized volatility $\sigma_{target}$ (for example, 10%).
- A max drawdown tolerance (for example, "we do not want a 30% peak-to-trough drawdown more often than once per decade").
- For multi-strategy portfolios, a fraction of total firm risk budget allocated to this sleeve.

Volatility is easier to work with mathematically, so we start there.

### Volatility Targeting: Scaling to a Volatility Target

Volatility targeting means scaling the portfolio so that realized volatility stays close to a target level. If the environment becomes more volatile, position sizes shrink; if volatility falls, they grow.

At time $t$, let $\hat{\sigma}_t$ be an estimate of the portfolio's annualized volatility if we used unit leverage (for example, computed from recent returns or from a risk model). Let $\sigma_{target}$ be our target. Then we set a leverage or scaling factor:

$$L_t = \frac{\sigma_{target}}{\hat{\sigma}_t}.$$

We then scale weights:

$$w_{i,t}^{final} = L_t \cdot w_{i,t}^{base}.$$

Intuitively:

- If the strategy's natural volatility rises (for example, because markets became choppier or signals became more aggressive), then $\hat{\sigma}_t$ increases and $L_t$ decreases, trimming exposures.
- If volatility falls, $L_t$ increases, allowing more exposure without violating the risk budget.

For AI strategies, this is especially important. Their behaviour can change sharply when signals react strongly to bursts of news or social media attention. Volatility targeting imposes a mechanical check on how much risk they can dump into the portfolio in such moments.

### Practical Considerations in Volatility Estimation

Estimation of $\hat{\sigma}_t$ can be done in several ways:

- **Realized volatility**: use an exponentially weighted moving average (EWMA) of recent portfolio returns.
- **Factor risk model**: estimate the portfolio's factor exposures and use factor covariances to compute forward-looking risk.
- **Hybrid**: blend realized and model-based estimates.

Shorter windows respond more quickly but are noisier; longer windows are stable but slow to adapt. Many practitioners use multiple horizons and put floors/ceilings on $L_t$ to avoid extreme leverage changes.

## Position Limits and Concentration Control

Risk management is not only about total volatility. Even a low-volatility strategy can blow up if it is overly concentrated in a particular name, sector, or theme.

### Single-Name and Sector Caps

A standard set of constraints includes:

- **Single-name limit**:

  $$|w_{i,t}| \leq w_{max}, \quad \forall i.$$

  This prevents any single asset from dominating the portfolio.

- **Sector or industry cap**:

  $$\left| \sum_{i \in \text{sector } k} w_{i,t} \right| \leq S_{max,k}.$$

  This caps exposure to each sector. It is important for NLP strategies that may cluster around sectors with high news volume (for example, technology or financials).

These constraints can be enforced through simple rescaling or, more robustly, by solving an optimization problem that maximizes some notion of alpha subject to these limits.

### Gross and Net Exposure Limits

Define:

$$Gross_t = \sum_i |w_{i,t}|, \quad Net_t = \sum_i w_{i,t}.$$

Typical constraints include:

- $Gross_t \leq G_{max}$,
- $N_{min} \leq Net_t \leq N_{max}$.

These guardrails ensure that your leverage does not drift upward unnoticed and that your net market exposure stays within acceptable bounds.

## Drawdown and Tail-Risk Management

Volatility targeting and exposure limits keep typical fluctuations under control. However, investors are particularly sensitive to *tail events*: large, sudden drawdowns and sustained periods of losses. Here we introduce explicit drawdown-based controls.

### Monitoring Drawdowns

Define the cumulative return of the strategy up to time $t$, $C_t$, and the running peak:

$$P_t = \max_{0 \leq s \leq t} C_s.$$

The drawdown at time $t$ is:

$$D_t = \frac{C_t - P_t}{P_t}.$$

We monitor $D_t$ and trigger actions when it crosses certain thresholds (for example, $-10\%$, $-20\%$).

### Drawdown-Based De-Risking Rules

A simple rule-based framework:

- If $D_t$ exceeds $D_1$ (for example, $-10\%$), reduce target volatility $\sigma_{target}$ by a factor (for example, to 70% of its normal value).
- If $D_t$ exceeds $D_2$ (for example, $-20\%$), cut risk more aggressively (for example, to 30–50% of normal), and freeze model updates to avoid frantic overfitting.

- If $D_t$ exceeds a critical level $D_3$ (for example, $-30\%$), invoke governance procedures: partial or full shutdown of the strategy, formal review, and potential redesign.

These rules reflect an important principle: *when the strategy is doing unusually badly, we do not simply "trust the model harder."* Instead, we assume that either the regime has changed or the model was overfit, and we reduce risk until we understand what is happening.

## Regime Detection and Regime-Aware Exposure Scaling

Markets are not stationary. Periods of low volatility and ample liquidity alternate with crises; news intensity ebbs and flows. Particularly for NLP and event-driven strategies, the environment in which text is generated and interpreted can shift quickly.

### Defining Regimes

A **regime** is a set of market conditions that are meaningfully different from others along one or more dimensions:

- **Volatility**: low, normal, high.
- **Liquidity**: normal, impaired.
- **News intensity or sentiment**: calm, noisy, panic.

You can detect regimes using simple threshold rules or more sophisticated unsupervised learning, but for risk management, transparency often matters more than complexity.

Examples:

- High-volatility regime if realized volatility of the benchmark index exceeds a threshold.
- Liquidity-stress regime if average bid–ask spreads or price impact per unit volume increase beyond a certain multiple of their long-run median.

- News-stress regime if the count of negative news headlines or social media posts crosses a high percentile of its historical distribution.

**Regime-Aware Risk Scaling**.

Once regimes are defined, we adjust risk budgets and constraints accordingly. For instance:

- In a **normal regime**, run at full target volatility $\sigma_{target}$, with standard gross exposure $G_{max}$.
- In a **high-volatility regime**, reduce $\sigma_{target}$ (for example, to 60–70% of normal), tighten single-name and sector caps, and increase transaction-cost estimates in the backtest and risk systems.
- In a **liquidity or news-stress regime**, further constrain gross exposure and turnover, and possibly restrict trading to the most liquid instruments.

For NLP strategies specifically, it can be useful to track where their historical alpha came from. If you know that most profits occurred in moderate-volatility, moderate-news environments, while performance in panic regimes was poor or unstable, then your regime-aware scaling should reflect that: the model is simply not trusted as much in panic regimes.

## When to Override the Model

No matter how sophisticated the model, there will be times when human judgment should override it. The challenge is to do so in a disciplined, pre-defined way, not as an ad hoc reaction to temporary discomfort.

### Pre-Defined Override Conditions

Examples of conditions that might justify overrides:

- **Data issues**: detected feed errors, vendor outages, or obvious mislabeling in critical alternative data sources.

- **Model out-of-domain**: the input distribution shifts far outside the training range (for example, unprecedented levels of negative sentiment or volatility).
- **Regulatory or structural changes**: new regulations, trading halts, or market structure breaks that invalidate some modeling assumptions.

For each such condition, you should define in your risk policy:

- Who is authorized to override.
- What actions are allowed (for example, reduce all positions by half, switch to a benchmark portfolio, stop opening new positions).
- How the decision and rationale are documented for later review.

### Balancing Discipline and Flexibility

Too many overrides undermine the whole point of systematic trading; too few may leave you exposed to avoidable disasters. One practical heuristic is to track:

- The frequency of overrides.
- The P&L impact of overrides vs. what the model alone would have done.

If overrides are frequent and usually harm performance, your risk framework may be overly conservative or reacting to noise. If overrides are rare but consistently save large amounts of capital in extreme situations, they are doing their job.

## A Practical Risk Policy Template

To tie these ideas together, it is helpful to think in terms of a **risk policy document** for an AI/NLP strategy. At a minimum, such a policy should cover:

**1. Strategy mandate and implementation.**

- Asset classes and instruments traded.
- Implementation type (directional, relative-value, factor-neutral).
- High-level description of signals used (for example, earnings-call sentiment, news-based topic models).

2. **Risk budget and scaling.**

- Target volatility and maximum allowed volatility.
- Gross and net exposure ranges.
- Single-name and sector caps.
- Volatility-estimation method and how $L_t$ is computed and bounded.

3. **Regime definitions and regime-specific limits.**

- How regimes are detected (which indicators, thresholds, and look-back windows).
- For each regime: target volatility multiplier, exposure limits, liquidity constraints.

4. **Drawdown and tail-risk management.**

- Drawdown thresholds and associated de-risking rules.
- Maximum acceptable drawdown before mandatory review or shutdown.

5. **Override governance.**

- Conditions under which overrides may be considered.
- Decision-makers and escalation paths.
- Documentation and post-event review process.

**6. Monitoring and reporting.**

- Daily and intraday risk reports (volatility, exposures, turnover, P&L attribution).
- Alerts for breaches of limits or unusual model behaviour (for example, extreme concentration, sudden change in trading patterns).

In subsequent sections, we will deepen the portfolio construction and risk modeling aspects, and later connect these to live deployment and governance frameworks. For now, the key takeaway is that an AI or NLP model becomes an *investment strategy* only when its outputs are wrapped in explicit risk budgets, volatility targeting, and regime-aware controls that are strong enough to keep drawdowns from becoming existential.

## 7.3 Portfolio Construction and Risk Models

So far we have focused on two questions: *Is the signal real?* (backtesting and bias control) and *How much risk should this strategy take at any moment?* (implementation and risk management). In this section we address the next practical question:

> Given several AI/NLP signals across many assets, how do we combine them into a *single, coherent portfolio* that respects risk limits, capacity, and turnover?

This is the realm of **portfolio construction**. It sits between your models and your execution engine:

*signals* ⇒ **portfolio construction and risk model** ⇒ positions and trades.

We will build up the ideas in five steps:

- Moving from single-signal strategies to multi-signal portfolios.
- Understanding the role of risk models and factor decompositions.
- Revisiting mean–variance intuition and constrained optimization.
- Respecting capacity and turnover through explicit penalties and constraints.
- Making the resulting portfolios stable, interpretable, and easy to govern.

## From Single-Signal to Multi-Signal Portfolios

The simplest strategy you can build from AI research is: choose one signal (for example, earnings-call sentiment), rank stocks by that signal, and go long the top decile and short the bottom decile. This is a *single-signal, single-sleeve* strategy.

In practice, a robust trading business will typically use:

- Several types of signals (for example, text sentiment, topic shifts, analyst revision signals, short-term technicals).
- A variety of horizons (from intraday to quarterly).
- Multiple asset classes or regions.

The naive way to combine signals is to average them, or to backtest each in isolation and then allocate capital by hand. This wastes diversification potential and usually ignores risk interactions. A better approach is to treat signals as inputs into a common *risk-aware optimizer*.

Before we get to optimization, it is useful to visualize the architecture.

Diagrammatic representation:

This diagram captures the concept of this section in one picture: many signals are blended into an *alpha vector*, passed to an optimizer together with a risk model and constraints, and out come portfolio weights.

## The Role of Risk Models

When you combine many assets and signals, risk can come from several directions:

- Broad market moves (equity beta, rates, credit spreads, FX).
- Common styles or factors (value, momentum, quality, size).
- Sectors, industries, countries.
- Idiosyncratic risk in individual assets.

A **risk model** helps disentangle these. Most institutional equity risk models (and many multi-asset models) follow a factor structure:

$$\Sigma = BFB^\top + D,$$

where:

- $\Sigma$ is the covariance matrix of asset returns.
- $B$ is a matrix of factor loadings (each row corresponds to an asset; each column to a factor).
- $F$ is the factor covariance matrix.
- $D$ is a diagonal matrix of specific (idiosyncratic) variances.

Why is this useful for AI/NLP-based strategies?

- It provides a stable estimate of risk even when the number of assets is large and history is short. Directly estimating a full $\Sigma$ from your own backtest sample will be unstable.
- It separates the risk you *want* (driven by your alpha) from risk that is just compensation for bearing generic factors.
- It lets you impose explicit exposure constraints, like "stay close to market-neutral" or "do not make big sector bets."

In this book we generally recommend: *manage AI and text-based alphas against an independent, well-tested risk model*, rather than trying to build a risk model from the same data and models that generate alpha. That separation helps reduce the chance that a modeling error or overfit structure in your alpha pipeline also contaminates your risk estimates.

## Mean–Variance Intuition for Portfolio Construction

With an alpha vector and a risk model in hand, it is natural to revisit the classic mean–variance framework. Let:

- $w$ be the vector of portfolio weights.
- $\mu$ be the vector of expected returns (derived from signals).
- $\Sigma$ be the covariance matrix (given by the risk model).

The canonical unconstrained mean–variance problem is:

$$\max_{w} \; \mu^\top w - \frac{\gamma}{2} w^\top \Sigma w,$$

where $\gamma > 0$ is a risk-aversion parameter. The first term is expected return; the second is a penalty for risk (variance). The solution, if there are no constraints, is:

$$w^\star = \frac{1}{\gamma}\Sigma^{-1}\mu.$$

There are two key insights here:

- The optimizer tilts weights toward assets with higher expected returns, but it does so more strongly when those assets are not too correlated with the rest of the portfolio.
- A "naive" strategy that only uses $\mu$ (for example, ranking by alpha and taking the top names) implicitly assumes $\Sigma$ is proportional to the identity matrix. That is rarely true; correlations matter.

Of course, real portfolios must obey many constraints. But it is helpful to keep the simple solution in mind: most practical portfolio construction schemes are constrained variations on this theme.

## Constrained Optimization with Risk Models

In realistic settings, the optimizer must handle:

- Box limits on individual weights (e.g., $w_i^{\min} \le w_i \le w_i^{\max}$).
- Factor exposure bounds (e.g., market beta close to zero; limited value or growth tilt).
- Sector, country, or asset-class limits.
- Turnover and transaction cost considerations.

A typical optimization problem for an equity long/short AI sleeve might look like:

$$
\begin{aligned}
\max_{w} \quad & \mu^\top w - \frac{\gamma}{2} w^\top \Sigma w - \lambda_{tc} \cdot \text{TC}(w, w^{prev}) \\
\text{subject to} \quad & \mathbf{1}^\top w = N_{target} \quad \text{(net exposure)} \\
& \mathbf{1}^\top |w| \le G_{max} \quad \text{(gross exposure)} \\
& w_i^{\min} \le w_i \le w_i^{\max}, \quad \forall i \\
& B^\top w \in [f_{min}, f_{max}] \quad \text{(factor exposure bands)} \\
& Cw \in [c_{min}, c_{max}] \quad \text{(sector / region limits)},
\end{aligned}
$$

where:

- $w^{prev}$ are current weights (before rebalancing).
- $\text{TC}(w, w^{prev})$ is a turnover or transaction-cost measure.
- $B$ is the factor loadings matrix, and $[f_{min}, f_{max}]$ are allowable factor exposures.

- $C$ is an aggregation matrix mapping asset weights to sector or region exposures.

This may look intimidating, but conceptually it only says:

> *Choose weights that trade off expected return against risk and costs, but stay within well-defined guardrails for exposures and diversification.*

For many AI-driven shops, this optimization is solved every rebalance (for example, daily), using current estimates of $\mu$, $\Sigma$, and transaction-cost parameters.

## From Multiple Signals to a Single Alpha Vector

So far we have treated $\mu$ as given. In a multi-signal AI setting, you might have:

- Short-horizon alphas from order-book microstructure models.
- Medium-horizon alphas from news and social media sentiment.
- Longer-horizon alphas from fundamental or topic-based NLP models.

How do we combine them into a single $\mu$ to feed the optimizer?

## Score Standardization and Scaling

A basic approach:

- Normalize each signal cross-sectionally at each time $t$ (for example, to zero mean and unit standard deviation).
- Rescale each normalized signal by a *signal strength* or *risk target* so that, historically, each contributes a controlled share of total risk/return.

- Add them up linearly:

$$\mu_{i,t} = \sum_{k=1}^{K} \beta_k s_{i,t}^{(k)},$$

where $s^{(k)}$ is the $k$-th standardized signal and $\beta_k$ is a weight reflecting its reliability and horizon.

The $\beta_k$ can be set using:

- Simple rules of thumb (for example, all equal, or proportional to long-run information ratios).
- A higher-level model (for example, a meta-learner that combines signals based on recent performance, with strong regularization).

The crucial point is stability: signal weights should change *slowly* relative to the trading frequency, or you risk creating a second layer of overfitting.

## Black–Litterman-Style Blending of Priors and Signals

Another perspective, especially in benchmark-relative contexts, is inspired by the Black–Litterman framework. The idea is:

- Start from a *prior* portfolio (for example, the market-cap benchmark or a diversified factor portfolio) and its implied equilibrium expected returns $\mu^{prior}$.
- Treat your AI signals as *noisy views* about relative performance between assets or groups.
- Blend the prior and your views, with the weight given to each determined by their estimated uncertainty.

Schematically:

$$\mu^{posterior} = \mu^{prior} + (\text{risk-adjusted effect of AI views}).$$

You then feed $\mu^{posterior}$ into the optimizer. Conceptually, this prevents your AI signals from dragging the portfolio too far away from a diversified starting point unless they are both strong and consistently reliable.

## Capacity and Turnover as First-Class Constraints

So far we have treated transaction costs and turnover as penalties in the objective. For AI strategies that may react quickly to news or microstructure, **capacity** and **turnover** deserve explicit, front-and-center treatment.

## Capacity Constraints

A strategy's **capacity** is the amount of capital it can deploy before its own trades significantly erode its alpha through impact and slippage. Roughly:

$$\text{Capacity} \propto \text{Typical ADV} \times \text{Acceptable Participation Rate}.$$

In portfolio construction, we translate this into constraints such as:

- Upper bounds on position sizes as a fraction of average daily volume (ADV), for example:

  $$|w_i| \leq \kappa \cdot \frac{\text{ADV}_i}{\text{Total Capital}},$$

  with $\kappa$ a small percentage.

- Limits on total daily turnover relative to market volume.

These prevent the optimizer from concentrating capital in small, illiquid names just because they have strong alpha scores.

## Turnover and Transaction-Cost Penalties

Transaction costs scale with turnover. Including a term like $\lambda_{tc} \cdot \mathrm{TC}(w, w^{prev})$ in the objective encourages the optimizer to make only those trades whose expected alpha meaningfully exceeds their cost.

A simple quadratic approximation for transaction costs is:

$$\mathrm{TC}(w, w^{prev}) = \sum_i a_i |w_i - w_i^{prev}| + b_i (w_i - w_i^{prev})^2,$$

with $a_i, b_i \geq 0$ calibrated from historical execution data. The linear term captures spread and fees; the quadratic term approximates impact, which grows faster than linearly with trade size.

In some cases you may also impose hard constraints on turnover:

$$\sum_i |w_i - w_i^{prev}| \leq T_{max},$$

so that even in a wild market your strategy cannot suddenly churn the entire book.

## Stability, Robustness, and Interpretability

Optimizers are powerful tools, but they can also produce portfolios that are fragile or counterintuitive if they are fed noisy inputs or left unconstrained. Three practical guidelines help maintain stability:

## Regularization and Shrinkage

Aggressive reliance on noisy alpha and risk estimates can lead to extreme weights that are highly sensitive to small perturbations. Regularization techniques include:

- Shrinking $\mu$ toward zero or a benchmark.
- Adding penalties on large deviations from a prior portfolio (for example, the previous day's holdings or a benchmark index).

- Adding a small multiple of the identity matrix to $\Sigma$ to avoid overreacting to weakly identified correlation structures.

These steps may reduce backtest Sharpe ratios slightly but usually improve out-of-sample robustness.

## Portfolio Diagnostics

After each optimization, you should compute and monitor:

- Factor risk contributions: how much of total risk comes from each factor?
- Active risk and tracking error versus benchmark (if applicable).
- Concentration metrics, such as the Herfindahl index of weights.
- Marginal contributions to risk and to expected return by asset and by signal.

These diagnostics help identify when the optimizer is doing something unexpected, such as concentrating an NLP strategy's risk in a single sector due to correlated signals.

## Alignment with Business and Governance Constraints

Finally, the portfolio construction process must align with:

- The firm's broader risk appetite and regulatory environment.
- Transparency requirements (for example, being able to explain to a risk committee why the optimizer chose a given overweight).
- Operational realities (for example, trading desks' ability to execute the recommended trades without excessive slippage).

In practice, this means keeping the optimization problem as simple as it can be while still capturing the essential trade-offs between alpha, risk, and costs. It also means documenting assumptions and choices so that the process is auditable—a theme we return to in the final section on deployment and governance.

In this section we elevated AI and NLP signals from isolated, back-tested curiosities to components of a disciplined, multi-signal portfolio. The key ideas were:

- Use an independent risk model to understand and manage factor and idiosyncratic risk.
- Translate multiple signals into a single alpha vector, with careful normalization and stable combination rules.
- Feed alpha and risk into a constrained optimizer that encodes exposure, capacity, and turnover limits, as well as transaction-cost penalties.
- Regularize and monitor the resulting portfolios to ensure they remain stable, interpretable, and compatible with the firm's risk appetite.

The next section will move one step closer to reality by focusing on transaction costs, market impact, and execution algorithms—the frictions that lie between the theoretical portfolios designed here and the realized P&L of live trading.

## 7.4 Transaction Costs, Market Impact, and Execution Algorithms

In the previous sections we moved from robust backtests to risk-aware portfolio construction. We assumed that, once the optimizer proposes a set of trades, you can execute them at some reasonable reference price—say, the mid-quote at the time you decided to trade. In reality, every trade you send to the market leaves a mark. The difference between your *model P&L* and your *realized P&L* is largely explained by **transaction costs** and **market impact**.

For fast-reacting AI and NLP strategies, this gap can be the difference between a profitable business and a money-burning research project. Signals that look strong in a zero-cost backtest may disappear once you account for spreads, fees, slippage, and the price impact of your own trading. Moreover, naive execution can *leak information* to the market, causing others to trade ahead of you and erode your alpha.

This section has three goals:

- Decompose transaction costs into components and show how each erodes model alpha.
- Introduce basic market impact models and how to incorporate them into portfolio construction and backtesting.
- Survey common execution algorithms and smart-routing techniques, with an eye toward preserving AI-driven alpha.

## From Gross Model Alpha to Net Realized Alpha

Suppose your research pipeline produces a strategy with a gross annualized information ratio of 1.0 when you ignore costs. Once you trade it live, you discover that after fees and slippage the realized information ratio is closer to 0.3. Where did the rest go?

It is often helpful to think of a waterfall from *gross model alpha* down to *net realized alpha*, with each layer representing a cost component:

- commissions and explicit fees,
- bid–ask spread,
- slippage versus your decision-time benchmark,
- market impact.

Right after introducing this decomposition, it is useful to visualize it.

The exact numbers will differ by asset class and strategy, but the qualitative message is durable: if you ignore these layers, your backtest is likely exaggerating true performance.

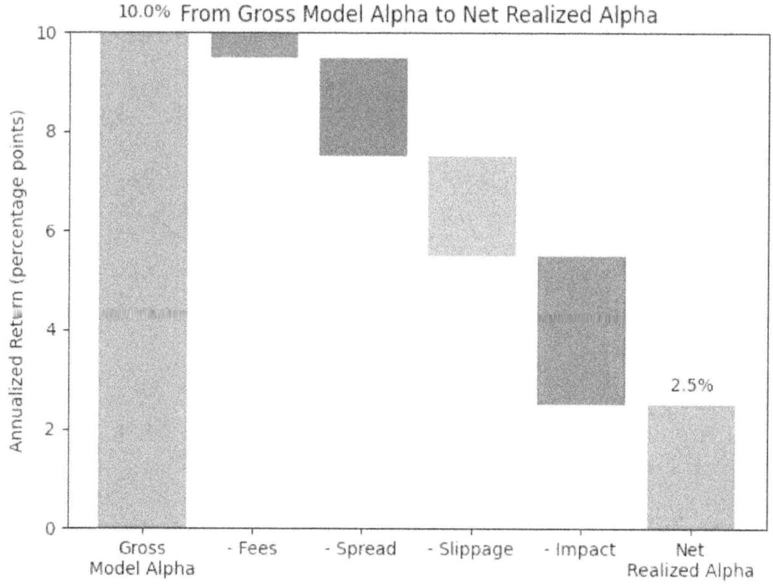


Figure 7.1: Illustrative waterfall from gross model alpha to net realized alpha.

## Components of Transaction Costs

We now define each component more precisely and connect it to observable quantities.

### Explicit Fees

**Explicit fees** are the easiest to grasp:

- broker commissions,
- exchange and clearing fees,
- transaction taxes (such as stamp duty or financial transaction taxes in some jurisdictions).

These are usually charged per share, per contract, or as a fraction of notional traded. In most liquid markets, explicit fees are non-negligible but not the dominant cost for institutional-sized trades. However, for very short-horizon AI strategies that trade often, even small per-trade fees can accumulate.

In a backtest, explicit fees can be modeled directly as:

$$\text{Fees}_t = \sum_i c_i^{fee} \cdot |\Delta q_{i,t}|,$$

where $c_i^{fee}$ is the per-unit fee and $\Delta q_{i,t}$ is the number of units of asset $i$ traded at time $t$.

**Bid–Ask Spread**

The **bid–ask spread** is the price gap between the best bid (highest price at which someone is willing to buy) and the best ask (lowest price at which someone is willing to sell). If you:

- buy by hitting the ask,
- sell by hitting the bid,

then, relative to the mid-quote, you lose half the spread each way, on average. On a full round trip (buy then sell) with no price movement, you lose the whole spread.

If $m_t$ is the mid-price and $s_t$ is the quoted spread, then an aggressive buy at time $t$ pays $m_t + s_t/2$, and an aggressive sell receives $m_t - s_t/2$.

In a backtest, assuming you always cross the spread, you can approximate spread costs as:

$$\text{SpreadCost}_t = \sum_i \frac{s_{i,t}}{2} \cdot |\Delta q_{i,t}|.$$

For highly liquid large-cap equities, spreads might be a few basis points; for small caps or less liquid instruments, spreads can be much larger.

**Slippage**

**Slippage** captures the difference between your execution price and a benchmark price, such as:

- the mid-quote at the time you decide to trade (arrival price),
- the day's volume-weighted average price (VWAP),
- the official close.

Even if spreads were zero, you would still face slippage due to:

- latency and queue position (orders being filled after the market has moved),
- partial fills and cancellations,
- other traders reacting to the same information.

In practice, slippage is often measured ex post by comparing realized trade prices with benchmarks. In backtesting, we must approximate it, often via a combination of spread, volatility, and participation rate assumptions.

### Market Impact

**Market impact** is the component of price movement that is caused by your own trading. Impact is especially important for:

- large orders relative to typical market volume,
- less liquid instruments,
- aggressive trading (high participation rates, short execution horizons).

A simple intuition: if you try to buy 20% of a day's volume in a stock within a few minutes, you will likely push the price up as you walk the book and attract short-term traders who front-run your demand. The more urgent and larger your order, the more you typically move the price.

Impact is central to capacity analysis: as you scale up a strategy, impact costs often grow faster than linearly, eventually erasing all alpha.

## Basic Market Impact Models

Impact modeling is a deep research area, but many practical uses rely on relatively simple parametric forms. A common idea is that the expected implementation shortfall (difference between execution price and decision benchmark) scales with the *participation rate* and *volatility*.

Let:

- $Q$ be the quantity traded,
- ADV be average daily volume,
- $\phi = Q/\text{ADV}$ be the participation rate,
- $\sigma$ be the asset's daily volatility,
- $P$ be the decision price (for example, mid at order submission).

A stylized impact cost (per share) model might be:

$$\text{ImpactCost} \approx k \cdot P \cdot \sigma \cdot \phi^{\alpha},$$

with:

- $k$ a calibration constant (often of order 1),
- $\alpha$ between 0.5 and 1, reflecting concavity (doubling participation less than doubles impact per share but increases total cost).

Total dollar impact cost is then ImpactCost $\times$ $Q$.

In a portfolio context, this extends to:

$$\text{ImpactCost}_t = \sum_i k_i \cdot P_{i,t} \cdot \sigma_{i,t} \cdot \left( \frac{|\Delta q_{i,t}|}{\text{ADV}_{i,t}} \right)^{\alpha_i}.$$

These models are calibrated from historical execution data. Even if the exact form is imperfect, using any conservative impact model in backtests is vastly better than ignoring impact altogether.

## Incorporating Costs and Impact into Portfolio Construction

Earlier we wrote a generic optimization problem that included a transaction-cost term $\text{TC}(w, w^{prev})$. We can now be more explicit.

Let $w$ be desired weights, $w^{prev}$ current weights, $V$ portfolio value, and $\Delta q_i = V\,(w_i - w_i^{prev})/P_i$ the number of shares traded. We can write:

$$\text{TC}(w, w^{prev}) = \sum_i \left[ c_i^{fee} |\Delta q_i| + \frac{s_i}{2} |\Delta q_i| + k_i P_i \upsilon_i \left( \frac{|\Delta q_i|}{\text{ADV}_i} \right)^{\alpha_i} \right].$$

This cost function can be plugged directly into the optimizer's objective:

$$\max_w \quad \mu^\top w - \frac{\gamma}{2} w^\top \Sigma w - \lambda_{tc} \cdot \text{TC}(w, w^{prev}),$$

subject to exposure and capacity constraints. The effect is intuitive:

- Trades in illiquid names or at high participation rates become more expensive in the optimizer's view, so it only undertakes them when the expected alpha is strong enough.
- Strategies that churn the portfolio excessively are penalized, naturally encouraging lower turnover and smoother paths.

For AI strategies with multiple horizons, this often leads to a balance: very short-horizon, reactive signals may get lower effective weight than their raw backtest Sharpe suggests, because their turnover and impact costs are higher.

## Execution Algorithms: From Schedules to Opportunistic Trading

Even with a good cost model, there remains the question: *how do we actually slice and route orders to minimize costs and information leakage?* This is the domain of **execution algorithms**.

Execution algorithms sit between your order management system (OMS) and the exchanges/venues. You specify an *order parent* (for example, buy 500,000 shares of stock X today), and the algo decomposes it into child orders over time and across venues.

### Common Algorithm Types

We briefly summarize the main families, in order of increasing adaptiveness:

#### TWAP (Time-Weighted Average Price).

A TWAP algorithm spreads the order evenly over a specified time window. For example, if you want to buy 100,000 shares between 10:00 and 11:00, a TWAP might schedule roughly 1,666 shares every minute. It is simple and relatively predictable, making it less suitable when others might infer your presence.

#### VWAP (Volume-Weighted Average Price).

A VWAP algorithm aims to match the market's natural volume profile over the day or period. If more volume tends to trade near the open and close, VWAP will schedule more of your order then. This reduces your participation rate at any moment and can reduce impact, but it does not adapt to intraday price movements beyond that pattern.

#### POV (Percent of Volume).

A POV or "participation" algorithm tries to trade a fixed fraction of real-time market volume. For example, you may specify "be 10% of volume," and the algo will chase that participation rate, speeding up when volume is high and slowing down when volume is low. This ties your trading to actual liquidity, which can be more impact-efficient.

#### Implementation Shortfall (IS) or Arrival-Price Algos.

IS algos are designed to minimize the difference between your execution performance and the price at which you decided to trade. They are more adaptive, often speeding up when market moves threaten to erode your expected alpha, and slowing down when price moves are favorable. They typically make explicit trade-offs between *market risk* (waiting too long and missing the move) and *impact risk* (trading too aggressively).

#### Liquidity-Seeking and Opportunistic Algos.

These algorithms actively search for hidden liquidity across lit and dark venues, adapt to order book conditions, and may opportunistically take advantage of temporary imbalances. They are valuable for larger or more sensitive orders, where leaking your intent would be particularly harmful.

### Choosing the Right Algo for an AI Signal

The appropriate execution style depends on the *signal horizon* and *decay*:

- **Short-lived signals** (minutes to hours): For example, AI models reacting to specific news headlines or order-book imbalances. Here, time is alpha: waiting too long destroys value. More aggressive IS or liquidity-seeking algos are often appropriate, even at the cost of higher impact.

- **Medium-horizon signals** (days): For example, daily sentiment from earnings commentary. You may have more room to work the order over the day, making VWAP or POV attractive.

- **Long-horizon signals** (weeks to months): For example, slow-moving thematic NLP signals. Execution can be patient and opportunistic; you can substantially prioritize minimizing costs over speed.

An important design choice is to *co-design* signal horizons and execution policies. There is little point in building a delicate intraday alpha that requires fills within seconds, if your execution and risk systems operate at daily granularity.

## Venue Selection and Smart Order Routing

Modern markets are fragmented across multiple exchanges and alternative trading systems. Prices and liquidity can differ across venues at any moment. **Smart order routers** (SORs) decide where to send your orders.

Key considerations include:

- **Lit vs. dark venues**: Lit venues display quotes and trades publicly; dark pools hide orders until they match. Dark pools can reduce information leakage but may entail higher non-fill risk or adverse selection.
- **Rebates and fees**: Some venues pay rebates for providing liquidity and charge fees for taking it; others have different structures. A good SOR considers net economics, not just raw price.
- **Latency and reliability**: For low-latency AI strategies, small differences in speed and reliability across venues matter for both execution quality and model performance.

From a research perspective, you do not need to model venue-level details in the first iteration of a strategy. However, for deployment at scale, understanding how your broker or in-house SOR behaves, and ensuring that your cost assumptions in backtests are compatible with that behavior, becomes critical.

## Monitoring Execution Quality and Closing the Loop

Execution is not a black box. You should monitor and evaluate execution quality continuously, feeding what you learn back into research and portfolio construction.

Common metrics include:

- **Slippage vs. benchmarks**: average and distribution of price improvement/deterioration relative to mid, arrival price, VWAP, or close.
- **Fill rates and completion risks**: how often do you fail to complete an order in the allotted time?
- **Impact footprints**: price movement during and after your trading, adjusted for market moves.
- **Venue performance**: breakdown of performance by venue, algo type, or broker.

These metrics should be analyzed by:

- instrument characteristics (liquidity, volatility),
- order size and urgency,
- signal type and horizon.

For AI and NLP strategies, one particularly important feedback loop is between execution and alpha modeling:

- If a strategy consistently loses more to costs than expected, consider:

- reducing its turnover in the optimizer,
- lowering its signal weight in crowded or illiquid names,
- lengthening its horizon or reducing aggressiveness.

- Conversely, if slippage is consistently better than modeled, your cost assumptions may be conservative; you can cautiously consider allowing more turnover or higher participation rates—but only with proper backtesting and stress testing.

This section has bridged the gap between theoretical portfolios and the messy reality of trading. The main messages are:

- Transaction costs are multi-layered: explicit fees, spreads, slippage, and market impact each play a role in eroding gross model alpha.
- Market impact, driven by order size, urgency, and liquidity, often defines the scalable capacity of an AI strategy and must be modeled explicitly in backtests and optimizers.
- Execution algorithms and smart order routing transform portfolio-level trade lists into actual fills; their design must be aligned with your signals' horizons and decay.

- Continuous monitoring of execution quality, and feeding those insights back into research and portfolio construction, is essential for preserving net alpha in production.

In the final section of this chapter, we will see how to embed all of this—backtesting discipline, portfolio construction, risk management, and execution—into a production architecture with monitoring and model risk governance that can withstand real-world scrutiny.

## 7.5 Deployment, Monitoring, and Model Risk Governance

Up to this point, we have treated your AI trading strategy as if it lived in a well-behaved laboratory: careful backtests, disciplined portfolio construction, realistic cost models, and thought-through execution tactics. In reality, none of that matters unless you can *run* the strategy reliably, day after day, in a production environment where data feeds break, models drift, and regulators or investors may ask, "Why did the system do that on Tuesday at 9:32 a.m.?"

This section is about turning research into a *service*: an AI trading system that can be deployed, monitored, and governed. The central themes are:

- **Deployment**: how code and models move from research to production using CI/CD (continuous integration and continuous deployment) patterns.
- **Monitoring**: how we observe infrastructure, model behaviour, and portfolio outcomes in real time.
- **Model risk governance**: how we keep humans firmly in control through validation, approvals, kill switches, and audit trails.

We will develop these ideas gradually, always keeping in mind the special challenges of NLP and alternative data: non-stationary language, shifting data vendor behaviour, and the risk of embedding opaque decision logic in models that directly move capital.

## 7.6 Separating Research and Production

A common antipattern is the "notebook-in-production" system: code written for exploration is run directly with live capital. This is fast but fragile. A better approach is to maintain *distinct* research and production environments that communicate through controlled interfaces.

**Research Environment**

The research environment is optimized for flexibility:

- Interactive notebooks and scripts.
- Fast iteration on data cleaning, feature engineering, and models.
- Access to large historical datasets and experimental tools.

It is acceptable—even healthy—for the research environment to be messy. What matters is that when a research artifact is considered for production, it can be *packaged* and promoted in a controlled way.

**Production Environment**

The production environment is optimized for reliability and reproducibility:

- Locked-down dependencies (libraries, OS versions, drivers).
- Strict access controls and logging.
- Clear separation between configuration (what model, what universe, what parameters) and code (how the model is implemented).

The same code and model should behave identically in staging and live trading, given the same inputs. To make this realistic, we typically use containerization and CI/CD pipelines.

## 7.7 Containerization and CI/CD for AI Trading

### Containerization

Containerization (for example, using Docker) bundles the model code, its dependencies, and configuration into a self-contained unit. This has several benefits:

- **Reproducibility**: the same container can be run on a developer's machine, in staging, and in production.
- **Isolation**: conflicting library versions between different strategies do not cause outages.
- **Versioning**: each production deployment refers to a specific container image hash, which can be rolled back if needed.

In an NLP context, a container typically includes:

- The trained model artifacts (for example, neural network weights, tokenizer vocabulary).
- The feature extraction pipeline (text cleaning, embedding computation, aggregation).
- Logic for forming signals and passing them to the portfolio construction layer.

### CI/CD Pipelines

Continuous integration (CI) and continuous deployment (CD) orchestrate how changes flow from research to production:

- **Code commit and review**: changes to the strategy code or configuration are committed to a version control system (for example, Git) and reviewed.
- **Automated tests**: unit tests, integration tests, and regression backtests are triggered. For AI strategies, tests should include:

- basic correctness (no look-ahead, correct label alignment),
- stability checks (does the new model behave sensibly on known edge cases?),
- performance comparisons against a baseline model.

- **Artifact build**: if tests pass, a new container image and associated metadata (model version, parameters, training data version) are built.
- **Staging deployment**: the new image is deployed to a staging environment that uses live or replayed data but does *not* trade real capital.
- **Production deployment**: if staging checks are successful and approvals are obtained, the new version is rolled out to production using safe patterns such as canary deployments.

A **canary deployment** sends a small fraction of traffic or capital (for example, 5–10%) through the new model while the rest remains with the old version. If the canary behaves well according to predefined metrics (for example, stable signal statistics, no unexpected exposures), the rollout continues; otherwise, it is rolled back.

## 7.8 Three Layers of Monitoring

Once in production, the strategy must be continuously observed. Effective monitoring spans three layers:

- Infrastructure and data.
- Model behaviour.
- Portfolio outcomes and risk.

### Infrastructure and Data Monitoring

At the lowest level, you need to know whether the system is *up* and receiving valid data:

- Process and container health: CPU, memory, disk usage, process restarts.
- Latency and throughput: how long does it take from data arrival to signal update and order generation?
- Data feed quality: are prices, corporate actions, and alternative data arriving on time and within expected ranges?

For NLP pipelines this also includes:

- Ingestion pipeline health for text sources (news feeds, social media, transcripts).
- Monitoring for missing or delayed documents from key vendors.
- Simple sanity checks (for example, daily document counts by ticker, language detection to ensure expected languages).

Alerts at this layer are usually operational (for example, "primary news feed delayed by more than 5 minutes"), triggering fallbacks or human intervention.

**Model Behaviour Monitoring**

Above the infrastructure sits the model itself. We care about how its inputs and outputs evolve over time.

Key diagnostics include:

**1. Input distribution checks.**

Compare current feature distributions to those seen in training:

- Means, variances, and quantiles of key features (for example, sentiment scores, embedding norms, text length).
- Frequency of rare tokens or out-of-vocabulary terms.
- Changes in language usage (for example, topic distributions, incidence of new jargon).

Large shifts may indicate **data drift**: the environment has changed in ways the model has not seen before.

**2. Prediction and signal stability.**

Track:

- Cross-sectional distribution of signals (for example, are 90% of names suddenly rated "strong buy"?).
- Time-series stability (for example, how often do signals flip sign from day to day?)
- Correlations with previous model versions.

Abrupt, unexplained changes can reveal bugs, data issues, or a model that has become unstable out of sample.

**3. Performance indicators.**

At the model level, you can compute:

- Realized hit rates or rank correlations between signals and short-horizon returns.
- Information coefficients (ICs), both raw and adjusted for risk factors.
- Breakdown by segment (sector, region, capitalization) to detect localized failures.

These metrics should be tracked with appropriate statistical noise in mind; short-term fluctuations are expected, but persistent deterioration is a warning.

### Portfolio and Risk Monitoring

Finally, at the portfolio level, we monitor:

- Current and projected volatility, drawdowns, and VaR-type measures.
- Factor exposures (for example, beta, value, momentum, quality) and whether they remain within policy bounds.

- Concentration metrics: largest positions, sector weights, liquidity buckets.
- Turnover and transaction costs versus expectations.

Many of these were defined as constraints or targets in earlier sections. Monitoring checks whether the live system is actually honoring them, or whether unanticipated interactions between signals, models, and execution are creating exposures outside the design envelope.

## 7.9 Drift Detection and Performance Decay

Financial markets are non-stationary. Language evolves, corporate communication styles shift, and the meaning of certain text patterns can change (consider how "subprime" acquired a different connotation after 2007). NLP models are therefore particularly exposed to **concept drift**.

**Types of Drift**

We can distinguish:

- **Data drift**: the distribution of inputs $X$ changes (for example, new topics, new slang, changes in documentation style).
- **Label drift**: the distribution of returns $Y$ changes (for example, volatility regime shifts).
- **Concept drift**: the relationship between $X$ and $Y$ changes (for example, optimistic language in earnings calls stops being predictive when management becomes more constrained by legal review).

Detecting concept drift directly is hard, but we can monitor proxies.

**Practical Drift Detection Techniques**

Common tools include:

- **Statistical tests on feature distributions**: for example, Kolmogorov–Smirnov tests comparing current feature distributions to training distributions.
- **Windowed performance diagnostics**: monitor rolling ICs or hit rates over different horizons and compare to historical baselines.
- **Stability of feature importance**: for interpretable models or with post-hoc explainers, track how often the same features appear as most influential. Large, sudden shifts can be concerning.

Thresholds for alerts should be set to balance sensitivity with robustness: too sensitive and you will be constantly chasing noise; too insensitive and you may miss genuine deterioration.

When drift is detected, the response may include:

- Reducing risk (for example, lowering target volatility or gross exposure).
- Freezing model updates of certain types or signals while investigating.
- Scheduling retraining with updated data, combined with backtesting to ensure changes do not overfit recent noise.

## 7.10 Model Risk Governance

All of the above supports, but does not replace, a formal **model risk governance** framework. Regulators and sophisticated investors increasingly expect that AI models moving capital are subject to processes analogous to those used for market risk or credit risk models.

**Model Lifecycle and Ownership**

Each production model should have:

- A clear **owner** (for example, a lead quant or model steward) responsible for its performance and documentation.

- A defined **lifecycle**: development, validation, approval, deployment, monitoring, periodic review, retirement.
- A unique **model identifier** and version history.

Documentation should cover:

- Model purpose and scope (what decisions it informs; what markets and instruments it applies to).
- Data sources (including alternative data), with notes on licensing, privacy, and MNPI (material non-public information) controls.
- Methodology: key modeling choices, feature engineering, and any known limitations or failure modes.
- Backtesting and validation results, including stress tests.

### Independent Validation

Independent validation means that a team or function separate from the model developers:

- Reviews the conceptual soundness of the model.
- Reproduces key backtests using independently sourced or audited data where possible.
- Challenges assumptions (for example, choice of horizon, robustness of signals across regimes).
- Evaluates implementation correctness (for example, checking that production code matches the validated research version).

For complex NLP models, validation may also examine:

- Sensitivity to particular keywords or document types.
- Potential biases (for example, whether the model systematically underweights or overweights firms in certain regions due to data coverage issues).

- Reasonable behaviour under adversarial or extreme inputs (for example, bursts of highly repetitive or obviously spam-like text).

**Change Management and Approvals**

Material changes to models or their use should follow a documented change-management process:

- Classification of changes (for example, minor parameter tweak vs. major architecture change vs. new data source).
- Requirements for impact analysis (for example, side-by-side backtests, stress tests).
- Approval workflows (for example, sign-off by model owner, validation, and risk committee).

Changes should not go directly from a notebook to live trading; they should pass through the CI/CD pipeline, staging, and canary deployment described earlier, with governance checkpoints aligned to the change's materiality.

## 7.11 Kill Switches, Circuit Breakers, and Incident Management

Even with careful design, things go wrong: data feeds break, exchanges misbehave, or a previously unseen market scenario triggers aberrant model behaviour. A robust production setup includes mechanisms to *stop or slow down* trading when necessary.

**Kill Switches and Circuit Breakers**

**Kill switches** are manual or automated controls that can halt trading activity quickly. For example:

- A global kill switch that stops all automated trading and liquidates positions to a defined fallback (for example, a benchmark portfolio or cash).

- Strategy-level kill switches that disable only specific models or sleeves.

**Circuit breakers** are pre-defined rules that automatically reduce or pause trading when certain conditions are met, such as:

- Portfolio-level losses exceeding intra-day or daily thresholds.
- Model diagnostics crossing extreme levels (for example, 99th percentile deviations in input distributions).
- Infrastructure or data feed failures (for example, loss of primary and backup price feeds).

These actions should be conservative and reversible: the priority during an incident is to protect capital and avoid compounding errors.

### Incident Runbooks and Post-Mortems

An **incident runbook** is a step-by-step guide for operators and quants when specific classes of problems occur:

- "What to do if the news feed fails."
- "What to do if realized intraday drawdown reaches X%."
- "What to do if model input drift exceeds threshold Y."

After an incident, a **post-mortem** should be conducted to:

- Reconstruct the timeline (what happened when; what the system did; who intervened).
- Identify root causes (technical, data, or design flaws).
- Propose and implement remediations (code changes, new checks, revised limits).
- Update documentation and training for future incidents.

The goal is learning rather than blame: improving the system without encouraging overfitting to a single episode.

## 7.12 Regulatory and Fiduciary Considerations

Finally, AI trading strategies must operate within regulatory and fiduciary frameworks. While specifics vary by jurisdiction and firm type, several themes recur.

**Explainability Proportional to Risk**

Highly complex NLP models (for example, deep transformer architectures) may be difficult to fully explain. Nevertheless, for material risk-taking decisions, you should be able to provide:

- A clear high-level explanation of how text and alternative data are used.
- Illustrative examples of model-driven trades and the patterns they exploited.
- Evidence that the model does not rely on obviously spurious correlations or prohibited data (for example, MNPI).

The standard of explainability should be *proportional to the risk*: the more capital at stake and the more concentrated the strategy, the higher the bar.

**Data and Privacy Controls**

Alternative data often include sensitive information (for example, web-scraped content, geolocation data, or anonymized transactional records). Governance must ensure:

- Proper licensing and terms of use are respected.
- Personally identifiable information (PII) is handled in compliance with privacy regulations.
- Data provenance is tracked so that, if needed, you can demonstrate that no MNPI was used.

These controls intersect with model governance: validators should know which datasets feed which models and what safeguards are in place.

## 7.13 Bringing It All Together

Deployment, monitoring, and governance complete the arc of this chapter. Taken together, the core ideas are:

- AI trading models must move from research to production through controlled, reproducible pipelines (CI/CD, containerization, staging, and canary rollouts).
- Monitoring must span infrastructure, model behaviour, and portfolio outcomes, with specific tools for detecting drift and performance decay.
- Model risk governance provides a formal structure around ownership, validation, documentation, and change control, ensuring that humans remain accountable for machine-driven decisions.
- Kill switches, circuit breakers, and structured incident management protect capital when things go wrong and create feedback loops that strengthen the system over time.
- Regulatory and fiduciary expectations around explainability and data use are not obstacles but design constraints that, if embraced, lead to more robust and trustworthy AI trading platforms.

With these elements in place, the AI strategies developed and evaluated in earlier chapters can be run not just successfully, but responsibly, in the real world.

www.ingramcontent.com/pod-product-compliance
Lightning Source LLC
LaVergne TN
LVHW052029200926
848481LV00005B/1628